WOMEN'S CHALLENGES
OF
THE NEW MILLENNIUM

WOMEN'S CHALLENGES OF THE NEW MILLENNIUM

Vibhuti Patel

GYAN PUBLISHING HOUSE
New Delhi-110002

WOMEN'S CHALLENGES OF THE NEW MILLENNIUM
[*Women Studies*]

Rs. 675

ISBN: 81-212-0806-8

Published in 2002 in India by
Gyan Publishing House
5, Ansari Road
New Delhi 110 002
Phones: 3261060, 3282060, Fax: 3285914
e-mail: gyanbook@vsnl.com
visit our website at: http://www.gyanbooks.com

Laser Typeset at: ALPHABET, Delhi
Printed at: Mehra Offset Press, New Delhi

Contents

Preface

Idea of writing this book emerged when I was Visiting Fellow at the Development Studies Institute of The London School of Economics and Political Science. During my tenure, I was invited to give seminars and presentations on wide range of subjects concerning women, for workshops and conventions at several universities in Sussex, Edenborough, London, Manchester, Bradford and York in the United Kingdom. I also presented papers at International Institute of Research and Education, Amsterdam, The Netherlands and University College of Los Angeles, California. For these presentations, I had to do great deal of research. During the last decade, I have been exposed to gender training of the decision makers in the academic institutions, policy-making and political bodies, judiciary and legal system and the criminal justice system. Their practical- down-to-earth approach made me examine women's problems in the context specific manner.

This book also owes its existence to the intellectually stimulating atmosphere provided by my neighbours, Dr. Tanushree Seth and Ms. Shilpa Seth and fiiends at Centre for Enquiry Into Health and Allied Themes (CEHAT), especially, Rai Duggal, Manisha Gupte, Dhruv Mankad, Padma Prakash, Amar Jesani, Neha Madhiwala, Sunil Nandaraj, Anagha Khot, Sumeeta Menon, Padma Deostaii, Dr. Sunita Bandewar, Dr. Anant Phadake, Dr.Abhaya Shukla and Dr. Sharadini Rath. It was really an enriching experience to discuss with them either individually or in their workshops. They inspired me with their spirited and selfless dedication to the defense of human rights, women's rights, freedom, equity, justice, democracy, secular humanism and all other human qualities that make us human. Volume of reference material provided by the CEHAT team over last IO years has enriched my database and enhanced the scope of this book. Many thanks are due to CEHAT team of Bombay and Pune. None of them, I need hardly add, is responsible for what I have written or necessarily agrees with it.

I would like to stress that this book tries to answer important questions raised by the social movements of the 20th century and challenges brought about by the massive changes due to globalisation in the 21 st century. At a juncture, when the secular fabric of our country is threatened due to xenophobia, women's predicament will be deplorable unless both, the state and the civil society take affirmative action to safeguard womews interest. This book makes humble effort to provide direction in this line. It tries to - contextualise women's survival struggles in the political economy perspective and offers worldview and analytical vision for engendering each and every area of human existence.

Vibhuti Patel

Acknowledgements

I am thankful to Dr. Amar Jesani, Ms. Lara Jesani and my parents who provided congenial atmosphere to pursue this work. I gratefully acknowledge moral support provided by Mr. Ravi Duggal, Coordinator of CEHAT. I express my deep sense of gratitude towards Dr. Asharaf, publications Officer of CEHAT who agreed to read the manuscript and helped me out with the layout of the final draft. Ms. Saramma (the Administrator of CEHAT), Ms. Margerette, Ms. Rajeswari Balaji, Ms. Sapna Pillai, Ms. Anagha Khot and Mr. Anirban Bose helped me out whenever I was stuck in computer work at CEHAT office. Mr. Raut, Mr. Tipse and Mr. Vijay - Librarians at CEHAT were helpful, generous and courteous when I was doing my reference work over a period of 1993-2001. I offer profuse thanks to Mr. Vijay Dhargalkar (Sophia Poly Technique, Bombay) for providing sketch of a woman for cover design of this book.

Section I

Political Economy of Gender

One

Introduction

This book aims to examine development issues from gender perspectives. Examination of gender relations in the development studies is relatively a new area. It is based on the presumption that the potential of women to play central roles in development has not been fully recognised by our governments. Household as a unit of analysis leads to policy risks and conceptual distortion because there are gender differences in intra household allocation of production and consumption. Women's and girls' interests in terms of food, education, care and health-needs are sacrificed if we presume that all members of the household have homogeneous interests. According to Dr. Amartya Kumar Sen, women face seven types of inequality - Mortality inequality, i.e., gender bias in health care and nutrition, natality inequality means sex selective abortion and female infanticide, basic facility inequality in education and skill development, special opportunity inequality in cases of higher education and professional training, professional inequality in the field of employment and promotion in occupation, ownership inequality in terms of home, land and property and household inequality in terms of sharing the burden of housework and childcare.[1]

Over and above cooking, cleaning and caring, women do unpaid family work, which augment family resources. Poorer the household, more time women spend on low income and labour intensive occupations. Middle class women do "status production work". All problems concerning women other than population problem are considered as personal problem or family problem. As women's concerns are classified under the heading of welfare, women get small as well as residual budgetary allocations.

This book has adopted an interdisciplinary perspective to examine gender relations.

Section I *Political Economy of Gender* focuses on women's predicaments in response to macro and micro changes in the economy. "The work women do contributes substantially to the well being of families, communities and nations. But work in the household, even when it is economic is inadequately measured".[2]

Chapter II, *Women and the Structural Adjustment Programmes in India* shows the implications of new economic policy on women by examining macro policies during the last decade. Pressure from women's groups and women studies forced the government to provide safety-nets in the field of public works programme, primary education and public distribution system. Women have to fight every inch for small concessions. The working class women are creating relentless pressure to change labour laws.

Chapter III, *Women's Issues-Economic Parameters* analyses women's economic role in the economic development. "India ranks 112 in gender related development index of global ranking."[3] During 1990-95, Indian Women's life expectancy at birth was 60.5.[4] India continues to record high levels of morbidity especially among infants, children, the elderly and women.[5] In 1993-94 India had 18.45 per cent of urban and 37.91 per cent of rural economically active female population in the age-group of 15 years and above. Economically active female children (Age-group 10-14 year) were 4.70 per cent in urban and 14.32 per cent were in the rural areas.[6] In 1997, female labour force participation rate in India was 31.0%. Among total workers women constituted 28.9 per cent in the urban areas and 31.6 per cent in the rural areas. Women constituted 35.3 per cent of agricultural, 34.4 per cent of industry and 27.9 per cent of service sector.

Chapter IV, *New social Movements and Gender in India- Lessons for Feminist Economists* highlights changing role of new social movements as a result of professionalisation of the new social movements and global competition for funding. Excluded from most political offices, many women have found a voice in Non-government Organisations (NGOs) at the grass roots, national and international level."[7]

Chapter V, *Budget 2000-Gender Analysis* reveals that investment priorities in the budget seem to reinforce women's image as that of caregivers and mothers. End of the women's

Decade Conference in Nairobi had highlighted the issue of women's unequal access to economic resources. Paragraph 345 of the Beijing conference, 1995 reiterated NFLS (Nairobi Forward Looking Stategy-1985)'s stance in these words, "Financial resources have generally been insufficient for the advancement of women. This has contributed to the slow progress to date in implementing the NFLS for advancement of women." It recommended integration of gender perspective in budgetary decisions on policies and programmes. Following this statement, the budget 2001 has allocated 30 per cent development resources for women and development schemes through women's component plans. It has increased budgetary allocation for schemes for girls' hostels. Twenty Four percent of allocation to the scheme for development of nursing services. Most beedi workers are women who need occupational diversification. Allocation is made in the budget for the wives of truck-drives who die on duty. There is no budgetary allocation for gender training of bureaucrats. The year 2001 was declared as women's empowerment year, which has provided innumerable schemes for employment of women.

Chapter XI, *Gender Economics* examines political economy of control of women's sexuality, fertility and labour of women in a patriarchal class society. It also explains the material reality which governs sexist bias in our customary and family laws which discriminate against women in matters concerning marriage, divorce, maintenance, alimony, custody of children, property and land rights. Three approaches of development of women - WID-WAD-GAD-Women in Development, Women and Development and Gender and Development are explained.

Chapter XII, *Women, Education and Social Development* examines problems faced in the field of women's education and gives case studies of successful models for literacy campaign. Thirty Three per cent reservation of seats for women in the Panchayati Raj institutions have also helped promotion of women's education. As per the 2001 census, 46 per cent of Indian Women were illiterate.

Chapter VIII, New *Reproductive Technologies and Gender Relations in India* gives a bird's eye view of population policy and infertility treatment in our country." 57.4 per cent of married women of reproductive age (15-49 years) are currently using contraceptives".[8] Many of the currently used contraceptives are harmful. But the women users are not informed about contra-indications. In the name of infertility treatment, women are given long acting hormone based drugs which have carcinogenic and mutogenic implications. The state is not doing public education to convey that solution to infertility can be adoption. Anaemia prevalence in pregnant women is 87.5 per cent and 31 per cent of all babies born are low-birth weight babies.[9] Providing balanced diet and nutrition are far more important than population control programmes or infertility treatment. For many women, high-risk activity can be simply being married. Almost one half of all cancers in men and one quarter of all cancers in women in India are believed to be tobacco related. With accent on NRT, genuine issues affecting women get sidetracked. E.g. occupational health issues, backaches, aches in shoulder and waist, stiffness in joints and extreme fatigue were reported by women workers in number of informal sector occupations in India.[10]

Antenatal care for pregnant women has a poor quality of care record. 66.4 per cent of urban, 57.6 per cent of rural and 58.5 per cent of total women in India reported that the antenatal care was not necessary. Only 3 per cent of Indian women smoke.[11] New Reproductive Technologies such as amniocentesis, chorion villi biopsy and pre implantation sex test are rampantly used not to allow the birth of female babies.

Section II provides an analysis of Social Change and Gender Relations.

Chapter IX, *Women's Movement in India* gives an account of the challenges faced by the women's movement in India. In the beginning of the women's movement, agitation and propaganda against violence were main issues around which women rallied. After two decades of struggle, women's issues have been visible in all sectors of the economy and polity. As a result of the women's movement, women's issues are taken up seriously by the decision-making bodies.

Chapter X, *Challenges of the New Millennium and Voluntary Organisations* are examining professionalisation of voluntary sector and their role in governance in the day-to-day matters of civil society. Financial institutions are expressing great confidence in NGOs. For (DRI) Differential Rate of Interest Schemes, (IRDP) Integrated Rural Development Programmes and SETUP-Self Employment Programme for Urban Poor, NGOs are requested to act as facilitators. NGOs role in credit recycle-assessment of credit needs, appraisal, disbursal, supervision, repayment, reduction in formal paper work, disbursal of credit to the poor is appreciated. For Gramin banks, NGOs involvement is sought for mobilisation of resources, lending policies procedures and recoveries.[12] NGOs as facilitators for project formulation by banks on the one hand and its effective implementation by beneficiaries on the other i.e. follow-up, supervision, achievement of expected results.

Chapter XI, *Effective Governance: Importance of Women's Leadership in Local Bodies* shows work of women leaders as networkers to establish connection of every person in the economy to nature and community and to reintegrate community with modernity. In the implementation of mega projects, plunder and displacement go hand in hand. In the agricultural development strategies men are cornering more profitable modern commercialised economy while women get less fertile land which has to be cultivated by traditional tools.

Chapter XII, *Rape Laws- Travesty of Justice* is a very important chapter so far as women's involvement in the development process is concerned. Sexual violence has proved to be the most effective tool for terrorisation, subjugation and humiliation of women. The paper makes a case in favour of broader definition of sexual violence over and above penile penetration. It demands reforms in the existing rape laws.

Section III is on Women in Decision Making processes in India. It also highlights how the decision-making bodies are co-opting women's issues in the mainstream of Indian polity, economy and other apex bodies of governance.

Chapter XIII, *Globalisation and Women's Question in India* shows that globalisation has proved advantageous for educated women of the upper strata of society. Market oriented economies and consumerist culture generate double disadvantage for poor women because of her underprivileged class and underprivileged gender. As compared to many south Asian countries India's score on

Human development is lower. Scarcity of essential services and increasing emphasis on consumerism has escalated violence. Shifting market consideration has resulted in unforeseen hardships for those states that don't have adequate IT professionals for forecasting about economically profitable projects. Globalisation has compounded the situation by using purdah ideology to push majority of women further down the occupational hierarchy. At the same time, teleworkers are gaining ground. *Fear of the unknown* coupled with legacy of colonialism generates insular feelings among the nation states in Asia.

Chapter XIV, *Women in Decision Making* gives the gist of several round tables (from 1990 to 2000) on women in decision-making processes of the social movements and the existing power structures. Publication of Towards Equality Report legitimised women's concerns in the state apparatus. Street fighting by women's groups around wide range of issues made Indian women visible in the media, educational institutions, criminal justice system and in the political arena.

Chapter XV, *Evolution of Women's Studies in India* gives a genesis of invisibility to respectability of women's studies as an interdisciplinary subject in the Indian academia. Main aim of women's studies in India has been - to bring women into the mainstream of development. Seventies brought women to the forefront of development concerns with formation of women's studies centres in SNDT Women's University and Tata Institute of Social Sciences in 1974. In the subsequent period several autonomous women's studies centres and women's units/ departments in the Indian universities brought visibility of women in statistics, indicators, policy planning, government programmes, mainstream media and political discourse.

Chapter XVI, *Dynamics of Women's Studies and Women's Movement in India* explores symbiotic relationship between women's studies that involve teaching, training, research as well as documentation and women's movement that encompasses advocacy, public education, interaction with the state apparatus and policy intervention.

Let us hope that this volume will make a worthwhile contribution in the Gender and development discourse.

Footnotes

1. Amartya Kumar Sen "Many Faces of Gender Inequality", an inaugural Lecture for the New Redcliff Institute at Harvard University, 24-4-2001.
2. The World's Women- Trends and Statistics, The UN, 1995, p. xxii.
3. Women of South East Asia, World Health Organisation, New Delhi, Regional Publication, SEARO, No. 34, 2000, p. 14.
4. *Ibid*. p. 21.
5. India - Human Development Report, NCAER, A Profile of Indian States in the 1990s, Oxford University Press, 1999, p. 133.
6. *Ibid*. p. 265.
7. The World's Women- Trends and Statistics, The UN, p. xx.
8. Women of South East Asia - A Health Profile, WHO, 2000.
9. *Ibid*., p. 255.
10. *Ibid*, p. 136
11. Women of South East Asia, WHO, New Delhi, 2000, p. 63.
12. DR. C. Rangrajan, "Banking with the Poor, Governor's Keynote Address at the Indian National Workshop for Bankers organised by the Foundation for Development Corporation Limited, Australia and Indian Banks Association at Bombay on Jan, 31, 1994, pp. 353-358.

References

Anjali Bhelande and Mala Pandurang (2000), *Articulating Gender*, Pencraft International, New Delhi.

Desmond A. D'Abrea (1995), *Social Worker looks at the New Economic Policy*, Dialogue Group, August.

Francis Green and Peter Nore (eds) (1977), *Economics- An Anti Text*, The Macmillan Press Ltd, London.

Haleh Afshar (ed.) (1985), *Women, Work and Ideology in the Third World*, Tavistock Publications, London.

Haleh Afshar (ed.)(1991), *Women Development and Survival in the third world*, Longman, Singapore.

Kalyani Menon Sen and K. Seeta Prabhu (2001), "The Budget – A Quick look through a 'Gender Lens'", *Economic and Political Weekly*, Vol. XXXVI Nos. 14-15, April 14-20, pp. 1164-1169.

Naila Kabeer (1994), *Reversed Realities - Gender Hierarchies in Development Thought*, Kali for Women, Delhi.

Noeleen Heyzer (1985), *Missing Women – Development Planning in Asia and the Pacific*, Asian and Pacific Development Centre, Kuala Lumpur, Malaysia.

Raj Mohoni Sethi (1999), *Globalisation, Culture and Women's Development*, Rawat Publications, New Delhi.

Rao N, Rurup L and Sudarshan R. (1996), *Sites of Change: The Structural Context for Empowering Women in India*, Friedrich Ebert Stiftung, New Delhi.

Seminar (2001), Special Number on Economic Turmoil - a symposium on the continuing slowdown of our economy, No. 507, November.

Vinay Kirpal (ed.) (1992), *The Girl Child in 20th Century Indian Literature*, Sterling Publications, New Delhi.

Two

Women and Structural Adjustment in India

Introduction

In response to a mounting burden of debt leading to a balance of payment crisis, the Government of India (GOI) adopted a structural adjustment programme (SAP) in 1991. It included reductions in public investment, devaluation, cutting food and fertilizers subsidies, the reduction of budgetary provision for developmental planning, capital intensive and 'high-tech' productive activities, economies in government expenditure, an increase in the bank rate, insurance charges and rail tariffs. Simply put, the policy aimed at capital, energy and import-intensive growth with the help of 4 "Ds" - devaluation, deregulation, deflation and denationalisation.

This policy has intensified the processes pursued in the last decade and a half (mainly in the post-emergency period), as a result of a new international division of labour between the advanced capitalist economies and the post-colonial economies of Asia, Africa and Latin America. In the late 1970s, national and multinational corporations in the USA and Europe realized that the best way to reduce the wage-bill and to enhance profit rates, was to move industrial plants to poorer countries like India, Sri Lanka, Bangladesh, etc. The cheap labour of 'docile', 'nimble fingered' and 'flexible' Asian women was found to be most attractive step to enhance profit margins. This policy was given the appealing title of 'Integration of Women in Development.'

During the Indian emergency rule in 1975, a major policy-shift took place where the slogan of 'import-substitution' was replaced by the slogan of 'export promotion'. The 'emergency rule' provided politico-repressive instruments to push through a new economic strategy to restructure its industrial sector by introducing a higher degree of mechanisation and rationalisation on the one hand and on the other hand, the expansion of an extremely exploitative informal sector. (Desai and Patel, 1985). A 14-country Alternative Asian Report on the Impact of the UN Decade for Women (1975-1985) at the Nairobi Conference stated, "The new strategy of 'Integration of Women into Development' meant in most cases getting women to work in some income-generating activities, integrating women into market oriented production and thus integrating women into the world market economy. It was not meant that women should expand their subsistence production and produce more for their consumption - for their own food and their clothes. Income-generation in this approach meant money income. Money income could be generated only if women could produce something, which could be sold. People who could buy these products live in western countries. This meant export-oriented production." (AWRAN, 1985).

The Impact of Globalisation on Women Workers in India

Women of the third world are seen as the most flexible of the world's labour force. The lower supply price of these women provides a material basis for the induction of poor working-class women into export industries such as electronics, garments, sports goods, toys and agro-industries. (Moser, 1978). Researches conducted under an Indo-Dutch Programme in the eighties revealed that in many of the poorer countries, "Women are rigorously socialised to work uncomplainingly, under patriarchal control, at any allotted task however dull, laborious, physically harmful or badly paid it may be. There are large numbers of poor and desperately needy women in many countries looking for work within the narrow confines of a socially imposed, inequitable demand of labour and strict taboos on mobility. These women have become ideal workers for this kind of international division of labour." (Banerjee, 1991). In the export-oriented industries, the production of leather goods, toys, food-products, garments, diamond and jewellery, piece-rate female labour is employed, working from sweatshops or from home. (Banerjee, 1977). In a similar way, the women of ethnic minorities - South Asians, Afro-

Caribbeans, Puerto Ricans and Mexicans living in the industrialised countries have been used as cheap labour by the world capitalism since the early 1980s. They face triple oppression as they are subjected to race and colour prejudices as well as class exploitation. (Mitter, 1986). The relationship between the formal sector and the decentralised sector is a dependent relationship where the formal sector has control over capital and markets and the 'informal' sector works as an ancillary (Harriss, 1982). In India, 96 per cent of women work in the decentralised sector, which has a high degree of labour redundancy and obsolescence. These women have less control over their work and no chance for upward mobility because of temporary, routine and monotonous work. In the agrarian sector, the cash crops - fruits, mushrooms, flowers and vegetables, are replacing the traditional subsistence crops where women had important role to play. This process has also intensified immiserization of working women in rural areas and has created tremendous food-shortages. (Patel, 1992).

Performance of the Indian Economy and Implications of 1991-92 Budget

As 1991-92 was a landmark budget as it set the tone for new economic policy in the subsequent years, a detailed examination is provided of the budget.

During 1991-92, the Indian economy's achievement was reported to be 1.5 per cent rate of growth of the Gross National Product (GNP). But, when the sectoral profile was examined, the picture was dismal.

This table reveals that there was recession in the agricultural and industrial sectors and growth in the service sector. The decline in agricultural and industrial production showed that millions of workers (both men and women) were retrenched and lost the purchasing power to procure the bare necessities of life.

The 1991-92 budgetary allocation and the projected 1992-93 budgetary provision had a direct bearing on women's survival struggle. Fiscal and monetary policies pursued under the stabilization programme demanded 'item-by-item' closer examination in terms of their gender implications.

TABLE - 1

(A)	Value addition in the agricultural sector - 0.8 per cent (Decline in foodgrain production from 176.2 m tonnes to 171m tonnes and coarse cereals, grown and eaten by the poorest, production from 31.1 tonnes to 29 m tonnes),		
B.	Growth in	Industrial production	–0.4%
		Manufacturing sector	–2.0%
		Electrical machinery production	–17.3%
		Metal products	–7.2%
		Leather and fur products	–5.4%
		Textile products	–3.6%
		Transport equipments and spare parts	–4.4%
		Rubber, plastic, petroleum products	–1.6%
		Wood products	–2.5%
C.	Growth in the service sector (finance, insurance, business, trade, storage, hotel, transport, the armed forces, public administration)		+5.2%

Source: Research Unit for Political Economy, Bombay, 1992.

(i) Prices of Essential Commodities and the Public Distribution System (PDS)

An IMF survey (May, 1992) in its report on Asian Developing Countries commented that south Asia recorded the highest inflation rates in the region, with Pakistan in particular, plus Bhutan, India, Myanmar and Nepal all recording higher inflation rates in 1991 than in 1990. Compared to 1990, India, Bangladesh, Myanmar and Sri Lanka experienced a slower growth. India had faced a steep rise in the price of essential items. As the following table shows, both the Consumer Price Index (CPI) and the wholesale price index had risen within a year.

On 29th September 1991, the annual price rise in cereals was running at 28.4 per cent, and it had risen to 33 per cent by June, 1992. The burden of galloping inflation, especially the spiralling prices of essential commodities, had fallen heavily on women who had to procure them for the sustenance of the household. The increase in the prices of fodder and transport, meant the price of milk had increased by 25 per cent. Hence more poor children were deprived of milk. The price rise in consumer durables had not deterred the 240 million Indians with purchasing power to indulge in conspicuous consumption. For the remaining 600 million the survival struggle had become acute because of the erosion of their purchasing power as a result of price rises as a result of a double digit inflation.

TABLE - 2

Price-Rise in	*1990-91*	*1991-92 (April to March)*
Wholesale Price Index	12.1	13.3
Consumer Price Index (CPI) for Industrial workers	13.6	13.9
CPI for Urban non-manual employees	13.4	13.6
CPI for agricultural Labourers	16.6	21.9

Source: Quarterly Review of Developments in the Indian Economy, RBI Bulletin, June, 1992.

India is well-known for its public distribution system (PDS) which averted mass death by starvation. In the 1991-92 budget, 12.3 per cent cuts in food-subsidy affected the Public Distribution System (PDS) in the subsequent years because of tremendous political pressure exercised by the trade unions and social movements efforts have been made to strengthen PDS in the extremely interior areas identified by investigative journalists and electronic media. The amount of food-grains needed to provide sustenance for the 'really poor' (according to the World Bank's standard, 235 million Indians) is 46.5 million tonnes. In reality, the distribution of food-grains in the PDS for 1991-92 was 19.1 million tonnes - a shortfall of nearly 59 per cent. Lifting of buffer stock from the Food Corporation of India (FCI) godown has been a major bottleneck faced by the administration.

(ii) Health-care

Studies on intra-household distribution of resources reveal that among the poorer households with gross malnutrition and nutritional deficiency, the deficiency among girls and women was

25 per cent more than among men. For every three men using health-care facilities in India, only one woman does so (Batliwala, 1984). According to the 1991 census, the sex ratio showed there were 929 women for every 1000 men in India, the lowest in the history of census in India. In the 0-19 age group, the death rate of girls is higher than boys. In this context, budgetary cuts in public health expenditure will have dire consequences for women and girls in India. In the budget, funds for the treatment of tuberculosis, malaria, phyleria and goitre eradication programmes have been reduced compared with previous years.

The inadequate funds for the rural sanitation programme in each and every budget through out the nineties for provision of clean water, toilets and sewerage, has given rise to higher incidents of water-born diseases and has increased the burden of women in terms of nursing. Also, the reduction in the quota of clean water resources by 38 per cent in the urban areas and 36 per cent in the rural areas, has increased the drudgery of working class women who have to stand in long queues for many hours to obtain one bucket of water (Dholakia, 1992). Concrete programmes for water management has to be given top priority in the annual budget.

The only items for which budgetary provision had increased in 1991-92 were family planning (34 per cent), defence expenditure (7 per cent) and the police force (14 per cent). In the subsequent budgets, they justified it in the name of cross border terrorism. Much has been documented on the coercive aspect of population control programmes that force poor women to adopt contraceptives without informed consent or proper follow-up by the medical staff. (See, Economic and Political Weekly, 1-1-1992, "Development for Whom"?; Radical Journal of Health - "Politics of Population Control", Bombay, 1985).

(iii) Educational Facilities

In the 1991-92 budget, educational funds were reduced by Rs 801.3 million. In the subsequent budgets they justified reduction of budgetary provisions for higher education by encouraging privatisation and collaborative ventures with the industrialised world. Cuts in funding for the mass literacy movement, in which women participate enthusiastically, were Rs. 10 million; which amounted to a 5 per cent reduction compared with the previous year. Government expenditure cuts of 14 per cent for primary education have forced many schools to approach private sources for funds. There was a massive opposition against these measure. Hence in the subsequent years, massive government sponsored advertisements were given in the national dailies about budgetary provision for education. As per 2001 Census, literacy rate for women and girls have improved to 54.16 per cent that makes 22.7 crores Indian women who are literate. The privatisation of educational institutions promoted by the SAP makes education an expensive proposition for poorer households who are already disinclined to allow their girls to pursue higher education, instead of helping in domestic chores and/or earning income. Cuts of 17 per cent in budgetary provision for non-formal education has forced the closure of many night schools and adult-education programmes in which working class women participate. Quality of education is extremely poor in the non-formal educational institutions. It badly needs an introduction of new information technology and distance education by television and radio programmes. According to the 2001 census, 51 per cent of Indian women are illiterate. In 1998-99, the school enrolment ratios for primary classes were 100.86 for boys and 82.85 for girls, and for secondary classes it was 65.27 for boys and 49.08 for girls. According to data given by the Department of Education, GOI, (1987-88) School Dropout Rates, at both primary and secondary levels, were much higher for girls than for boys. (43.28 and 49.42 respectively for primary classes boys and girls, and 58.80 and 67.55 respectively for secondary classes boys and girls). Privatisation in education promoted by the SAP will further increase the dropout rates for girls. In higher education, women are segregated into traditional streams such as Humanities, Arts and Commerce. Women constitute 43 per cent of the total faculty enrolment in Arts and only 6 per cent in Engineering. Reduction in government expenditure on higher education and encouragement towards private colleges will reduce women's opportunities for higher education, as private education promotes only the more lucrative professional and technical courses. Women students will be affected by the reduction in the number of colleges providing studies in the Arts and Humanities. Special scholarships, fellowships and study grants for women and girls are needed on a war footing .

(iv) Poverty Alleviation Programmes

The budgetary provision for a poverty alleviation programme and for the welfare and economic security schemes for the working people were slashed by 12 per cent. But because of tremendous pressure exercised by the left, poverty alleviation programmes were restored. In drought-prone districts and desert areas various schemes for poverty alleviation are now finding better budgetary allocation. NEP had suggested 20 per cent to 25 per cent cuts. Indian army has taken up several development projects in which the rural folks pick up new skills. In these schemes, generally 1/3 of the workforce constitute poor women, and almost their entire earnings go to feeding the family. The resource cuts for the poverty alleviation programme affect poor women and their children the hardest, in terms of their access to food, health care and energy expenditure on work. This distressing reality had forced some scholars, who were generally appreciative of the NEP, to comment, "It cannot be emphasised too strongly that the New Economic Policy of deregulating or freeing the industrial economy, however desirable in itself for the longer-term health of the economy, will do nothing in the short-run to provide more employment in the rural areas or to reduce poverty in general. In political terms, therefore, it leaves vast sections of the society virtually untouched. If there is to be sufficient support for the policy of liberalisation and even more for its extension, a great deal more has to be done simultaneously to infuse a new vigour in the anti-poverty programmes. And it is here that the problem of internal resources becomes most relevant because a great deal of that additional employment opportunity will have to be created in public works of one kind or another." (Patel, 1987). In an appeal to Members of Parliament on the NEP prepared by economists, trade-unionists, social scientists, media-persons and social activists this was the most criticized aspect. (WGAS, 1992)

(v) Employment of Women

The 1991 census showed the work participation rate (WPR) of women as 23 per cent. For the rural women the WPR is 27 per cent and for the urban women it is 10 per cent. Compared to the 1971 and 1981 censuses, this rise in WPR is considerable.

TABLE - 3

Year	*Female Work Participation Rate (WPR)*
1911	33.73
1961	27.96
1971	11.86
1981	14.44
1991	22.69

Source: Census of India, 1991.

A sectoral profile shows that most women workers in rural areas are in occupations such as weaving, handicraft, tailoring, forestry, sale of fish, silk and poultry farming. In urban areas, the majority of women workers are either in the construction sector or in the nursing and teaching professions, working either on a contract-basis or self-employed.

According to UN estimates, in 1970, India had 60 million economically active women and in 1990 the number had risen to 76 million. Out of the total workforce of women, 2 per cent are administrative and managerial workers, 11 per cent are clerks, sales and service workers, 15 per cent are industrial and transport workers and 31 per cent are agricultural and hunting workers. In predominantly tribal states like Sikkim, Arurachal Pradesh, Nagaland and Manipur, the WPR of women is higher but the quality of employment, in terms of wages or income from self-employment and work-condition, is deplorable.

Subcontracting, home-based production, family labour system, and the payment of wages on a piece-rate basis, are jobs earmarked for women. According to the 1991 census, 19 per cent of the total female workforce constitutes unpaid family labour. Even in a state like Kerala, only 17 per cent of the women are gainfully employed.

Women in the Unorganised Sector

94 per cent of the total women workers are in the 'informal' (dependent) sector. The NEP reinforces the trend of informalisation for the female workforce. The formation of a 'flexible' labour force is the key concept of NEP. A shift from a stable/organised labour

force to a flexible workforce has meant hiring women on a part-time basis and the substitution of highly paid male labour by cheap female labour. The NEP provides congenial state support for the large corporate houses who are closing down their big city units and using ancillaries which employ rural and tribal girls (without responsibilities for families and children) on a piece-rate basis. In the post riot milieu, home-based work by women and girls get easily legitimised. This is called an increase in 'efficiency' and 'productivity' of labour.

In the name of increasing marginal efficiency of financial capital, there have been attacks on women's access to credit, extension services and input subsidies. The same concern for efficiency and the proper management of public funds, however, was not to be seen when it came to stock market speculators. The nationalised banks, indicted in the country's biggest financial scam, talked of increasing their interest rates, to the detriment of self-employed women who are dependent on loans. This had affected the small businesses of self-employed poor women. To continue their business, these women now had to approach private money-lenders who charge compound rates of interest. Now there have been improvements because of initiative of the Reserve Bank of India.

The liberalisation of the economy has not liberated working women. The elimination of 7000 licences, the scrapping of MRTP limits and the reduction in customs duty on capital goods have given free grazing grounds for foreign capital. Following the liberalisation of the economy, the right to fish in Indian waters has been given to several foreign firms, including Union Carbide. As a result, 50,000 fisher-folk families have lost their jobs. Food processing industries with foreign collaboration are being established. There has already been a major shift in the cropping pattern from subsistence production like rice, millet, corn, wheat to cash-crop production such as fruit, mushrooms, flowers and vegetables. This process has affected women's employment in the agrarian sector. Several studies have shown that a shift from subsistence to cash-crop production invariably leads to women being the first to lose their jobs. (Agarwal, 1985; Chatterjee, 1989; Krishnaraj, 1988, Shramshakti, 1981) As a result of shrinking self-employment prospects for women, the large majority of them join the rural and urban reserve army of labour. Use of women in the informal sector of electronics, diamond, garment manufacture and pharmaceutical industries has increased. Here again, the underlying reality is disturbing. With globalisation of production and the introduction of assembly-line production, research and management is being controlled by the first world, while strenuous, monotonous, 'unskilled' or 'semi-skilled' work is being done by third world women. Commenting on this situation, the UN Report, Third World Women: 1970-90 states, "The informal sector is by no means a panacea for women. It is far less secure than formal sector work and it generally pays less than the minimum wage."

Employment Profile in the Public Sector

The NEP has declared 200 public sector units 'economically unviable' and 'sick'. Consequently, millions of workers have lost their jobs. Disinvestments in public sector units, closures and retrenchment rendered 6.6 million workers (7 per cent to 9 per cent of them women) unemployed, within a year of the introduction of SAP, according to the Annual Survey of Industries, 1991. 50 per cent of the factory employees who were supported by the National Textile Corporation are now unemployed. Now, new job opportunities are provided by the information technologies. The Information Technology (IT) profession has created an army of teleworkers.

In the rural areas, some states like Madhya Pradesh and Andhra Pradesh have generated massive employment in the IT sector which provide services in the fields of telemedicine, literacy programme and science education.

TABLE - 4

DAILY STATUS UNEMPLOYMENT RATE OF INDIAN WOMEN

Year	*Rural*	*Urban*
1972-73	11.2	13.7
1977-78	9.2	14.5
1983	9.0	11.0
1987-88	6.7	12.0

Source: Sarvekshana, Journal of National Sample Survey Organisation, Vol. IX, No. 4, April, 1988 and special No., Sept, 1990.

In the last decade, new recruitment in railways, banks and insurance companies has virtually stopped. Following the SAP, the GOI had declared 4 lakh workers as surplus in the nationalised banks. Out of 900,000 bank employees in India, 20 per cent are women. Plans for retrenchment in the Indian Railways, announced by the GOI, has made thousands of women typists, telephone operators, and clerks' jobless. The post and telegraph department has declared 200,000 workers as 'excess'. The women-dominated profession of nursing has been greatly affected by the SAP. Recruitment of nurses in the public hospitals of Maharashtra has decreased by 15%. Vacancies are not filled because of budgetary cuts in public health expenditure. Nursing was an occupation that had experienced virtually full-employment in India. This is now changing. One of the largest government hospitals in Bombay, the J.J. Hospital, has not filled 217 vacant staff-nurse posts. In the Employment State Insurance Scheme (ESIS) hospitals, 500 nurses have been declared surplus. Consequently, the workload of employed nurses has increased tremendously. According to the nursing council, the nurse: patient ratio is 1:4 but in these changed circumstances nurses work at a ratio of 1:15. Though there are 15 sanctioned beds per nurse, because of staff shortages they end up caring for 40-50 patients.

Reduction in educational funds by the government has created job-redundancy in the teaching profession, where women constitute 22.8 per cent of teachers. Encouragement to the private sector in the education has eroded the rights provided by the labour laws, as private institutions hire teachers on a contract basis and often terminate employment before staff becomes legally entitled to a permanent post.

In the organised sector of the overall economy and in private enterprise, the growth rate of employment during 1980-1990 was 2 per cent and 1.5 per cent respectively. Now it has been reduced to 0.60 per cent.

Employment Profile in Agriculture

The employment elasticity of output in agriculture has reduced to 0.64 per cent. Reduction of subsidy and credit in agriculture has affected small and marginal farmers negatively. Unemployment and underemployment in the rural areas have gained serious proportion because, in the NEP, schemes for rural development and rural industrialisation have not been given any importance. (Dholakia, 1992). As per Economic Survey 2000-2001, budgetary allocation under several employment schemes has to absorb the backlog of the unemployed and the new additions to the labour force.

Urban Unemployment

Between 1980 and 1990, the number of persons registered as unemployed in the Employment Exchange Bureaus of the country doubled. At present, India has 34 million registered unemployed and every year it increases by 12 per cent to 13 per cent. The number of women professional workers, such as executives, decision-makers in government departments, lawyers, doctors and engineers has increased and will continue to increase, but their strength in the overall economy is miniscule.

Recent Debates on the Part-time Work for Women

The government finds it difficult to dismiss permanent staff in public sector enterprises, as they are well organised, vocal, articulate and visible. To create an ideological justification for segmentation in the labour market on the grounds of gender relations, a debate on the issue of part-time work for women employees has begun. The argument in favour of it is that working women shoulder the burden of domestic duties as well as office-work, so a reduction of working hours will give them some relief. The majority of employed women have refused this offer feeling it will deprive them of promotion and responsible assignments, as well as providing a weapon to discriminate against women, by projecting women as "supplementary earners". Moreover, often the most strenuous part of work is commuting back and forth, and whether a person works part-time or full-time, the same amount of time and energy is spent commuting. The argument in favour of part-time work for women does not question the existing gender-based division of labour in the family. It throws the whole burden of child-care and housework on the individual woman. The long-standing demand for the socialisation of family functions to be supported by the state is also negated here. The women's movement in India has suggested that the best way to reduce the double burden for women is to inculcate the ethos of housework shared between both male and female members of family, the provision of cheap and safe eating facilities, child-care centres that provide both custodial care and developmental inputs for children, and better transport facilities, etc. (Gotoskar, 1989)

(vi) Environment and Forest Development

The most ironic impact of the SAP is on the environment and forest development. In last few years, the environment has become one of the most debated political issues. At the Rio Summit, government organisations (GOs) and non-government organisations (NGOs) from India made their presence felt by making passionate presentations. In reality, however, there has been an overall budgetary cut of 18 per cent for the environment and forest development.

Women are employed in wasteland development, social forestry and desert development programmes on a large scale. In these areas the budget has been cut by 23.5%. Smokeless 'chullas' have been enthusiastically promoted among rural and urban poor women because they are less harmful to women's health. The Government's budget for funding this project has reduced by 18.5 per cent.

In the context of a wood-fuel crisis, alternate energy resources like biogas and solar energy equipment gain major importance. The Government, however, has reduced the budget for these alternate energy sources by 26.3 per cent and 25.4 per cent respectively. Further funds allocated for research on alternate energy resources have been reduced by 26.3 per cent. On the one hand, a resource "crunch" is created where environmentally regenerative programmes are concerned, while on the other hand, millions of rupees are made available for controversial mega projects like the Sardar Sarovar, Dabhol Power Plant and Narmada Dam. The Morse Committee, noted environmentalists, most of the NGOs outside Gujarat, within India and internationally, have criticized the latter projects which are supported by the World Bank. This is because they will harm 240,000 people and create major environmental problems.

(vii) Female Headed Households (FHHs)

Feminisation of Poverty: Studies have shown that the burden of poverty falls more heavily on women than on men. Agarwal (1985) provided a review of literature on poverty, which shows the inequality in income and consumption levels between women and men. Of the total households, around 11 per cent are supported by women's income alone. In other words they are 'female-headed households' i.e. households supported totally by widows, single unmarried women, deserted or divorced women. The female headed households are the poorest of the poor. The combined effects on these households of price rises, reduced quotas for PDS, reductions in health-care facilities and educational facilities are deplorable. The fact that the FHH and poverty go hand in hand has been established by studies of Parthsarathy (1982) and Visaria (1985). In a study examining the incidence, characteristics and standards of living of FHHs in India, Visaria concluded that FHHs expenditure on survival needs was half that of male-headed households. Parthsarathy revealed that, among the poor households of every section of the agricultural community and the peasantry the proportion below the poverty line for females was considerably higher.

Children of the FHHs will suffer more from nutritional deficiency and inadequate primary health care facilities and cuts in expenditure for the primary and non-formal education. State support to FHHs had been one of the central demands of the women's movement since 1975. In the National Perspective Plan (NPP) for Women (1988-2000), the GOI had responded quite positively. But the SAP has worked against the objectives of the NPP.

(viii) Sex-tourism as an Integral Part of Globalisation

Sex-tourism in India has reached massive proportions with globalisation. A new type of publicity material for foreign tourists shows scantily dressed women waiting for tourists at the beach or in the foyer of five star hotels. Worsening economic conditions force young, poor and lower middle class women to become prostitutes - either for survival or by brute force.

In last two decades, rich men from the Middle-East had been

the main clients of the sex-industry. Now it is being geared up to accommodate an international clientele. (D'Cunha, 1991) Goa especially is being developed, for this purpose. The Industrial Development Bank of India (IDBI) is providing large loans to the hotel industry to develop land near the seaside in Goa. Yet when the women's group "Bailancho Saad" approached the IDBI for Differential Rate of Interest (D.R.I.) loans to start an employment generation programme for women in distress, they were told that there was no need for women's groups to initiate such programmes because tourism in Goa provided these women opportunities for work as bar-maids and entertainment workers (Bailancho Saad Newsletter, 1990). This subject needs serious examination. The available literature on Gender implications of SAP in other Asian, African and Latin American countries has also neglected this issue.

(ix) SAP V.S. SAARC Decade of the Girl Child (1991-2000)

In terms of educational opportunities and health care SAP has done great damage to female children. During the SAARC Decade of the Girl Child, millions of young girls were forced to do back-breaking work in hazardous and inhuman work-conditions.

India has the largest population of working girls who do not go to school. In 1988, there were 7.6 million girl-child labourers in India. In rural areas, their struggle to collect fuel, fodder and water will become sharper. In the urban areas, the number of girls working in the informal/unorganised sector for precarious wages has increased. Multinational corporations operating in the Free Trade Zones (FTZs) and the Export Processing Zones (EPZs) of India employ girls in their production units or hire them on piece-rate basis for home-based work. High production quotas create mental and physical stress among the workers. Chemical hazards, improper ventilation and lack of health and safety provision in the EPZs make these girl-workers victims of respiratory ailments, burns, ulcers, deteriorating eyesight. Young unmarried girls are of primary interest to the MNCs and TNCs, they will not fight for their rights because of family pressure to earn money. "Catch them in loop" is the motto of the MNCs and TNCs. Using girl-child labourers is the cheapest way to increase the profit margin. Corporate houses follow the same practice. Many of them have closed down their large units in industrial towns and cities, using instead tribal and rural girls and paying them on a piece-rate basis. Hindustan Lever Ltd, Godrej and multinational pharmaceutical industries have begun to use this employment strategy. (Deshpande, 1992).

Lessons of Latin America

The experience of Latin American countries which adopted SAP in the 1980s shows that in the name of 'flexible jobs' women's jobs in the formal sector were reduced. Further, because of reduction in the state welfare support, women had to depend on informal exchange network with neighbours and relatives for childcare, care of old and sick members of the family, etc.

The IMF-World Bank pressure to eliminate food subsidies in Latin American countries together with the reduction of real wages affected the consumption of the poor. (Sheahan, 1987). In the Amazon region, malnourished women outnumbered malnourished men in a ratio of 2:1. In Jamaica, women have suffered more from the cuts in health expenditure. In Brazil, female children get less food to eat, as family incomes drop. In Costa Rica large numbers of women have lost jobs.

With reduction of family incomes, the unpaid domestic work of women increased. A UNICEF study of Latin America showed that because of SAP, the decline in the standard of living had a great impact on women's lives as they struggled to balance their priorities for the survival of their households. "This means a permanent search for ways of resolving the problem of consumption from what to give the children for supper when there is no money in the house, to how to look after a sick person when the hospitals are in crisis (which means standing in long queues for attention or looking for other alternatives when hospital is not an option, difficulties in access to medical attention because of lack of money for travel, etc. The deterioration of domestic equipment is also a fact of daily life." (Carmen and Jelin, 1987).

African Experience

During the eighties several African countries adopted adjustment programmes in response to economic crisis reflected in decline in growth of GDP, budgetary deficits and balance of payments crises. To reduce public expenditure, a policy of rationalisation of the public sector was adopted. The industrial working class had to accept wage-freeze/wage-cuts. Urban women faced difficulties because of loss of jobs and erosion of real incomes.

Export-oriented production led to massive shift in crop-cultivation where production of subsistence crops, mainly managed by women, were replaced by the production of cash crops such as coffee, cocoa, fruits to serve the interests of the agro-business of Europe. This, not only rendered the mass of toiling women unemployed, but it also created food shortages leading to mass starvation. The women and children of Africa suffered the most. (Dennis, 1991).

In Zambia, the drop out rate of school-going girls increased drastically because of cuts in the government's educational expenditure. In Africa, generally the SAP has increased women's drudgery without increasing their income or decision-making power. (Jolly, 1987). The experience of Zimbabwe shows that the adverse effects of stabilization policies and SAP were countered by health care programmes that included free health care for poor people administered through provincial and district hospitals and rural clinics, immunisation programme, diarrhoea disease control programme, National Nutrition and Children's Supplementary Feeding Programme, The National Village Health Worker Programme. Although, overall government expenditure on health decreased after the IMF stabilization programme came under operation in Zimbabwe, the health profile of women and children improved because the Government increased the allocation of resources to preventive services and reduced the resources in medical services. (UNICEF, 1988)

Women Beneficiaries of the SAP

In India, upper-middle class, educated, city-based women with substantial salaries were very enthusiastic with the new budget as it gave more tax-exemption to them. These women - in the higher echelons of the public service, top executives in private business, local agents of foreign business, partners and consultants to foreign businesses, MNCs and TNCs, advertisement industries, owners of export industries (such as government, diamond, food-processing units who get benefits of the higher producer prices, low-wage policy and privileged access to state-provided infrastructure services and inputs) have definitely benefited from the SAP. A wide range of consumer goods from the international market have pleased these women (both middle class housewives and professional women). Through the SAP, they are given opportunities to take part in global conspicuous consumption. But, as the following table shows, these women are a minuscule proportion of the total population of women in India.

TABLE - 5
WOMEN AND MEN IN DIFFERENT PROFESSIONS IN INDIA

Profession	*No. of men*	*No. of women*
Advocates	18083	10493
Chartered Accountants	43700	934
Judges in High Court	380	11
Judges in Supreme Court	610	1
Indian Railways	157266	42974
Indian Administrative Services	4209	339
Indian Police Service	2418	21
Indian Foreign Service	480	53
Other Central Govt. Service	9939	571

Source: Women in India, Statistical Profile, Government of India, Delhi, 1988.

Thus austerity for majority of Indian women has existed side by side with higher luxury consumption of a few rich women.

Women Victims of the SAP

As already mentioned, the SAP has increased women's drudgery and hardship in the struggle for survival. The inflationary impact of the SAP reduces the purchasing power of a household which in turn increases unpaid labour of women. For example, buying cheaper food requires more time for procuring, cleaning and preparation. The unpaid labour of women for cooking, cleaning, caring and doing those chores which augment family resources (like collection of fuel, fodder, water, looking after livestock, poultry farming and processing of agricultural goods) is regarded as elastic by the IMF stabilisation and the World Bank SAP. The reduction in paid work for women makes women hunt for the cheapest resources for sustenance of the household. Casual employment of urban working class women in the organised manufacturing industry (textile is a glaring example) has forced thousands of women to eke out their subsistence through petty trading activities (officially known as an 'informal sector' occupation).

In Bangladesh, which falls under the category of the Enhanced Structural Adjustment Programme (ESAP), the increase in the price of rice resulted in a rise in the child mortality rate. The situation will become worse if the demand of GATT for 20 per cent cuts in agricultural production subsidies is accepted. (Economist, 17-10-92 "Free Trade with luck").

GATT's pressure to amend the Indian Patent Act that is based on process-patenting will make essential drugs very expensive. Poor women will find it impossible to avail themselves of medical facilities. Finally, ten case-studies based on the experiences of Botswana, Brazil, Chile, Ghana, Jamaica, Peru, Philippines, Korea, Sri Lanka and Zimbabwe suggest that unless the governments ensured compensatory policies in terms of public works, nutritional support, public education alongside the SAP, women suffered the most. (Cornia, Jolly, Stewart, 1988).

SAP vs. Democratic Rights of Toiling Women

It is very important to convince the policy makers working for national and the international bodies, that economic decision-making processes should be in tune with the democratic decision-making process in that the right to dignified life and bodily integrity of women must figure prominently.

In SAP, poor women are seen as just 'a mass' or a target of 'population control'. The tenth five year plan will try to achieve population stabilization with the help of a Net Reproduction Rate of 1 (NRR_1) i.e. a mother should be replaced by only 1 daughter. This concept has an inherent sexist bias as the projected birth-rate to achieve population stabilisation is 2.1 i.e. 1 daughter and 1.1 sons. To achieve it, a number of scientific technologies are available readily in the medical market of India such as amniocentesis, chorion-villai-biopsy, sex-preselection techniques. Moreover, in the post-emergency period, women have been the main target of the 'population control' programmes using hormone-based and long-acting harmful contraceptives. Targeting males for sterilisation operations proved politically counter-productive for the Congress government during the Emergency rule of the mid seventies.

Each year the budgetary provision for a 'population control' programme is increasing. Technologies which are more invasive, such as long-acting, hormone-based contraceptives, e.g. Net-O-En, Norplant, anti-pregnancy vaccines have been introduced. Poor women seeking employment in the state supported poverty alleviation programmes are coerced to accept this devices. In the 1991-1992 budget, the only item concerning women for which the allocation of funds had increased was 'population control'. Substantial sums have been provided by USAID to encourage the use of controversial contraceptives like Norplant/Net-O-En/Depo-provera, banned in most Western countries.

'Population control' has been a crucial concern of NEP-SAP. Poor women are blamed for the environmental crisis by breeding like 'cats' and 'rats'. No-one asks the policy-makers, to what extent top-down population control programmes, which violate the basic human rights of Indian women, can be justified? Further, by victimising the victims of a patriarchal class society and by focusing narrowly on the 'population explosion', we ignore other fundamental causes of environmental crises, such as industrial toxic waste, chemical fertilizers, nuclear armaments, space research programmes, over-consumption by the affluent in both the first as well as the third world. Out of the total Indian population of 844 million, 240 million Indians have a purchasing power equivalent to that of Europe. (The Economist, June, 1991). And, of course, there are first world countries where the population growth rate has declined, yet the environmental conditions have deteriorated.

The SAP is increasingly forcing working women into the unorganised sector, thus depriving them of their trade-union rights. By doing this, the women fall outside protective labour laws such as The Maternity Benefits Act (1961), The Employees State Insurance Scheme, Factories Act (1948), Equal Remuneration Act (1976), The Bombay Shops and Establishment Act (1984), The Plantation Labour Act and the Child Labour (Prohibition and Regulation) Act, 1976. In any discussions of SAP, these issues must to be considered.

Dissenting Voices

Between 1947-1975, Indian economy attained 3.5 per cent annual rate of growth (economists called it a Hindu rate of growth), between 1976 and 1991, it was 5 per cent and in the post SAP period of 1992-2001 the Indian economy achieved 6.5 per cent annual rate of growth. (Basu, 2001). Still, The SAP has been criticised not only by individual academics and trade-unionists but also by the UN also. UNDP Report 2000 had recommended SAP with human face and avoid the past mistakes as a result of SAP.

"No adjustment policy is acceptable which allows children to be sacrificed for the sake of financial stability. Yet it has happened, and it need not happen." (UNICEF: The state of the World's Children, 1987). Based on the findings of ten case-studies of the impact of adjustment policies in Botswana, Brazil, Chile, Ghana, Jamaica, Peru, Philippines, Korea, Sri Lanka, Zimbabwe, UNICEF declared that most of the measures under the SAP are 'not only unnecessary', but 'economically inefficient' also. (Jolly, 1987).

Articles in the World Bank's own publication concerning this issue have been critical of SAP because of its accent on cuts in expenditure on nutrition, health and educational level. (Streetan, 1987). On 18th August 1992, an appeal to Members of Parliament (MPs) by noted economists, trade unionists, social scientists, Media-persons and social activists, stated that "the policies currently being followed will lead to greater concentration and centralisation of economic power and facilitate India's integration into the world economy on humiliating and iniquitous terms. They go against the trend towards decentralisation of our polity. They will further polarise as never before an already unequal, divided and strife-torn society. They can only weaken the basis of our democracy and strengthen authoritarian trends. India because of its democratic legitimacy, history, geography, size and population, has an acknowledged potential for pursuing endogenous and relatively independent development even more so than Russia and China. The North knows that the undermining of this Indian potential will be a decisive blow against the South as whole."

Safety-net Approach

There is a section of intelligentsia and development workers who accept inevitability of the SAP and recommend a 'safety-net approach' to protect the interest of vulnerable sections of society. Economists, social-scientists and demographers, who have made pioneering contributions in the field of development policies affecting women, submitted a memorandum to the Finance Minister about this. UNICEF and other international agencies have sponsored nutritional support programmes. Aid organisations such as Oxfam, Save the Children Fund and Health Action International are supporting education, public health, rural water and sanitation programmes. The International Labour Organization supports food for work programmes. Non-government organizations supported by smaller funding agencies are organizing employment generation programmes and drought relief programmes.

This safety net is inadequate to cope up with the damage done by macro economic policies that lead to large scale retrenchment of workers, the withdrawal of health-care and educational facilities, worsening environmental crisis. Moreover, the macro policies have a global dimension. What can an individual country do in this situation? This question has been asked in different forms (Frank, 1984; Hayter of Watson, 1984). One-sided propaganda about inevitability of SAP needs to be countered with data on the actual experience of the SAP in different countries. On the basis of such concrete empirical work, region-specific solutions must be sought ensuring ecologically sustainable growth with 'social justice' and 'enhanced participatory democracy'. It is sad that these two concepts never appear in those documents circulated by advocates of SAP.

It is very important to place the economic crisis and the NEP-SAP within the matrix of the political economy of India and to analyze their repercussions on internal socio-political and cultural conditions in the short and long run. Austerity measures are opposed by the majority of toiling masses and also by a large section of intelligentsia in the third world.

In India this dissent has been expressed in public by the women's groups - in leaflets, an open letter to the Finance Minister by Forum for Women and Politics and on 8th March 1992 in rallies in different towns and cities of India. The forthcoming National Conference of Women's Movement in India will concentrate on gender implications of SAP.

In most of the countries where SAP has been implemented, democratic institutions are almost non-existent. Then what happens to dissenting voices? Commenting on the African situation Sawyer (1990) states, "It is hardly surprising that military regimes and authoritarian civilian governments whether of the one-party, no party or multiparty variety-provide the political conditions most conducive to the maintenance of the current crop of SAPs in Africa."

In Latin America the situation is more or less the same. The regimes in Asia, Africa and Latin America resort to ruthless repression when the urban and poor working class raise their voice against price-rises, unemployment and cuts in public services. Democratic institutions in India, especially the print-media and the plural politics have allowed open debate on this issue from which, it is hoped, a developmental model will emerge that is ecologically sensitive, women friendly and ensures sustainable development with distributive justice.

References

Agarwal, Bina (1985) "Women Poverty and Agricultural Growth", Journal of Peasant Studies, Vol. 13, No. 4, July.

AWRAN (1985) The Alternative Asian Report on the Impact of the UN Decade for Women, Asian Women's Research and Action Network, Philippines.

Banerjee, Nirmala (1977) "Exports and the Indian Economy", Economic and Political Weekly, Bombay, Vol. X11, No. 15 16 April.

Banerjee, Nirmala (1992) *Indian Women in a Changing Industrial Scenario*, Sage Publications, London.

Basu, Kaushik (2001) "India and the Global Economy-Role of Culture, Norms and Beliefs", Economic and Political Weekly, Vol. Xxxvi, No 40, October 6.

Batliwale, Srilata (1984) "Rural Energy Situation - Consequences for Women's Health", Bombay, Socialist Health Review, Vol. 1, No. 2.

D'cunha, Jean (1991) Prostitution in India, Joint Women's Programme, Delhi.

Dennis, Carolyne (1991) "'Constructing a Career' Under Conditions of Economic Crisis and Structural Adjustment: The Survival Strategies on Nigerian Women: in Haleh Afsher (ed) Women, Development and Survival in the Third World, Longman.

Desai, Neera and Vibhuti Patel (1990) *Indian Women-Change and Challenge*, Popular Publications, Bombay, See Introduction.

Deshpande, Sudha (1992) "New Economic Policy and Future of Indian Women-Employment Duplications", Seminar paper, Dept. of Economics, SNDT Women's University, Bombay.

Dholakia, Jitendra (1992) "New Economic Policy and the Toiling Masses of India", C.G. Shah Memorial Lecture Ahmedabad, 15th August.

Frank, A. G (1984) "Economic Crisis, Export Promotion and Political Repression in the Third World" in Ngo Manh-lam (ed): *Unreal Growth-Critical Studies in Asian Development*, Vol. 1, p 54, Delhi-Hindustan Publishing Corporation.

Gotoskar, Sujata (1989) "Part Time Work for Women, Economic and Political Weekly, Vol. XXIV, No. 46, 18th November.

Harriss, John (1982): "Character of an Urban Economy, 'small scale' production and labour market in Coimbtore", Economic and Political Weekly, Vol. XVII, Nos. 23-24.

Hayter, Terassa and C. Watson (1984): *Aid-Rhetoric and Reality*, London of Sydney, Pluto Press.

IMF Survey, (1992): "Asian Developing Countries Record Impressive Growth" - A Publication of the International Monetary Fund, Washington D.C., Vol. 21, No. 11, May 25, p. 172.

Jolly, Richard (1987) "Women's Needs and Adjustment Policies in Developing Countries, Women's Development Group of the OECD, Paris.

Krishnaraj, Maithreyi (1988) *Women and Development*, Dept. of Sociology, SNDT Women's University, Bombay.

Mitter, Swasti (1988) *Common Fate, Common Bond*, Pluto Press, London.

Moser, Carolyn (1978): "Informal Sector or Petty Commodity Production. Dualism or Dependence in Urban Development?" World Development, Vol. 6, Nos. 9/10.

Parthsarathy, G (1982): "Rural Poverty and Female Heads of Household-Need for Qualitative Analysis", Paper presented at Technical seminar on 'Women, Work and Employment', Delhi, .

Patel, I.G. (1987): On Taking India into the Twenty-first century (New Economic Policy in India)", Modern Asian studies, 21,2, pp. 209-231.

Patel, Vibhuti (1992): "NEP's Gender Implications," Business and Political Observer, Bombay 4 July and Paris-International View Point, September.

Research Unit for Political Economy (RUPE) (1991) Aspects of Indian Economy, July-Sept.

Sawyerr, Akilgpa (1990): *The Political Dimension of structural Adjustment Programmes in Sub-Saharan Africa*, Ghana University Press, Accra.

Sheahan, John (1987) *Pattern of Development in Latin America-Poverty*, Repression and Economic Strategy, Princeton University Press, USA.

Shramshakti (1988) Report of the National commission on Self-employed Women and Women in the Unorganized Sector, Government of India, Delhi.

Vanayak, Achin (1990) *The Painful Transition, Bourgeois Democracy in India*, Verso, U.K. Visaria, Pravin and Leela Visaria (1985): "Indian Households with Female Heads – Their Incidence, Characteristics and levels of living", in Devaki Jain and Nirmala Banerjee –Women and Poverty - The Tyranny of Household, Vikas Publishing House, New Delhi.

WGAs (1992) - Working Group on Alternative Strategies, India, 1992. India. Bombay 4 July and Paris-International View Point, September.

Three

Women's Issues: Economic Parameters

There is a need to examine women's issues affecting their material life from the perspective of social movements of the last two decades. Massive changes in the course of economic development have sharpened the polarization of economic interests among various contending economic forces with, mostly, mutually exclusive, and at times, complimentary interests. Escalating violence against women, rising prostitution among dalit, tribal and poor women, increasing proportion of female-headed households in the areas of economic, social and political tensions have made it imperative to understand women's survival struggle from the perspective of collective wisdom of the women's movement (WM). During the seventies WM was highlighting marginalisation of women in the economy.[1] This approach is known as 'WID'-Women in Development. Three major findings of Towards Equality (Status of Women in India) Report, 1974, which sensitized the decision-makers of our country were:

- Continuously declining sex ratio of women.
- Declining work-participation of women.
- High rate of mortality and morbidity among women.

During the eighties, women's groups made an effort to integrate women in the economy. But the means of production, exchange and distribution being controlled by men allowed women very limited space to evolve a development alternative with women (DAWN).[2] In this approach, articulate-urbane-highly educated and politically connected women got prominence as the spokespersons of women from the marginalised section. In this period, the Indian economy was most ferociously attacking the survival base of the mass of poor women in the rural, tribal and urban areas.[3] While women employees in the white-collar occupations, women professionals such as lawyers, doctors, scientists, educationists, teachers, chartered accountants, women employees in the central and state government as well as in the corporate world and financial institutions managed to get some economic gains. This decade witnessed some of the most militant mass mobilizations of women on wide range of issues – water, drought, caste riots, communal tensions, police-brutality against forest people, agricultural labourers, industrial workers, white-collar women employees problems about promotion and transfer, sexual harassment at workplace, harassment for dowry and bride price, witch hunting, widow burning, sexual violence against women, coercion in the family planning programmes, selective abortion of female foetuses, female infanticide, child-care facilities, woes of women workers in the development schemes supported by the state and central governments as well as by the international aid agencies and the voluntary organisations.[4] Several alliances and collaborative ventures of this period, engendered trust among different stake groups dealing with these issues from different positions of power. This approach is known as WAD-Women and Development. This approach focussed on a patriarchal control over women's sexuality, fertility and labour. In this phase, women's groups established rapport with pro-women individuals (men and women) in the government, the state apparatus, the criminal justice system, the legal system, the political parties and the professional bodies. The decade of nineties is marked by an approach of Gender and Development (GAD). Here the focus is on the power relations determined as a result of interplay of complex class, caste, ethnicity, religion, races and gender. This is an era of PARTNERSHIP with a clear-cut understanding that women constitute half of the world population, 2/3 of the world's workforce and get only 1/10th of the world's income and own only 1/100th of the world's wealth.[5] With these resource-base women decision-makers will have to empower the mass of toiling women who are struggling to survive.

Nearly 1/3 of Indian women and 1/6 of Indian girls are a part of the labour force. In the low productivity segments of the economy, the choices before the girls have been child-marriage, child- prostitution or child-labour (CM, CP, and CL). Grooming of girls in different parts of the country determines whether they would be part of the SS side of the CM, CP or CL or grow as empowered women. Studies on this process from the political economy perspective are handful but they throw light on the areas of active intervention by the state, civil society and the social movements.

TABLE - 1
LABOUR FORCE IN 1995 IN INDIA

Workers age group 15-64		*Average Annual Growth rate of the Labour Force*		*Labour Force Participation rate in 1995*			
				Age Group 15-64		*Age Group 10-19*	
Male	*Female*	*1965-1995*	*1995-2025*	*Male*	*Female*	*Male*	*Female*
26 Crores	8.4 Crores	2.1 %	1.6 %	90 %	31 %	30 %	16 %

Source: World Development Report, 1995.

National Campaign Against Child Labour has carved out phase-wise programme of rehabilitation of child-labour and integrating them into the formal/ non-formal educational institutions. Homes for street-children have been established in the cities like Delhi, Banglore, Bombay, Ahmedabad, and Calcutta. Public interest litigation cases against inhuman conditions in the rescue homes, by social organisations have forced the iron wall of secrecy fall. Employers with modern outlook have realised that without healthy and educated\skilled labour-force, they can't attain high productivity. But, in spite of this awareness, condition of girl child labour is deplorable. In match industry in Shivkashi, out of 45000 children, 90 per cent are girls.[6] Highest numbers of girl-children are sold either as child-brides or as bonded labourers or as child-sex workers in the drought-prone areas.[7] Brutalisation of girl-victims of CM-CP-CL is more pronounced because their male counterparts have to face control of their labour and sexuality while girl children have to bear multiple burdens of control of sexuality, fertility and labour and consequences of teenage pregnancy are faced by girls alone. Sociological studies examining material basis of this phenomenon have helped to sensitize the professional bodies to make the state intervention more effective.[8]

TABLE - 2
WORK PARTICIPATION RATE, ENROLMENT AND DISCONTINUATION OF GIRLS EDUCATION IN RURAL INDIA

STATES	*WPR*	*Enrolment*	*Discontinuation*
Kerala	0.5	98.0	2.0
Himachal Pradesh	0.6	90.0	2.2
Uttar Pradesh	0.8	53.4	5.6
North East Region	1.0	76.3	4.1
Rajasthan	1.1	41.9	6.6
Bihar	1.2	51.2	4.1
Haryana	2.3	72.3	4.6
West Bengal	2.3	65.1	6.5
Punjab	3.0	84.4	6.1
Madhya Pradesh	4.1	55.8	9.0
Orrisa	4.2	63.4	9.3
Gujarat	5.0	74.5	9.5
Maharashtra	5.8	82.0	8.4
Tamil Nadu	7.5	84.3	14.8
Karnataka	7.8	75.1	9.1
Andhra Pradesh	10.3	73.8	12.1
Rural India	**3.5**	**64.8**	**7.6**

Source: NCAER, 1994. Taken from Seminar no. 464, April 1998.

The above table reveals that the enrolment ratio is much lower in the BIMARU states, which are known as the lowest literacy (for women and girls) states. States known for child prostitution, right from the colonial days to the present, have been Himachal Pradesh, Rajasthan, Gujarat (tribal belt), West Bengal and North Eastern states, Orissa, Kerala (Malabar region) and Goa. Percentage of Girl-children involved in the agrarian and non-agrarian economic activities has been above 5 per cent in Gujarat, Maharashtra, Tamilnadu, Karnataka and Andhra Pradesh. In the segments of the economy where the adult population enjoys food-security and better quality of life as well as commitment towards women's development, the girl children can easily avoid the vicious circle of CM-CP-CL. Girls from the female headed households (i.e. households which are headed by unmarried, divorced, widowed and deserted women) are the most vulnerable in this regards.[9] In the last two decades of women's movement, they have been empowered through collective efforts of the women's movement.

TABLE - 3
WORK PARTICIPATION RATE, 1991

	Total Workers	*Main workers*	*Marginal Workers*
Total	38	34.2	3.3
Male	52	51	0.6
Female	22.3	16	6.2
Rural	40	36	4.3
Male	53	52	0.7
Female	27	19	8.0
Urban	30	30	0.7
Male	49	49	0.4
Female	9	8	1.0

Source: Tata Service Limited, Department of Economics and Statistics, 1995, p. 46.

In the 1980s women constituted 14-17 per cent of the total work force, within a decade, it has risen to 22%. Due to globalisation, work participation of women and young girls have increased drastically in the industrial sector. Recruitment of women in the electronic, garment, diamond – gems and jewelry, dairy, food processing, horticulture and floriculture sectors have multiplied. Availability of home-based work for women has opened more avenues for women of all class backgrounds to use their abilities, skills and education more productively. Home-based work ensures flexitime, secured environment and freedom from travelling to the mass of women with domestic responsibilities such as child-care, nursing of the old, sick and disabled members of the family.

New approach towards recruitment, where on the job training for skill upgradation is provided to the new entrants, is conducive for human resource develcpment. Domestic work is the only area where deskilling and cabbagification of the workforce is the highest because the domestic worker loses his/her verbal skills, traditional skills of his/her occupation and at the same time, does not gain any new skills for upward mobility. In the last two decades, women's organisations/ rescue homes working for the women victims of violence in the developing countries have become the main recruitment centres for domestic workers. Domestic work does not require any investment for human resource development. Moreover, due to its lowest opportunity cost in the economy, the labour concentration camp approach can be effectively utilised to control the workers. It is the most feudal sector of the economy that demands wage-labour-contract relations aided by development inputs of education, skill development, assertiveness training and the government initiative.[10] Women's involvement (as owner cultivators, agricultural workers and unpaid family workers who augment resources of the household by collection of fuel, fodder and water and looking after the live-stock, poultry and kitchen-garden) in the economic activities of the agrarian sector is the highest.[11]

TABLE - 4

ESTIMATES OF EMPLOYMENT OF WOMEN IN THE PUBLIC AND PRIVATE SECTORS

Year	*Public Sector*			*Private Sector*			*Total public + Pvt. %*
	Lakh Persons		*% of the total*	*Lakh Persons*		*% of the total*	
	Female	*Total*		*Female*	*Total*		
1990	23	188	12	14	76	18	14
1991	24	191	12	14	77	19	14
1992	24	192	13	15	78	19	14
1993	25	193	13	16	79	20	15
1994	26	194	13	16	79	20	15
1995	26	193	13	17	81	20	15

Source: Economic Survey, 1995-96, Government of India, Delhi.

The above table reveals that women constituted 15 per cent of the workforce in the public and private sector establishments. 1/8th of the workforce in the public sector and 1/5th of the workforce in the private sector are composed of women, majority of whom happen to be in the lowest rung of the hierarchy. More and more women are joining public and private sectors as accountants, computer operators, administrators and public relations persons. Only 6 per cent of the workforce in these sectors is part of the organised sector workforce i.e. only 6 women employees out of 100, in the public and private sector enjoy benefits of the labour laws. The rest are casual/contract workers who face insecurity of job. In a highly segmented private and public sector labour markets, women with connection, recommendation or qualification only, can manage to enter, as in these sectors women are expected to handle equipment/property of the establishments. In other words, these are employers' markets. One or two women with efficiency + and with readiness to work in the midst of extremely adverse circumstances manage to acquire top positions in these sectors.

Women in the Informal Sector

The law of jungle prevails in the informal sector market. 94 per cent of women workers work in this sector.[12] This sector is marked by the lowest wages, uncertainty of work, seasonal variations, interpersonal and state violence and backbreaking work, occupational hazards.[13] Double standard of sexual morality coupled with utter helplessness of women make them more vulnerable in the informal sector market and force them to seek an illusionary protection from men.[14] Culture of sex-segregation and limited access to familial and societal resources force them to remain in female ghettos.[15] Most of the political parties have neglected this sector. The state apparatus has brutalised and criminalised this sector. Only social movements' sphere-headed by non-party political formations have done careful examination of their problems with participatory action research perspective.[16] Their advocacy on the plight of women workers and girl-child labour has helped build public opinion in favour of social justice. Large NGOs (Non-government Organisations) of women such as Self Employed Women's Association (SEVA- Ahmedabad), Annapurna (Bombay), Working Women's Forum (Madras) and Sakti (Banglore) have been able to provide employment generation activities in a subsistence sector, micro-credit facilities and defense mechanism to combat day-to-day harassment from petty officials and the local bullies.

Women artisans' cooperatives networking under the umbrella of DASTKAR has ensured craft-women in the subsistence sector to pursue their traditional art and crafts without harassment and control of the local and the city-based male-agents. Women artisans involved in family-based work of production of leather-goods, pottery, handicrafts, handloom, bamboo products, wood-work, ready-made food-items, dairy products, live-stock-raising, floriculture find themselves increasingly vulnerable because men have total control over the cash nexus in the context of erosion of kinship-based support network. To some extent, the women's organisations tried to fill in the gap on an ad-hoc manner. For the long-term and sustained support to the artisan class proper networking between the dependent sector and the mainstream market is needed. While undertaking any employment generation activities in the community, the social workers and activists are invariably confronted with eight issues concerning gender-justice—

- Domestic violence
- Alcoholism among men and in some communities among women
- Drug abuse among men and boys, adolescent girls and housewives
- Psychological atmosphere conducive for child prostitution of both varieties- male child prostitution and female child prostitution
- Polygamy among upwardly mobile men and polyandry among upwardly mobile women and the resultant family feuds around the issues such as restitution of conjugal rights, rights over parental or matrimonial home, share in property, land rights, custody of child/ children, maintenance for a divorced wife, alimony.[17]
- Deplorable condition of female-headed households as subcontract workers who are controlled by men of the community.
- Distorted use of customary laws to disempower women by the patriarchs of different castes, religions and tribes.
- Misuse of literacy by the relatively more educated segments for super exploitation of the rest of the community members.

These octopacy clutches have demoralised most of the women activists to work in the community. They find it more fruitful to work from a secure and neutral place where highly motivated, intellectually versatile and professionally equipped men and women gather to discuss the area development issues. Collective wisdom generated through such discourses can be disseminated to concerned authorities so that effective policy intervention and / or changes in the policy can be ensured.

Handloom and Khadi units have enjoyed the patronage from the state since independence. The pattern of power relations in this sector is not different from the rest of the unorganised sector where the caste-based kinship-networks play predominant role to maintain statuesquo. Report on Socio-economic Conditions of Women Workers in Selected Handloom and Khadi Units in Gujarat, 1994[18] reveals that 25 per cent of them were unmarried/ widowed/ divorced/ separated. 58 per cent of them were illiterate. As compared with Handloom industry, Khadi industry provided more opportunities for home-based work for women. In the handloom units, majority of women weavers were from S.C., while in the cooperative sector, only 39 per cent of women weavers were from S.C. Unlike in the Northeast, tribal women of Gujarat don't do weaving in the handloom units. Pattern of women's employment is not different in the Khadi Industry of Gujarat. Predominantly SC women are employed as weavers but women from all communities are employed as spinners, weavers and pooni-makers.

None of the evaluation reports on KVIC and handloom industry has made a systematic critique of highly labour intensive, low productivity and low-income model of women's development, which is averse to science and technology (S & T), and Research and Development (R & D). This economic model can be termed as Development model for the helpless lot. The younger generation of the working class males ridicules this approach by calling it Majboori ka naam Gandhi. It was O.K. during the colonial regime as the British rule had put several constraints on the indigenous economic development. But, now things have changed. Abolition of license-permit raja, multilateral trade agreements, management cadre with modern outlook and our pool of scientifically and technologically advanced human resource can help the process of humanization of KVIC and other occupations in the informal sector.

TABLE - 5
WOMEN WORKERS BY INDUSTRIAL CATEGORIES – 1991

	Industrial categories	*Millions*	*%*
Primary Sector			
I	Cultivators	22	34.0
II	Agriculture Labourers	28	45.0
III	Livestock, forestry, fishing, plantations and allied activities	1	1.6
IV	Mining and Quarrying	0.2	0.3
Secondary Sector			
V	Manufacture, processing, servicing of which in household Industry	4.7	7.5
VI	Construction	0.4	0.7
Tertiary Sector			
VII	Trade and Commerce	1.4	2.2
VIII	Transport, storage and communication	0.2	0.3
IX	Other services	5.2	8.3
Total Main Workers		62.9	96.3
Total Marginal Workers		2.4	3.7
Total Workers		65.3	100.0

Source: Census of India, 1991.

Increasing number and intensity of ethnic, caste and communal tensions have made it imperative for the local self-government bodies, state and central governments to make strategic intervention to secularise factor, labour and product markets. Women decision-makers need to take affirmative action to counter gender-based segmentation in the local, regional and global markets. To achieve this goal, we need more women in the local self-government bodies. At present, women's participation in the mainstream political and economic bodies is quite limited. In 1995, women constituted only 2 per cent of total administrators and managers, 21 per cent of professional and technical workers, 6.1 of the government employees, 4.2 per cent of the ministerial level and 6.3 per cent of the subministerial level staff.[19] They occupied 7.3 per cent of seats in the parliament and had 19.2 per cent of share in the total earned income of our country.[20] It is difficult to survive in these decision-making bodies without intellectual versatility, connections and protection.

The highest number and percentage of Indian women workers are agricultural labourers and the second highest are the cultivators. Rural women augment family resources by free collection of fuel, fodder and water.[21] Agricultural mechanisation has relieved women of drudgery prone tasks of agricultural and allied occupations in some parts of Punjab, Gujarat and Maharashtra. Intellegentia of these states is bringing all modern technologies from the industrialised western world. Hundreds of writings of women's studies scholars have given an impression that high work participation of women as agricultural laborers and cultivators per se makes them economically independent as they are supposed to be part of social production. But, careful examination of nature of women's work-participation in the agrarian sector has revealed that men are controlling capital-intensive cash crop cultivation and women are left to look after labour intensive subsistence sector. "Ignoring women's role in agriculture in designing agriculture extension, input and credit policies leads to lower real income of women and may shift household resource allocation away from food-intake and nutrition of women and children."[22] Children earn nutritionally when women earn more compared to men.[23] Policy makers need to understand that changes in gender-specific control of income translate into changes in expenditures. Men spend a greater proportion of the income they earn on goods such as alcohol, cigarettes, gambling, status consumer goods and 'female companionship'. By contrast, women spend 65 per cent of their incomes for basic necessities of the households such as food, clothes, medicine, etc.[24] Women's rights organisations all over the world have demanded specific policies targeting macro economic factors as well as an individual household are needed to alter intra-household distribution of income so that supply and expenditure on food –items increases and on the other hand production of and expenditure on alcohol and tobacco products reduces. Networking of like-minded gender-aware policy-makers, politicians, legal experts, economic advisers with expertise on monitory and fiscal policies as well as agrarian and industrial development, industrialist and scientist with enlightened outlook towards food processing industry and rational use of biotechnology can change the scenario of perennial food shortage among poverty groups.

Meaningful Indicators of Women and Development

Comparative data of 130 countries regarding gender-related development index (GDI) reveals that gender-equality does not depend entirely on the income level of society. The human development approach which focuses on demographic, health, educational and human rights profiles have revealed that there is an urgent need to reexamine this approach by conducting participatory action research and rapid rural appraisal not by social scientists alone, but in collaboration with other professionals such as scientists, doctors- occupational health and safety experts, engineers and lawyers who believe that like them, citizens from subsistence sector also have right to enjoy fruits of modern science and technology in terms of food security, safe transport, clean environment, secure housing and healthy life. India ranks 103rd in GDI and 104th in the HDI as, the Indian women enjoy nearly 1/5th of the total earned income, life expectancy of 60.4 years and 35.2 per cent adult literacy rate and combined primary, secondary and tertiary Gross enrollment ratio (GER) of 45.8. While their male counterparts enjoy 4/5th of the earned income, life expectancy of 60.3 years, 63.7 per cent adult literacy rate and combined primary, secondary and tertiary GER of 63.8. HDI for India is 0. 398 and GDI for India is 0.401. There is a gender gap of 0.003. [25] As compared to their male counterparts women in India have higher life expectancy because women from the middle and upper classes live in a secure environment, produce one or two children and control food (kitchen) of the household.

References

S, Murthy (2001), *Women and Employment*, RBSA Publishers, Jaipur.

Subhashini Mahapatra (2002), *Women's Participation in Labour Force*, Rajat Publications, New Delhi.

Footnotes

1. Pioneering work in these regards has been by Esther Boserup (1970), *Women's Role in Economic Development*, Aberdeen George Allen and Unwin, London.
2. Geeta Sen and Caren Grown (1985), *Development Alternative with Women*, DAWN Network, Monthly Review Press, 1987.
3. Shirin Kudchetkar and Sabiha Al-Issa (eds.), *Women Against Violence-Violence Against Women*, Pencraft International, Delhi, 1998.
4. Documentary evidences of the mass mobilisations of women are available in the issues (1985 onwards) of Economic and Political Weekly (Bombay), Social Action (Delhi), Mainstream (Delhi), Seminar (Delhi), Manushi (Delhi) and Samya Shakti(Delhi), Lokayan Bulletin (Delhi).
5. This data is culled out from the country reports submitted during Women's Decade (1975-1985) to The United Nations, INSTRAW and UNIFEM, New York, 1990. Conceptual basis of the same lies in the debate around paid and unpaid work, wage-work and housework (cooking, cleaning and caring), unpaid family labour of rural women which augments family resources such as collection of fuel, fodder and water, invisiblised work of women and girls who are working for family\ households businesses among the artisan classes such as potters, weavers, handloom and powerloom owners, lacemakers, brassworkers, carpet industry, owner cultivators.
6. Neera Burra Born to Work-, *Child Labour in India*, Oxford University Press, Delhi, 1997.
7. Girl Child- A Status Report, UNICEF, SAARC Decade for a Girl Child (1990-2000 A.D.), Delhi.
8. Jean D'cunha *Prostitution* Joint Women's Programme, Delhi, 1990.
9. (a). Pradeep Kumar Panda: "Female Headship, Poverty and Child Welfare-A Study of Rural Orissa", Economic and Political Weekly, October 25, 1997, WS-73.
   (b) John Hoddinott and Lawrence Haddad "Does Female Income Share Influence Household Expenditures? Evidence from Cote D' Ivoire," Oxford Bulletin of Economics and Statistics, Vol. 57, No.1, 1995, pp. 305-9049.
10. Domestic Workers' Union of Sevaniketan, SPARC (Bombay) and Molkarin Sangathana (Pune and Nagpur) have done pioneering work of articulating needs and demands of domestic workers. Documentary evidences based on the survey reports on the domestic workers have appeared in Labour File, Delhi, 1998.
11. Country reports of the developing countries to the UN-INSTRAW reiterate this fact.
12. Graphic description of labour processes and labour relations in this sector is available in Shramshakti Report (1988) by Committee on Self Employed Women and Women in the Unorganised Sector appointed by Government of India.
13. Nirmala Banerjee (ed.) *Indian Women in a Changing Industrial Scenario- Indo-Dutch Studies on Development Alternatives*, Sage Publications, New Delhi, 1991.
14. Johanna Lessinger, "Work and Modesty: The Dilemma of Women Market

Traders in Madras". In Leela Dube and Rajani Palriwala (ed.) Structures and Strategies- Women's Work and Family, Women and Household in Asia-3, Sage Publications, 1990, pp.129-150.

15. Haleh Afshar (Ed) *Women, Work and Ideology in the Third World*, Tavistock Publications, London, 1985.
16. (a) Jana Everett and Mira Savara: *Women and Organisations in Informal Sector*, Himalaya Publishing House, Bombay, 1994. :
    (b) Rohini P.H., Sujata S.V. and Neelam C. *My Life is One long Struggle- Women, Work, Organisation and Struggle*, Pratishabda, Belgaum, 1983.
    (c) Sujata Gotoskar (Ed) Struggles of Women at Work, Vikas Publishing House and IAWS, Delhi, 1992.
    (d) Nandita Shah, Sujata Gotoskar, Nandita Gandhi and Amrita Chhachhi, "Structural Adjustment, Feminisation of Labour Force and Organisational Strategies", Economic and Political Weekly, Vol. 29, No. 13, April 30, 1994, WS 39- WS 48.
17. (a) Jyoti Gupta "Class Relations, Family Structure and Bondage of Women" in Leela Dube and Rajni Palriwala Structures and Strategies- Women, Work and Family, Sage Publications, 1990, pp. 129-150.
    (b) Vasudha Dhagamwar: *Personal Laws in India*, Indian Law Institute, Delhi, 1990.
    (c) Vasudha Dhagamwar, " Obstacles to Empowerment of Women- Culture, Custom and Religion" in Sites of Change- The Structural Context for Empowerment of Women in India edited by N. Rao, L. Kurup, R, Sudarshan, Friedrich Ebert Stiftung, N. Delhi, 1996.
18. This report is published by Shram Bureau, Shram Mantralaya, Bharat Sarkar, Chandigarh/Simla.
19. Human Development Report, UNDP, OUP, 1996.
20. Human Development Report, UNDP, OUP, 1995.
21. Bina Aggarwal "Neither Sustenance nor Sustainability- Agricultural Strategies, Ecological Degradation and Indian Women in Poverty" in Bina Aggarwal (Ed) Structures of Patriarchy- State, Community and Asia, Kali For Women, Delhi, 1991, pp. 83-120.
22. Shubh K. Kumar "The Economics and Politics of Food Policies", International Food Policy Research Institute, Washington D.C., 1994. p .101.
23. Cheryl Doss and Ben Senaver " Strengthening Agricultural Resource Policy Through Intrahousehold Analysis- Discussion", International Food Policy Research Institute, Washington D.C., 1994,p. 1227.
24. Several studies by International Labour Organisation published in International Labour Review have corroborated this fact. Recent study of Cote D' Ivoire provides systematic analysis on the subject. See John Hoddinott and Lawrence Haddad, "Does Female Income Share Influence Household Expenditure Evidence From Cote D' Ivoire", Oxford Bulletin of Economics and Statistics, Vol. 57, No. 1, 1995, pp. 305-9049.
25. Human Development Report, UNDP, OUP, Bombay, 1995, p. 33.

Four

New Social Movements and Gender in India

Lessons for Feminist Economics

In the eighties, sharp polarisation took place in the new social movements due to gender issues. Entry of gender-blind male professionals who controlled powerful positions, political agenda (which deliberately invisiblised women's concerns) and finances made competent women (who were *deliberately made to do the tasks which would deskill them*) feel powerless. Women experts and the activists were treated as worker bees and/or comfort women without decision-making power, dignity and recipients of crumbs thrown at them by the accountants of the funding agencies or by their male leaders. Democratic rights movement targeted only state violence and maintained conspiracy of silence on domestic violence and reproductive rights of women. Civil liberties organisations did not acknowledge violence against women by the civilians in the name of caste, communal or male identities. Environment movement did not highlight women's survival struggle for collection of fuel, fodder and water. Tribal movement did not pay attention to the tribal women's demand for land-rights. Witch-hunting of educated dalit and tribal women needed urgent attention. Women leaders who verbalised these problems found themselves isolated in these social movements and at times witch-hunted. In the absence of family support due to their involvement in militant actions, women in these social movements had to create their own support systems by establishing independent and special interest women's institutions to deal with domestic violence and their reproductive rights.

Early nineties brought tremendous anxiety as a result of new economic policy. Initial years of structural adjustment programme created tremendous fears among spokes-persons of the women's movement as horror stories based on the experiences of Latin America and Africa in the eighties were fresh in their minds. Women economists lobbied and saw to it that budgetary provision for women's development programmes were not curtailed.

Aftermath of the nationwide communal riots in 1992-93 has made all social movements to concentrate on development of their constituency in which different classes obviously have many mutually exclusive priorities. NGOs (Non-Government Organisations) receiving foreign, government and private funding are under tremendous pressure as they have to be constantly vigilant about which project to support and cleanse their staff from the harmful habits which they have picked up from the community-work such as use of unparliamentary language, violent methods to settle differences, misogyny and debilitating addiction to narcotic drugs, consumption of dangerous varieties of liquor, cancer generating tobacco products and viewing of pornographic literature and films . Vested interests pressurise them to support activities such as child-marriage, ostentatious wedding ceremony, sex-determination tests to get male child, alcoholic binges and unsafe sex, use of children in drug and weapons trafficking, opening of informal alcohol dens with women caterers, supply women victims of violence as domestic workers, baby-minders, concubines, actresses in the pornographic films or call girls. *Virtual absence of public transport in most of the cities makes women and children's position really miserable.* The local elite wants exclusive recreation clubs, boarding schools, private swimming pools, privately controlled vehicles (symbols of male pride and male power- machismo), marriage halls and private gardens. Isolation of the social activist makes them helpless when they are under pressure from these two contending patriarchal, self-seeking and sectarian forces. One is rooted in the poverty groups and among relatively less educated people and the other one is highly educated and upwardly mobile with strong connections with the state apparatus. But, both have only one way of self-actualisation i.e. consumerism and both support tyranny of market.

Advantages of Democratic Structures

The parliamentary democracy of India allows free debate on women's involvement in the public life so far as they remain mere decorative objects. But those who take stand have to face victimisation. At this juncture, pioneers of various social movements are facing marginalisation, invisibalisation, trivialisation, terrorisation, intimidation, isolation and humiliation. Those who decided to do drudgery- prone tasks as silent workers are totally cabbagified. Those who have adopted the laws of the market have been able to institutionalise their agenda in benevolent patriarchal terms. Women's equality is a distant dream. Veterans of many social movements (democratic rights, youth, women, tribal, dalit, working class) have either turned to film-making, writing or teaching professions. Some of them are also running library, documentation and training centres. Many of them had to change their residence, accept desertion from their children and husband. Many unmarried women activists have been thrown out by their family members because of their involvement in the social movements. They are perceived as deviant. Women who demanded their rights within existing personal laws or opted for inter-caste or inter-religious marriages had to face social boycott from custodians of racial purity. Hence, the need for an institutional base, which would ensure job-security, self- actualisation and meaningful leisure-time activities to women activists and which, can enable them to serve the constituency in the area development programmes. In this context, the professional bodies of women such as International Association of Feminist Economics (IAFE) can play a very important role in protecting endangered species namely "women's rights activists".

Development Media and New Social Movements

Development media is gaining place of prominence to give voice to the politics of petitioning and protest. Several private television channels are showing interest in the development issues such as environment, human rights, education and health. They have acquired respectability in the eyes of liberal bourgeoisie and the world capitalism. In the nineties, women's movement's agenda is being executed by both, enlightened women and men. Focus of the intervention is on the practical, down-to-earth, day-to-day survival issues with the use of modern science and technology and the management techniques.

Politics of 3 Ps - Petitioning, Protest and Public Interest Litigations (PIL)

You can avoid market in politics of petitioning and protest as these activities can be managed with the resources generated by the volunteers of social movements-placards, posters and people to shout slogans, hold banners and give speeches. Politics of PIL is more expensive as it involves research, lawyers' fees and travel cost to the High Court and Supreme Court. But, the most important implications of these 3 Ps are in terms of rise in the expectations of the masses from the movement activists. To go beyond advocacy and to fulfil the expectations of the stake groups, institution building is inevitable. This is a costly affair. Moreover, the activists are forced to give up their sectarian approach and end up dealing with all sorts of people who may have ideological differences.

Ideological Problems and Material Conditions

As the material condition is changing at a rapid speed, India 's experiencing ideological problems regarding course of economic development and cultural issues. The sharp divide in the thinking is between, those who have enjoyed fruits of Hindu rate of growth (3.5 %) by using pre-capitalist power relations based on subjugation of women, lower castes, minorities and tribal population, and those who want better quality of life, drudgery-relieving labour processes, active labour market policy and multi-cultural life-styles through interaction with the industrialised world.

Table 1 reveals that even in the relatively more prosperous states problems of housing, safe-drinking water, toilets and electricity have not been addressed. They can be solved only if the NGOs are rooted in the skilled proletariat and the construction industry. Or else all crorepati and lakhpati NGOs end up generating hostility of the toiling poor whose slave labour is utilised for area development. Wealthy voluntary organisations should direct their energies to create more educational institutions for technical training, value-based education and modern management of multicultural civil societies.

TABLE - 1
AMENITIES AVAILABLE TO HOUSEHOLDS BY STATES

Percent of households

States	*Mud, grass, bamboo owning house*	*Electric connection*	*Tap water*	*Toilets*
Andhra Pradesh	44.7	63.1	31.20	15.2
Bihar	71.7	9.8	3.6	7.3
Gujarat	37.4	71.9	59.7	21.9
Haryana	13.8	81.9	44.3	8.0
Himachal Pradesh	57.5	88.0	70.6	16.2
Kerala	25.2	61.1	16.7	63.1
Madhya Pradesh	60.7	50.4	11.0	5.5
Maharashtra	55.7	59.7	43.3	5.4
North Eastern Region	66.5	44.1	8.7	68.7
Rajasthan	44.4	49.1	28.4	4.0
Tamil Nadu	22.4	63.0	49.9	11.1
All India	55.4	42.9	34.8	15.3

Source: Indian Human Development Report, NCEAR, published in Indian Express, 27-8-2000.

The new social movements are forced to examine area development from these points of view. In the first approach, women have to be in the shadow of men and will be the losers in a long run and in the second approach women will have to find their development through hard-work and intellectual self-sufficiency.

Where is Women's Agenda in the New Social Movements?

Fight against child-labour, child-prostitution and child-marriage and advocacy for women's education and professional proficiency are two sides of the same coin. Fight against exploitation by moneylenders can't be successful without providing alternate financial security through women's banks. Fight against female foeticide and female infanticide can't be successful without providing shelter-homes for women who refuse to kill their daughters. Without one's own premises, women's development organisations can't function independently. In today's context, if women's groups want to survive, they need to have ability to sustain their institutions in terms of finances, crisis management, administrative skills, campus security and dealing with the outside world. Just by sending press release or issuing leaflet, you can't achieve anything. Making of video-documentary can help in mobilising financial, material and human resources.

(a) Educational Needs of Women

Non-formal education has been able to give limited empowerment to women. It is important to establish more educational institutions which give women formal education and which will enhance their opportunity cost. Technical training for women can be effective only after team building among women activists.

(b) Health Needs of Women

Health Issues have received limited attention in health economics due to the pre-dominance of private sector in the minds of the policy-makers. These have made tasks of the activists of the social movements much difficult. Right from the beginning of the women's movement adverse sex-ratio, high mortality and morbidity rates and nutritional deficiency of women have been areas of major concerns. But, without questioning patriarchal power-relations within the family, it is not possible to solve these issues. New concerns in the field of health movement have been abortion, HIV- AIDs (The official records reveal that over 200 children get infected by HIV everyday), female infanticide, reproductive health of women, health implications of violence against women, ethical codes for bio-medical researches. PIL against harmful contraceptives was filed by Saheli in Delhi. Now, the government bodies and mainstream medical associations are showing great interest in these issues.

Prerequisite for Launching a Movement

Thorough research and accurate details of the issue is a must before launching any social movement. Controversy around BIG

DAMS, Nuclear Energy, Environmental issues, mega-development projects, rice research, contraceptive technologies demand accurate scientific and technical information base from the specialists who also have in-house lab- facilities and reference libraries.

Beyond Guilt Tripping

New awareness among the funding institutions about utilisation of funding is as a result of intense debate on corruption, leakage and misappropriation of funding in the Asian and African countries. In the early 1990s, there was a fear that the global funding might get diverted to the East European countries. This debate in the development studies circle brought massive changes in the functioning of the social movements in the post colonial countries which were subsidized by the outside funding. Mostly, activists and experts from the minority communities and women are made to accept foreign funding. Rest of the social movements derives benefits of these funding without acknowledging the source. New dialogue with the funders based on mutual respect has helped to get rid of the anxiety that the developing world would be left out by the aid agencies. Induction of highly qualified professionals from developing countries as consultants to screen the proposals for funding has reduced wastage and vested interest. A Case-study of NOVIB- Oxfam International reveals that funding for these countries amounts to around 90%. 2/3 of the total budgetary provision is for direct poverty eradication. Discussion on transparency and accountability of handling funding is directly linked with democratic conduct, regular publication of accounts and progress report. Those NGOs which were secretive about their functioning and instrumentalists towards their supporters lost their credibility within 5-7 years.

Electoral Politics and New Social Movement

Though the social movements have thrown up new band of educated, sincere and hardworking women as leaders, their participation in the electoral politics is quite limited.

Credibility of new social movements has been commodified by the electoral market. Women social activists who are ready to give thumb-impressions are promoted by the mainstream politicians. Women who stick out their necks have to create their own safety nets- financial security, gainful employment, credit-worthiness and self- sustaining life-style. Women in public life need to have special skills to scrutinise budgetary provision in favour of empowerment of women. English educated articulate and aggressive women are tolerated by the mainstream, only, if they remain silent about budget. International Association of Feminist Economics (IAFE) has 550 members working in 31 countries. Women leaders with mandated power should interact with the women economists of IAFE as they can provide "insights into the relationship between gender and power relations in the economy" (Economic and Political Weekly, Bombay, 24-6-2000, p. 2280).

TABLE - 2
THE GENDER ADVANTAGE

Year	*No. of seats available*	*Total No. of contestants*	*Male*			*Female*		
			Contested	*Elected*	*% winning*	*Contested*	*Elected*	*% winning*
1952	489	1874	—	—	—	—	—	—
1957	494	1518	1473	467	31.7	45	27	60.0
1962	494	1985	1915	459	24.0	70	35	50.0
1967	520	2369	2302	490	21.3	67	30	44.8
1971	520	2784	2698	499	18.5	86	21	24.4
1977	542	2439	2369	523	22.1	70	19	27.1
1980	542	4620	4478	514	11.5	142	28	19.7
1984	542	5574	5406	500	9.2	164	42	25.6
1989	529	6160	5962	502	8.5	198	27	13.6
1991	521	8699	8374	492	5.9	325	39	12.0
1996	543	13952	13353	504	3.8	599	39	6.7
1998	543	4750	4476	500	11.2	274	43	15.7

Note: Gender-wise data for 1952 not available.
Source: Times of India, 2-9-99.

The following table reveals that around 44 educated women have to represent 44 crore Indian women's interests in Loksabha.

TABLE - 3
EDUCATIONAL QUALIFICATION OF THE MEMBERS OF THE 12TH LOK SABHA

Educational Qualification	*Male*	*Female*	*Total*
Doctorate	26	4	30
Post Graduates	127	16	143
Graduates	227	19	246
Sr. Cambridge	1	0	1
Under Graduate	8	1	9
Matriculate	43	1	44
Under Metric	11	2	13
Intermediate	44	1	45
Diploma	1	0	1
Illiterate	0	0	0

Source: The Times of India, 1-10-99.

Elected Women Representatives and Area Development: Elected women representatives can be successful in promoting women's development agenda only when their trusted soldiers and family members share their vision and don't force them to make unprincipled compromises. Each (Member of Parliament) M.P. gets government funding. Moreover, personal charisma of the M.P. and M.L.A. (Member of Legislative Assembly) brings investments for area development. MPs use these funds according to their political and personal priorities. Limited personal demands of the women politicians ensure maximum resources for the area development. Female headed households have been most successful in all social movements right from the pre-independence days. Elected woman representative whose decisions are taken by others is not respected by her constituency. It is very important for her to be aware of labour relations and labour processes in her constituency.

Rs. 2 crores allocated to each M.P. for the development of the constituency as per (Member of Parliament) MP local Area development Scheme.

TABLE - 4
THE CONSTITUENCY FUND SCHEME ROLLING SINCE 1993 REGIONAL VARIATIONS IN EXPENDITURE

State	*Percentage of utilisation*
Mizoram	91.0
Megahalay	83.0
Nagaland	82.8
Andaman and Nicobar	80.8
Orissa	57.4
Punjab	57.3
Himachal Pradesh	47.5
Jammu and Kashmir	46.0
Lakshadeep	39.5
Pondicheri	17.6

Source: Department of Statistics and Programme Implementation, GOI, 1999.

The above table is quite revealing. Utilisation of government funding is maximum in the North- Eastern states because of strong horizontal and vertical networking. The prosperous states depend more on the private funding to avoid bureaucratic hassles. If poorer areas in the state don't have a highly motivated administration or an NGO network, then too the funding remains unutilised. In the areas dominated by the lower middle class and the poverty groups, there are demands for more schools, libraries, bridges, toilets, drains, tube wells, community centres and crematorium. While in the prosperous areas, the demands are for road repairs and schools. Private sector of the economy demands banks, hospitals and shopping plaza. The (Members of Parliament) M.P. and M.L.A. (Members of Legislative Assembly) have to strike balance by keeping into consideration immediate needs and long-term considerations for the constituency.

Conclusion

Women's contribution in Social movements in India has been effective in the southern states because of horizontal and vertical networking with the forces in favour of gender justice. In the Northern states horizontal networks of women through mahila mandals and bhajan mandals are giving them some breathing space to deal with the statusquo. Though visibility of glamorous women in media is extremely high in the Northern states, in these states the male social reformers, especially senior citizens can be effective change agents. Women's contributions in the mass movement and in the decision-making bodies, both are valued by senior citizens as they don't perceive them as threat. Career women and women professionals have provided an umbrella for women in the social movements who lead crisis-prone lives. Now, the state apparatus also views their work favourably. It is such a contradiction that on the one hand we notice strong resistance to 33 per cent reservation for women in the electoral bodies, but at the same time, more and more women are getting elected in the local self- government bodies because the nature of work in this sector is nothing but an extension of housework and it can be performed along with shouldering family responsibilities.

References

Domestic Violence (1999), MASUM and CEHAT, Pune.

Health Watch Trust (1999): "The Community Need-based Reproductive and Child Health in India- Progress and Constraints", Health Watch Trust, Jaipur.

Jean Draze (1999):"Health, Development and Economics", The National Medical Journal of India, Vol.12, No. 1, Jan-Feb, pp. 2-5.

J. Kishore. (1999) National Health Programme of India- National Policies and Legislations Related to Health, Century Publications, Delhi.

John Chisholm (1998), "Domestic Violence- A Health Care Issue ?", Paper presented at CEHAT International Conference on Preventing Violence- Caring for Survivors, November.

Lawyers' Collective: Domestic Violence Against Women (Prevention) Bill, 1999, Women's Rights Initiative, Research & Documentation Cell of Lawyers Collective, B-5 Jangpura Extension, New Delhi-110014.

Novib-Member of Oxfam International, Annual Report,1998.

The ICMR Consultative Document on Ethical Guidelines (2000), a Critique and Some Recommendations- Saheli Women's Resource Centre, Delhi, Forum For Medical Ethics-Bombay, January- March.

T. D. Dogra and Pravir Bodka (1999), "Sex Oriented Torture- An Overview" & P.R. Pathak- "Gender Bias Torture in Place of Work", Journal of the Indian Medical Association, Calcutta, Nov.

Thomas Janoski and Alexander M. Hicks (1994), *The Comparative Political Economy of the Welfare State*, Cambridge Studies in Comparative Politics, Cambridge University Press.

Five

Budgetary Policy - A Gender Analysis

Women's status and women's bargaining power in the economy have a major bearing in the budgetary policy. Yearly analysis of the budget from the point of view of women is a must to enhance women's economic interest and socio-political standing in the economy. Analysis of budget from gender perspective makes us understand what are the nature, character and content of share of development cake for women. This contribution is based on the study of full text of budget document of 2000- 2001. In terms of its approach, it suggests major departure from the earlier budget documents. It also proves that if the economists interested in women's issues work seriously on the subject, it is possibly to change the focus of our budget in favour of women.

It is quite encouraging to know that some of the longstanding demands of the women economists and development organisations have been incorporated in the Union Budget 2000-2001 of our country. But, at the same time, we must highlight the missing points, which are crucial, for women's day-to-day survival needs.

A case study of Budget 2000 reveals that in the section on *Quality of Life* (point 17), specific needs of women vis-a-vis health, education, drinking water, housing and roads should be taken care of. They are as follows:

(a) Health (point 18)- Special budgetary provisions for women patients (separate from family planning budget) in the Primary health centers and public hospitals. Tax-exemption for sanitary pads and napkins for babies' etc. is welcome. It will enhance mobility of rural women and women from the working class background.

(b) Education (point 19): It is found that in the regions where safe and reasonably priced public or private transport is available, women's participation in educational and economic activities is higher. Hence, safe transport for working women and school and college-going girls should find place of prominence in the Block Development Plan. In 'Sarva Shiksha Abhiyan', 30 per cent of budgetary provision should be made for girl's school and women's colleges, so that parents who discontinue their daughter's education due to fear of teenage pregnancy and male aggression are encouraged to allow their daughters to attend schools and colleges.

(c) Drinking water (point 17): Dalit and tribal women find it very difficult and at times impossible to get water from the common taps. Common taps are in the center of the villages. While their dwelling places are in the margin of the villages. Hence, separate taps for dalit and tribal women, in their hamlet should be provided by the state.

(d) In all housing schemes (point 21), 10 per cent of houses should be allocated for women headed households (WHH) i.e. widows, divorcees, single unmarried women and deserted women. In a war torn and riot ridden pockets, 30 per cent houses should be allocated for WHH as in these crisis prone areas percentage of WHH is around 30 per cent of all households.

(e) At every 2 kilo meters, one public toilet should be provided in the urban centres. To avoid contagious disease, Indian-style toilets should be provided.

(f) Cheap and safe eating facilities in the district, tehsil and rural areas for the dalits, minorities and tribal population and judicious distribution of goods allocated for public distribution system should be emphasized in the budget.

Declaration of 2001 as Women's Empowerment Year (point 23) can be meaningful only if the programmes are targeted at children and youth through NSS, NCC, and *Scout and Girls Guides*. At present, they are focussing only on food, fun, Aids Awareness and physical training. Comprehensive Gender studies programmes with interdisciplinary perspectives should be organized for school and college students and youth in general. Government controlled media should focus more on educational programmes concerning women's issues either through documentaries or docudramas.

In a National Population Policy (point 24) a clear-cut mandate should be given that the government resources should not be used for promotion of female foeticide and unsafe contraceptives. Budgetary allocation for human trials of controversial biomedical researches involving women, whether it is an anti-pregnancy vaccine, Depo-Provera, Net-o-en should be withdrawn immediately.

In SSI (Small Scale Industries) sector (point 27), concrete plan of action for empowering women entrepreneurs and safeguarding women workers interests should be spelt out. Budgetary provision should be made for occupational health and safety of women workers should be spelt out clearly. While granting license to new establishment, an inquiry should be made about basic amenities for women workers such as ladies room, separate toilets for women workers/employees.

In a section on Industry and Capital market (point 31), affirmative action by the state to protect women producers in the factor market (i.e. loan facilities, land allocation etc.) and women employees and workers in the labour market and self employed women (who are facing innumerable difficulties) in the product market should be mentioned with specific details.

In a section on Science and Technology (point 36) special policies should be envisaged for WRD (Women Resource Development) with one module on assertiveness training and another one on culture.

In Banking and finance (point 39), schemes for women entrepreneurs and women industrialists should be spelt out. Especially, the terms and conditions for differential rate of interest facilities should be mentioned the way they have mentioned the policies concerning micro credit facilities.

In the North-East Region (point 59), in the industrial training institutes and computer information centres, women dominated sectors such as sericulture, horticulture, floriculture and weaving should be targeted for introduction of advanced technology.

Special budgetary provisions should be made for modernisation of labour processes in which scheduled caste and scheduled tribes (point 60) are involved. These include better equipment and better management of economic activities.

In plan expenditure (point 65), special consideration should be given for women specific tasks such as collection of fuel, fodder and water. In communications, special radio and television programmes for women in regional languages should be budgeted.

In the Non-Plan expenditure (point 67), in a budgetary provision for food and fertiliser subsidies, female headed households should be given special considerations. Labour reducing technologies in the subsistence sector (especially rice cultivation and animal husbandry in which women are doing the most drudgery prone tasks) should be introduced.

Reduction of duty burden on contact lens solution is welcome, as it will help young women and men who are working in computer industry and other tele-workers. The finance minister should be congratulated for totally ignoring tourism industry, as the world market is too willing to look after travel and tourism.

In conclusion, I must mention that use of gender aware language in an official document like budget is quite heartening. Gender sensitive statement by the finance minister must be appreciated when he says, "a budget is easier than that of an average house-wife struggling to manage the family budget. As a token of appreciation and recognition of women as productive contributors to the economy, I propose an additional rebate of Rs. 5000 for women tax payers from their tax liability".

Budget analysis from gender perspective should be introduced and promoted in all educational and research institutions. Public debate on Gender Perspectives on budget will help the country to tilt the balance in favour of area development and peaceful use of resources in the present atmosphere of jingoism.

Six

Gender Economics

Analytical tools provided by Gender Economics (GE) are extremely useful to deal with the socio-economic and legal issues concerning marriage, divorce, custody of children, guardianship rights, alimony, maintenance, property rights of mother, sister, daughter, legally wedded wives and her child/ children, co-wives and their children, keeps and their children and the issues concerning adoption. GE has a special significance in the subsistence economy, which uses the kinship networks, institutions of polygamy and polyandry for concentration and centralisation of wealth and capital by either the patriarchs or the matriarchs. Domestic animals, women and children are the main assets in the subsistence sector where collection of fuel, fodder, water are important components of daily life over and above agrarian chores, live-stock rearing and kitchen gardening.

GE has drawn heavily from all mainstream disciplines and innumerable social movements of the last three decades. GE provides insights to examine budgets of Government Organisations (GOs) and Non-Government Organisations (NGOs) from the point of view of gender justice. Priority areas being women's education, health and nutrition, skill development, accounts, financial and commercial viability, legal standing, asset and corpus building. GE contextualises day to day survival struggles of women in the family, in the households, in the community and in the micro, meso and macro economy with the perspective of power relations which control women and girl children's sexuality, fertility and labour.

To explain this concept, I would like to give some examples from popular culture:

1. Control of women's sexuality

(A) Dress code which, restricts mobility of women and girls, does not allow her to do those chores which require flexible body movements, reduces her efficiency and employability in non-conventional occupations.

(B) "Tool" as a phallic symbol, not being allowed to be used by menstruating women as it is supposed to have contaminating influence. Hostility towards women who ride bicycles, drive cars and scooters, operate machines and use ploughs for farming, wheels for pottery, saw for carpentry.

(C) Women being treated as repository of custom and tradition and cultural practices, dedicated as *devdasis, jogtis* and forced to undergo series of masochistic fasting, scarification and self infliction of pain which make them unemployable and perpetually dependant on the patriarchs. They enjoy only subversive power of a comfort woman that too, is mediated by men, as they don't have any legal rights. In the commercial context, the same happens to women beneficiary of *Maitri-Karar* (friendship contract) and *Seva-karar (Service contract).*

(D) Need for male escorts, bodyguards for dainty, sickly and weak women who see their identity as anorexic women. Billion-dollar beauty business thrives by controlling young women so that they are incapable of using their body for manual chores. Here, women's insecurity about their looks is used by the cosmetic industry.

(E) Women eating last, the least and the left over. Nourishing and balanced diet as a male prerogative. Daughters and brides kept on starvation diet. Food secure middle-aged women as honorary men.

Inference of A, B, C, D and E - Declining sex ratio – As per 2001 census (933 women per 1000 men), high mortality and morbidity rates.

2. *Control of Women's Fertility*

(A) Women being treated as male-child producing machine. Customary practices of female infanticide and neglect and abandonment of girl child, scientific techniques of sex determination tests used for female foeticide, pre-conception elimination of female embryo with the help of sex-preselection techniques.

(B) Population policies targeting women for unsafe contraceptives and harmful hormone based contraceptive researches, which violate bodily integrity and dignity of married and unmarried girls and women.

(C) Laws on prostitution penalising and persecuting women victims of sexploitation running a parallel economy of as much as 200 billion rupees.

(D) Social boycott of unwed mothers. Illegitimate children being stigmatised by society and deprived of economic, social and educational opportunities. They are further marginalised in the economy, which is undergoing massive structural adjustments and instability. Facilities like identity card, ration card and other legal documents which are a must for citizenship rights are not provided to them.

Inference of A, B, C and D, can be named as *brothel model of economic development* which thrives on unpaid and invisiblised labour of women. It perpetuates the vicious circle of Child marriage, child prostitution and child labour (CP, CM and CL). Super-exploitation of female headed household and domestic workers get sanctity in this model. Women have to shoulder this added burden along with the burden of the vicious circle of poverty, over-population and unemployment.

3 Control of Women's Labour

(A) Use of women in the economy for the occupations which, are extensions of housework, i.e. 3 Cs (cooking, cleaning and caring). Only 6 per cent of women are in the organised sector which guarantees protection of labour legislation and ERA (Equal Remuneration Act). 94 per cent of women are in the informal sector which does not guarantee job-security, regular income and personal safety.

(B) Demonisation of highly qualified, efficiency plus and career women. Witch hunting of intellectually independent and verbally articulate women workers, employees, technicians and decision-makers.

(C) Sexual harassment as an occupational hazard to crush the confidence of women and to keep them in the state of perpetual terrorisation, humiliation and intimidation.

Inference of A, B and C, can be limited opportunities for women and ghettoisation of women in non-challenging, routinised and low-status jobs known as "women prone industries" in the official discourse. Most of the economic activities done by majority of women are non-marketed and non-monetised and reward for labour does not reflect the value of their labour. In such a situation, to gauge economic worth of their work Time Use studies are the most effective tools to identify their opportunity costs.

Within this framework, now, we will examine efforts at empowerment of women by 550 feminist economists who are functioning in 31 countries under the banner of International Association of Feminist Economics to provide DAWN (Development Alternatives with Women).

(a) Visibility of Women in Statistics and Data System

For effective execution of macro policies such as National Perspective Plan for Women, Maharashtra State Women's Policy, we need an accurate data-base, area studies and time allocation studies, studies on energy expenditure and food consumption patterns among women of different communities, public utility services such as safe transport, public urinals, women's room in the office. Gender economists have done pioneering work to understand demographic profile of women and sex-ratio. Formulation of gender aware data system on literacy, education level, employment and earnings, health and well-being helps proper planning and policy making for empowerment of women. Inter -district, Inter-state and Cross country comparisions of women's empowerment are obtained from Gender related Development Index(GDI). GDI owes its origin to its precursor, the HDI (Human Development Index), three main components of which are per capita income, educational attainment and life-expectancy which is a proxy for health attainment. .Gender disparities are measured keeping these three indicators into consideration. "An additional measure, gender empowerment measure(GEM) has been formulated to take into account aspects relating to economic participation and decision-making by women. The indicators used in GEM are share in income, share in parliamentary seats and an index that includes share in administrative and managerial jobs and share in professional and technical posts." (K. Seeta Prabhu, P.C. Sarkar and A. Radha). This exercise is done with a philosophical understanding that without engendering, human development is endangered. (UNDP, 1995)

(b) Economic Profile of Special Needs Population

Female headed households (Divorced, deserted, widowed, separated women), home based workers, women workers in the family enterprise, self-employed women, and women entrepreneurs.

(c) Analysis of Nature of Occupational Diversification

Among women, industrial classification- Implications of office automation, computerisation, flexi-time, job-sharing, tele working, and part time work.

(d) Effects of Structural Adjustment on Market Segmentation

segmented factor market affects self-employed women directly when they want to buy raw material and other services. Segmented labour-market has direct bearing on the daily grind of women workers in the informal sector. Segmented product market makes unorganised women workers and women's collectives without networking insecure and vulnerable as sellers.

(e) Economic Basis of Customary Laws and the Family Laws

When the customary laws get codified, we must be vigilant about the fact that women's interests are not sacrificed. Women's land rights and property rights need special mention at the time of codification of personal laws. Except for Andhra Pradesh and the North Eastern states, women have lost their customary land rights due to Land Reform Act.

(f) In Mega Development Projects

Which displace the native population, care must be taken to see to it that women get equal share in monetary compensation, land-rights and right to shelter. The same applies to the social and natural disaster management programmes.

(g) Political Economy of GET RICH QUICK Formula

in the name of dowry, sati (widow burning), Bhootali (witch hunting) for land grab, house-grab or to deprive women of their legitimate property rights should be examined with a consideration for avoiding violence against women.

(h) Women's Empowerment by Men Decision Makers

In a situation where women's agency is virtually non-existent, the benevolent patriarch wedded to the cause of Women's empowerment become project coordinators. In such a situation, guidelines for Utilisation of Constituency Development Funds of Members of Parliament and Members of Legislative Assembly and Area Development Fund of corporators for women's education, employment, training, capacity building should be drawn by gender economists.

WID-WAD-GAD

There has been a coexistence of three approaches for women's development in India. WID- Women in Development model explains the reasons for women being treated as beneficiaries of the crumbs thrown at them, in the margin of the economy, as consumers and an auxiliary labour force to be utilised in the crisis period and eased out the moment men are ready for take over. The WID discourse revolved around the economic growth paradigm. WAD- Women and Development model integrates women in the development work as active change agents. Affirmative action by the state and pro-active approach by the civil society through NGOs and women's groups are advocated by these models for empowerment of women against the forces of patriarchal class society. NGOs-voluntary organisations implementing this approach have become powerful force during 1990s. GAD - Gender and Development model is based on an understanding of gender relations and empowers the weak (he or she). Gender is socially constructed and gender relations are power relations. Here power is an important analytical category. Explicit measures of gender inequalities are sex-ratio, literacy rates, health and nutrition indicators, wage differentials, ownership of land and property. "The implicit relations are those embedded in relations of power and in hierarchies and are more difficult to measure. Located in the household, in custom, religion, and culture, these intra-household inequalities result in unequal distribution of power, control over resources and decision-making, dependence rather than self-reliance and unfair, unequal distribution of work, drudgery and even food."(Asha Kapur Mehta) Super women who are able to look after the interests of each and every stake group are survivors in this model. In the Indian context, gender relations are determined by the complex interplay of power relations based on class, caste, ethnicity and religion.

References

Amarja Nerulkar and Vibhuti Patel (1995), *Women and Development*, Text Book for MA Part 1 & 2, Department of Distance Education, SNDT Women's University.

Asha Kapur Mehta (1996), "Recasting Indices for Developing Countries- A Gender Empowerment Measure", Economic and Political Weekly, October 26, WS 80-WS86.

Cheris Kramarae and Dale Spender (2000), *Routledge International Encyclopedia of Women- Global Women's Issues and Knowledge*, Vol I,II,III,IV, Routledge, New York.

Devki Jain (1996), "Valuing Women's Work: Time as a Measure", Economic and Political Weekly, vol. XXXI, no 43, October 26,WS-46-WS 57.

K. Seeta Prabhu, P.C. Sarkar and A. Radha (1996), "Gender Related Development Index for Indian States- Methodological Issues", Economic and Political Weekly, Vol. XXXI, No.43, October,26, pp. WS 72-WS79

Krishnaraj, Maithreyi (1988), Women and Development, PG Department of Sociology, SNDT Women's University, Bombay.

Krishnaraj, Maithreyi(ed) (1991), "Women in the Data Systems", Research Centre for Women's Studies, SNDT Women's University, Mumbai.

Martha C Nussbaum (2000), *Women and Human Development- The Capability Approach*, Kali For Women, Delhi.

Marilyn Carr, Martha Chen, Renana Jhabwala (ed) (1998), *Speaking Out, Women's Economic Empowerment in South Asia*, Vistaar Publications, New Delhi.

Mira Seth (2001)', *Women and Development-The Indian Experience*, Sage Publications, New Delhi.

Mukul Mukherjee (1996), "Towards Gender -Aware Data Systems- Indian Experience", Economic and Political Weekly, Vol. XXXI, NO.43, October 26, WS 63-WS71.

Naveen Mishra (2001), *Poverty in South Asia*, Authors press, Delhi.

Neera Desai and Usha Thakkar (2001), *Women in Indian Society*, National Book Trust, Delhi.

Ranjani K Murthy (2001), *Building Women's Capacities, Intervention in Gender Transformation*, Sage Publications, New Delhi.

Seven

Women, Education and Social Development

Marginalisation of women from the mainstream socio-economic, political and cultural scenario is mainly duo to gender-biases in the entry of the educational institutions, options for education and training available to girl-students and employment opportunities available to the educated and qualified women. If less educated and untrained women occupy the decision-making bodies, they have to depend mostly on men (with all their anti-women prejudices) for their day-to-day functioning. If highly qualified women have no mandatory power, their talent remains unutilised or underutilised and in due course of time, they become cretins. If we want to avoid both the types of situations, we will have to critically examine the monolithic structures of the formal educational institutions with their class, caste, communal and sexist biases and provide concrete alternatives in terms of:

(a) an increased outreach of the educational (both, of formal and non-formal variety) institutions,

(b) reforms in the existing curricula with commitment to social justice, gender justice, communal harmony and peaceful governance.

(c) more allocation of resources in terms of land, money and human resources.

Reason for recent enthusiasm about women's education in the official discourse is due to the fact that several area studies have shown that educated women are able to avoid child marriage, command more autonomy in their reproductive rights and produce less number of children[1].

A Statistical Profile

Five decades of independent India have generated different patterns of male and female literacy due to different priorities of different state governments and different cultural legacies determining women's autonomy and control of movements. As per Economic Survey, 2000-2001 of the Government of India, in the 53rd Round of National Sample Survey Organisation, 50 per cent of Indian women were found literate in 1997. Kerala scores the first rank in female literacy, thanks to the active collaboration of voluntary organisations such as Kerala Sastra Sahitya Parishad (KSSP) and Library Movement, university supported National Service Scheme (NSS), the state government supported Literacy Mission and an efficient private and KSRTC (Kerala State Road Transport Corporation) supported transport, over and above railways and waterways used for transporting the students at extremely reasonable rates. Sex segregation, caste hostilities and unsafe transport have resulted into tremendous restrictions on women's mobility in Bihar, Madhya Pradesh, Rajasthan and Uttar Pradesh which keeps 75 per cent of the female population illiterate. Alcoholism among men resulting into domestic violence in the urban working class areas and rural and tribal areas actively promoted by the economic and political vested interests has been a single major impediment in the literacy programmes in Andhra Pradesh, Gujarat, Haryana, Karnataka, Maharashtra, Orissa, Punjab and Tamil Nadu[2]. It is sad to notice conspiracy of silence concerning violence against women (in the domestic arena, while going to and returning from school, in classroom situations and in the school-college-university campuses) in all discourses about women's education in India[3].

Ethnic tension in Assam and paucity of funding for educational purpose in West Bengal prevent literacy missions to be successful. Against such hostile forces, women teachers are expected to achieve the targets of universal literacy.

As per the world Development Report[4] 62 per cent adult women and 35 per cent adult men in India are illiterate. This fact is alarming because the social fabric which provided the family-based safety-net, is getting eroded and the day to day governance of society can not be handled without literacy and systematic paper-work.

TABLE - 1
LITERACY RATE, 2001

State	*Total*	*Male*	*Female*
Andhra Pradesh	61	71	51
Assam	64	72	56
Bihar	48	60	34
Gujarat	70	81	59
Haryana	69	79	56
Karnataka	67	76	57
Kerala	91	94	88
Madhya Pradesh	64	77	50
Maharashtra	77	86	68
Orissa	64	76	51
Punjab	70	76	64
Rajasthan	61	76	44
Tamil Nadu	73	82	65
Uttar Pradesh	57	70	43
West Bengal	69	78	60
All India	65	76	54

Source: Final Population Total of 2001 Census, Series 1, paper no. 2 of 2002, The Registrar General of India.

TABLE - 2
GROSS ENROLLMENT RATIO (GER)

		Primary (I-IV)	*Upper Primary (V- VIII)*
Gujarat	Boys	136.4	75.5
	Girls	109.6	51.4
	Total	123.4	63.9
All India	Boys	113.8	77.1
	Girls	91.5	52.9
	Total	103.0	65.5

Source: Ministry of Human Resource Development, quoted in Economic Survey, 1995-96, Government of India, Ministry of Finance, Economic Division, Delhi.

As per Table 2, GER for Gujarat is higher than All India GER in the primary education. Mid-day Meal Scheme introduced and successfully implemented by the Government of Gujarat can be one of the reasons for this. But, in the upper primary education, the GER for Gujarat is lower than the national average for both, boys and girls. This reveals that, V std. onwards the drop out rate of girls is higher in Gujarat. Use of literate children with basic understanding of computing, for family business and use of child-labour for home-based work, farm-work or in the petty business are the crucial factors determining withdrawal of children from schools. In Gujarat, girls who discontinue studies are roped in for various income generation activities at a very young age, e.g., food processing and food-production, embroidery, tailoring, managing shops, account keeping. They are doing this along with routine housework[5]. Centre for Social Studies (Surat) researches also prove the same[6].

National Family Health Survey (NFHS) based on a representative sample of 3832 ever-married women, in the age-group of 13-49 from 3875 households was conducted between February 9 and June 11, 1993; by Population Research Centre, Faculty of Science, M.S. University of Baroda and Indian Institute of Population Sciences, Bombay. Its findings on women's education are important for policy-makers and educationists.

TABLE - 3

SCHOOL ATTENDANCE AMONG GIRLS IN GUJARAT (%)

Age	*Urban*	*Rural*	*Total*
6-10	84	64	71
11-14	78	58	65
6-14	82	62	68

Source: NFHS, 1993.

Table 3 shows that in primary and upper primary school levels, discrepancy in the school attendance rate is quite sharp. Less number of schools, violent discrimination against girls from the poor economic background, unsafe journey in the overcrowded state transport are some of the factors preventing girls from rural areas to attend schools. Though fear of teenage pregnancy has been one of the major stumbling blocks in the way of teenage girls' education, none of the mainstream research organisations have highlighted this fact. Only participatory action researches conducted by women's organisations have focused on this aspect[7].

TABLE - 4
PERCENTAGE DISTRIBUTION OF EVER-MARRIED WOMEN IN THE AGE-GROUP OF 13-49 YEARS BY EDUCATION, 1992-93

Educational level	*Gujarat*	*India*
Illiterate	55	63
Literate< Primary complete	9	7
Primary School complete	13	12
Middle School complete	7	7
High School complete	12	8
Above High School	4	3
Total	100	100

Source: NFHS, 1993.

Among ever-married women, at every level of education, Gujarat scores higher than the national average. At the same time, 55 per cent illiteracy among ever-married women is quite alarming.

Need for Multifaceted Approach in the Context of Unevenness in Different States

We need to learn a lot from the 19th century social reform movement to effectively manage literacy mission with the help of the state apparatus and progressive sections of the civil society. In the official documents one hardly finds legitimization of difficulties faced by women animators, anganwadi and balwadi workers in the Northern parts of India where they are increasingly facing backlash of violence by statuesquoist forces in BIMARU states. In these areas, if more men from different caste, ethnic and religious backgrounds are involved in the literacy programmes, it will be easier to negotiate women's concerns with the patriarchal forces (here I would like to clarify that both, women and men are carriers of patriarchal hostility against women's education). One of the reasons for the success of the literacy mission in Kerala and Maharashtra has been active involvement of male animators and male decision makers from different caste backgrounds who have been able to convince the caste and community panchayats to support women's education. They have been able to discuss prevalent stereotypes against the educated women i.e. "Education makes girls hostile to manual work, arrogant, disrespectful towards elders, uncontrollable, unruly and irresponsible towards domestic responsibilities (cooking, cleaning and caring)."

In the middle level literacy areas, vocational training programmes under TRYSEM and Industrial Training Institutes (ITIs) have been introduced for women. "Although 1887 ITIs throughout the country also enroll women, to improve their access, 132 separate women's ITIs were established along with 98 separate women's wings in the general ITIs[8]. But these vocationally trained women are not given any training in crisis management, assertiveness and self-defense. Women technicians' cooperatives with regular meetings for discussion of their day-to-day problems should be formed. As per Economic Times (3-4-2002), girls account for over 40 per cent of the enrollment in universities in arts and education faculties. But their share in engineering and technical courses is only 17 per cent.

Which are the factors responsible for the success of Mahila Samakya (Programme for education for women's equality) in Karnataka, Gujarat and Uttar Pradesh[9]. The most important factor for its popularity is its persuasive approach and democratic handing of the programme, both horizontally and vertically. Women animators working in the community are at ease with the managerial cadre due to relationship of mutual respect and all women employees are provided secure environment and personal safety by the government apparatus (top down) and the beneficiaries (bottom up). These factors seem to be missing in the Women and Development Programmes (WDP) in Rajasthan[10]. There is insecurity all around- among the village heads, among the animators and among the beneficiaries.

In the high literacy areas, there is a need to identify potential women decision-makers and efforts should be made to groom them to fulfill the tasks of social development.

Highly educated women who can compete in the global market should be provided the gender-just and secure environment to realise their full potential. Deskilling is the major casualty with the Indian educated Women. Patriarchs of, both Government Organisations (GOs) and Non Government Organisations (NGOs) systematically encourage deskilling of highly qualified women by making them do monotonous, routine chores, which could have been easily done by moderately educated and skilled persons. This has prevented professional women from taking decision-making roles, which demand abilities for critical evaluation, immediate response to unfolding realities and strategic thinking.

Section of women which is either hostile towards classroom teaching or can't learn from the teacher either individually or in the classes can be reached out only through television, video-films or radio and wall papers, charts. Married women fall in this category. One-to-one teaching is a luxury, which can be afforded by the economically secure individuals and institutions.

TABLE-5

EXPOSURE TO MASS MEDIA, 1992-93

Percentage ever married women (age 13-49) who	*Gujarat*	*India*
Watch television at least once in a week	39.4	32
Listen to radio at least once in a week	47	44
Visit a cinema/ theater at least once a month	10	15
Are not regularly exposed to any media	45	47

Source: NFHS, 1993.

Dissemination of information through listening to radio is highly popular among the toiling poor and the housewives. Increasing the slot on educational programmes on wide range of themes such as gender-justice, legal awareness, credit, minimum wages, environmental protection, employment generation schemes, scholarships, technical training, entrepreneurship training etc. Doordarshan Centres and All India Radio's regional-language programme officers should keep live contact with teaching faculties in the universities and schools to upgrade the knowledge base of today's EKLAVYAS in the dalit bustees (popularly known as

Harijanwas), in the Muslim ghettoes and in the tribal areas who are extremely diffident to approach caste Hindu teachers. In this context, it is an important duty of all Panchayati Raj institutions to reach out to 45 per cent of women in Gujarat and 47 per cent of women in India who are not exposed to any electronic mass media.

TABLE - 6

PERCENTAGE DISTRIBUTION OF EVER-MARRIED WOMEN IN THE AGE-GROUP OF 13-49 BY HIGHEST LEVEL OF EDUCATION ATTAINED, ACCORDING TO SELECTED BACKGROUND CHARACTERISTICS AND RESIDENCE, INDIA, 1992-93

Religion	*Illiterate*	*Literate <primary Complete*	*Primary School Complete*	*Middle School Complete*	*High School Complete*	*Above High School*
Hindu	64	6	11	7	8	3
Muslim	66	10	12	6	5	1
Christian	33	11	15	15	19	8
Sikh	51	3	19	8	14	5
Jain	10	7	14	12	33	24
Buddhist	59	11	13	9	6	1
Caste/tribe						
S.C.	81	4	7	4	3	0.5
S.T.	84	5	5	3	2	0.7
Total	63	7	11	7	8	3.4

Source: NFHS, 1993.

For a successful implementation of literacy mission and women's education and training, SAFE public transport for both women teachers and girls/women students is a MUST. Areas earmarked for purdah culture (of both, Hindu and Muslim varieties) and areas notoriously famous for eve-teasing/sexual harassment of women should provide **women- special buses** during school/college hours. Development of public transport, safety on roads and clusters of girls/women traveling together can create congenial atmosphere for women's mobility. For ensuring this, community-based networking and formation of special interest groups are a must. Careful nurturance of clusters of girls who are ready to do cerebral work, skilled work, semi-skilled work, unskilled work with a perspective of community's immediate and long-term needs has so far been a prerogative of the upwardly mobile sections of the society. Educationists and social workers need to adopt this approach to guarantee social development of economically, socially, culturally and educationally deprived sections of society. While doing this, we have to be extremely sensitive to the fact that religious feelings of each and every community are not hurt. Instead of lecture method, if the dialogical method is introduced in the educational institutions, we can create a human resource, which has qualities like verbal articulation with democratic behavior.

Illiteracy among married women is the lowest among Christian and Jain women because these communities are mostly based in the urban areas, which have an easy access to co-education and girls' school. Moreover, they have to spend less time in doing monotonous drudgery-prone tasks. They can easily hire labour of the native poor women for routine housework. Level of illiteracy is more or less the same among Hindu and Muslim women i.e. 64 per cent and 66 per cent respectively. The most distressing factor is extremely high level of illiteracy among women of the scheduled castes and the scheduled tribes. 69 per cent of S.C. and 84 per cent of S.T. girls in Gujarat and 74 per cent of S.C. and 81 per cent of S.T. Girls in India who manage to attend school dropped out in 1989-90[11]. Slashing of budgetary allocation for education in the post- structural Adjustment Programme (SAP) period has adversely affected women's education[12]. Committed male animators with mandated power from their respective panchayats can facilitate the task of: Getting young girls out of the clutches of matriarchs and patriarchs in the family and in the kinship network who thrive on the labour of girl-children and young women. 'Respect for elders' plays crucial role in hampering women from attending schools. Even when they are allowed to attend schools, the moment they return from school they have to forget about studies. We have reached a stage where boys and young men shun studying in the public libraries and more and more girls and young women are taking advantage of studying in the reading rooms and college libraries.

1. Taking active interest in mobilizing support for girls and women's enrollment in schools and colleges. This can happen when the male animators adopt the 19th century social reform policy i.e. 'Reform begins from home', not with narrow casteist/communal perspective but with the multicultural perspective. Women teachers who are powerless in their own families and in the community don't command moral legitimacy in the eyes of heads (male as well as female) of the household who take decisions about education of their daughters, sisters and daughters-in-law. They say, "She can't manage her personal life, how can she manage teaching our children?" Community leaders and village elders thoroughly scrutinize personal lives of gram-sevikas, anganwadi teachers, school teachers, head-mistresses, principals of schools and colleges, wardens (men and women) of hostels before enrolling their girls/women in any educational institutions.

Two major problems faced by Muslim girls have been—

- Tremendous fear in the minds of Muslim parents to send their girls out as a result of insecurity generated due to recurrence of communal conflicts in the recent past. This factor comes in the way of Muslim girls attending secular schools[13].
- Lack of employment opportunities and difficulty in finding marriage partners for educated Muslim women in India[14].

Successful NGO Models in Non-formal Methods of Imparting Education

1. Youth for Unity and Action- YUVA, Bombay

Main thrust of *Anubhav Shikshan Programme* of YUVA is conscientization of community-based youth through critical examination of the first hand experience, learning from literature produced by marginalised sections of society, unlearning sexism, casteism and communalism through exercises such as role-play and role reversal, mutuality in the relationship between the teacher and the taught. Band of youth trained in this manner after years of sincere efforts at community level start stagnating in the absence of more challenging tasks of new institution building, state-national-regional- global level work-experiences. Special branch of YUVA, which does budget analysis with human development perspective, has proved to be an effective tool for advocacy.

2. Stree Mukti Sangathana (SMS) and Granthali, Maharashtra

Since 1974, SMS has been involved in public education about women's rights through songs, skits, music ballets, plays, carnival and mobile exhibition in the first decade of its existence. Three male animators (who were hero-worshipped by women members of SMS) from the fields of media, education and social movement played crucial role in this phase. Main strength of this organisation is long lasting team building and absence of hedonism. By 1985, end of the UN decade, SMS managed to go high-tech by marketing its productions through series of audio and videocassettes, by making headway in the mainstream media (Radio and television), several publications and a mouth-piece in Marathi. Its plays on socialisation of girl-child, dowry, Pandita Ramabai were staged all over Maharashtra. Many non-Maharashtrians also expressed their interest in organising the shows. This encouraged them to go for their Hindi production and allow other groups to perform these plays in several Indian languages. Spartan life-style of the performers who could also handle discussions, sell books and explain posters to common citizens and villagers won the hearts of people across the class, caste and political boundaries which represent 85 per cent of the population. In the post-1992 period, SMS has made special efforts to reach out to the minority communities (Muslims- 11 per cent, Sikhs- 2 per cent and Christians- 2.4 per cent of the population) through their active participation in the Literacy Mission.

Granthali is a library movement spear-headed by secular-minded intellectual elite of Maharashtra, which imbibed the ethos of liberal humanism of 19th century social reform movement. Publication of original Marathi works, translations from English and other regional languages, celebration of the book-release function in an educational and non-threatening manner and their distribution through exhibition-cum-sale-cum-discussion by celebrity intellectuals are the most attractive aspects of this movement. It conveys the message that intellectual stalwarts are not in their ivory towers but they are rooted in the local culture. They don't despise ordinary mortals but respect them as socially useful human beings. Educational material generated by Granthali has been found useful for classroom teaching and teachers' training on social development issues.

3. All India People's Science Movement, Women's Desk

This organisation has made more and more girls interested in application of knowledge of physics, chemistry, botany and zoology in their day-to-day life. Its chapter in Madhya Pradesh is looked after by EKLAVYA, which is actively, working with schools, department of science and technology and its journal in Hindi called *Chakmak* is extremely popular among the school children. They have made effective use of computers-internet facilities for area development.

In Kerala its chapter is known as Kerala Shashtra Sahitya Parishad KSSP) which works with educational institutions and voluntary organisations to impart science education through exhibitions, posters, booklets, demonstrations and jathas.

Inspiring Projects for Girl Students

Young, underprivileged girls in the age-group of 9 years to14 years are getting education about real life issues, postal address, a place of their home in the map and an identity of their own due to **Vacha**, Bombay's Bal Kishori Action Research Project. Vacha regularly organizes educational melas for adolescent girls in which knowledge about their health, difficult subjects like mathematics, accounts and English language is given. *Prerana,* NGO based in the red light area, is trying to rescue the innocent children of commercial sex-workers from being sucked into the cesspool their mothers were dragged into, by educating the children and by providing shelter. CEHAT, Bombay initiated an informal school, *Sahayog* for adolescent girls who had dropped out of middle and senior school in June 2000. These girls are preparing for an open school exams. In two years time, it has focused its attention to create space and opportunity for adolescent girls, to revitalize community structures, to give direction for building an institution.

Health Education for Women

Two decades of grass-roots women's movement has made health education for women a topmost priority. Modules for health education prepared by Chetana (Ahmedabad) in Gujarati, Hindi and English, Masum-Cehat (Pune) in Marathi, Jagori (Delhi) in Hindi, Voluntary Health Association of India in several Indian languages have been found very useful for school health programmes. Material on fertility awareness by Mahila Samooh (Rajasthan), Search (Gadchiroli- Maharashtra) and Stree Multi Sangathana (Bombay), Forum for Women and Health (Bombay) is useful for teachers' training and education of girls. Foundation course of SNDT Women's University has a course on *Women in Changing India* in which there is a module on health.

Role of Distance Education in Women's Social Development

Correspondence Courses offered by over 100 Indian universities and newly established open universities have facilitated the tasks of girls and women who are unable to attend schools and colleges.

Contact Lectures conducted by University Grants Commission are watched by women and educational documentaries on women's studies telecast by Education Media Research Centre (EMRC) are found useful educational aids. There is tremendous shortage of regional language educational programmes on women on AIR and television. Individual women documentary makers and women filmmakers' collective such as Mediastorm (Delhi) should make a united effort to get more television time for women's education and educational programmes on gender issues.

Educational Input of the Social Movements against Dominant Discourse

Social movements have critiqued the dominant discourse, which refuses to examine power-relations while examining the existing education about socio-economic and cultural issues specific to women. At the same time, they have provided alternatives in terms of non-hierarchical methods of education, linkages between formal and non-formal education, input in curriculum revision, preparation of text-books for teaching totally new subjects such as environment and women, human rights, gender justice, methods of counseling, etc. Moreover, the social movements have adopted different approaches to reach out to differently abled human beings, those who are totally disinclined to cerebral work, those who are ready for basic education and skills, those who are ready for higher learning. Non-hierarchical functioning and mutual respect are answers to harmonious functioning among these three sets of people working in the same institutions.

Globalisation has made several conventional skills nonmarketable, e.g., labour intensive and drudgery-prone skills of artisan classes which are extremely important as home-based activities (especially for women with small children and elderly, handicapped or ill family members) which can be done when the basic survival issues are sorted out. At the same time, it has opened new vistas for social development through multilateral economic/trade, educational, professional , cultural collaborations, provided we are able to generate proper human resource to handle this. We will have to encourage courses on language learning, translations/transliterations, travel and tourism, museology, development studies, comparative cultures, religious studies, diplomacy with human face, systemic analysis and strategic thinking, human rights.

Dealing with Gender-biases in the Educational Institutions

In the early eighties, Government of Gujarat appointed Committee of Experts to identify sexist biases in the school textbooks[15]. In response to Narendra Nath Kalia's Ph.D. thesis, National Council of Education, Research and Training had done similar work with regard to Syllabi of Central Schools. In the late nineties, we find actual changes taking place to some extent. Scarcity of gender-sensitive text-book writers with knowledge of parent discipline and ability to weave women's concern within the subject matte is the main bottleneck. The course content also needs to provide education in crisis management, confidence building, dealing with anorexia and bulimia and assertiveness among girl students.

Introduction of Women's/Gender Studies as a Special Discipline

Research-work under the banner of women's studies began immediately after the discussion of ***Towards Equality Report*** (1974) in the parliament. Indian Council of Social Science Research (ICSSR) and UGC provided research grants to several institutions, university departments and individual scholars to conduct researches on women's issues. On the basis of these research material several text-books have been prepared[16]. In some universities special women's studies (WS) departments are formed and in several universities/colleges WS is introduced as a subject within parent-discipline such as sociology, economics, psychology, literature, history, home-science, polytechnic. WS as a special discipline is taught in the Police Academy (Hyderabad), Institute for Management in Governance-IMG- (Trivandrum), Institute of Economic Growth (Delhi), Shastri Institute (Masoori), Indian Law Institute -ILI (Banglore), Institute of Rural Management- IRMA (Anand), National Institute of Rural Development - NIRD and Indian Institute of Technology- IIT (Bombay), Academy of Defense Studies, autonomous institutions running courses of journalism and other mass communication techniques have incorporated gender studies in their syllabi. Only medical and engineering colleges, schools of architect, music colleges, school\faculty of fine arts and FTII (Film Institute- Pune) have miserably failed in this direction. There is a need for both, Gender studies, which focuses on analytical category, ***power*** and women's studies, which focuses specifically on ***women***.

Several NGOs are also offering courses on women's studies, gender justice and Gender and Development. YWCA (Bombay), Sakti (Banglore), SEARCH (Banglore) and Indian Social Institute (Delhi and Banglore) have been active in these fields for over a decade.

Need for New Initiatives for More Educational Institutions

Interaction between educational trusts and enlightened funders can establish formation of more educational institutions for teaching, training and need-based research. This can be achieved only when all stake groups (board of trustees, funders, education management people and representatives from local self-government body) discuss this issue in an ambiance of transparency in a seminar/ workshop. Education and training on gender issues have gained much importance because of the mandate from the top. But to find gender -sensitive trainers is very difficult. NGOs wedded to the cause of gender-just society will have to bring major shift in their priority in favour of gender-issues so that qualified women in these NGOs are not used as dancing dolls to maintain status quo. Moreover, there has to be shift in the paradigm, from paternalism and philanthropy to social justice and human rights[17].

Crisis in Educational Institutions

New Education Policy, 1986 has made a realistic analysis of crisis in the existing educational institutions and recommended democratisation of its functioning.

If it happens, it will be truly beneficial to women's cause. It will encourage more and more highly talented educated women to take up teaching profession. Dialogical approach in teaching methods can reduce alienation of girls from their studies. Skill upgradation of the existing staff to teach courses on development studies, environmental science, gender justice and human rights have begun in the big cities where they have been able to find highly motivated teachers who are ready to put in extra efforts to learn these subjects (which are interdisciplinary in nature, hence more demanding) and later on, teach these subjects over and above their regular work.

To facilitate inter-state, interregional and international trade, collaborative ventures in the fields of fine-arts, cultural activities, diplomatic ties, international conferences on women-specific issues; tolerant and emotionally mature women should be encouraged to learn more and more languages so that they can act as facilitators. For this, more courses on different languages should be introduced. Diploma courses to suit the needs of fast changing economy should be identified according to specific needs of the area. To achieve quick results in this direction, A-V medium should be promoted, as absorption of information is easier.

Experiences of the Open School

Rehabilitation centers for street children, child workers and ex-child prostitutes have experienced that formal education is very difficult to cope up with, for these special needs children. Hence many NGOs and social work institutions have started open schools which offer wide range of creatively designed courses. Here along with functional literacy, vocational training is given. Teaching aids are devised to suit the inclination and abilities of the students. Special coaching is given to students who want to appear for the exams of the formal education systems. If students find mathematics, science or English very difficult to cope up with, they can avoid these subjects. In Bombay, Jeevan Nirvah Niketan (JNN), an Open School was started by a retired principal of the mission school under a tree in the slum in the early nineties. Snehasdan, which established 15 homes of street-children in the same area had to adopt multi-pronged approach for education of the children. Those who managed to pick up fast, were admitted in the formal school. Those who could not, were admitted in the open school. In 1996, the Bombay Police executed series of raids in the red-light areas and rescued child-prostitutes were sent for rehabilitation in a shelter homes in the same area, which also needed open school for the girls who could not adjust with the formal education. Third category of students for the open school came from the child workers in the locality. The shelter homes constructed new building in their premises to house the open school in their premises. Now, the open school has a huge building with all modern amenities, well-equipped units for the technical training and vocational courses, placement of students from professional social work institutions and school buses. JNN is situated in the premises of two shelter homes for women situated in the same campus. Constructive approach of the Nirmala Niketan College of Social Work, the management of the shelter homes, retired bureaucrats and police officers, social activists and print media is the main reason for the success story of the open school. Initial opposition to JNN (because some of its students were ex-child prostitutes and street children) by the middle class neighbourhood was neutralised in due course as all measures were taken to keep the pimps, procurers and the mafia dons away from the vicinity of JNN[18] .

Role of Panchayati Raj Institutions in Promotion of Women's Education

Women's empowerment through education about handling of day-to-day problems of the community, maintaining accounts, dealing with financial institutions, legal literacy, awareness about the functioning of governmental structures, record keeping, writing of minutes, voting pattern- supporting, opposing, abstaining, non-voting, systematic methods of discussion/ debate, role of a chairperson, mock-parliament, mock-legislative assembly, mock court trials, social audit, social accountability, basic knowledge about national history, economic affairs, diplomacy, multicultural outlook etc., has posed major challenge to our educational institutions.

Priority issues for village, Tehsil and district Panchayats have been education, employment generation, housing, labour relations, human rights' and environment. Involvement of educated senior citizens who are economically secure, for education and training on the above subjects is the only answer to reduce the burden of teaching faculty.

"The Department of Women and Child Development has decided to give cash assistance of Rs. 10000 to each voluntary agency, college, school or social welfare organisation which takes up the task of educating women contestants to Panchayat bodies[19]." This amount should be used for reference material for the participants to build reference library on social development issues and high protein diet for the participants.

Functional Literacy to Handle Day-to-day Survival Needs of Women from the Socially and Economically Marginalised Sections

Adult education programmes should adopt a need-based approach, which should include the following items,

- reading of sign-boards
- handling transport system
- managing bank accounts
- handling official papers, records, ration cards, licenses
- mainstreaming of tribal/rural women's knowledge of forest resource management

- identification of secular minded teachers to work among the marginalised sections from different religious groups.

Educational Needs of Environmental Refugees

The most difficult area of educational work is among the victims of floods, famines, displaced population due to mega projects, nomadic tribes, sex-workers and the underworld. As this population constitutes nearly half of our population, add our educationists will have to give up their ivory tower approach. NGOs working with these sections of society will have to get legitimate space in the mainstream educational bodies so that realistic curriculum can be developed.

Conclusion

Induction of increasing number of highly educated women with direct experience of activism in the women's movement in the mainstream educational bodies, literacy mission, departments of women and child development of state and central governments and research institutions is a welcome step to promote women's education and social development.

References

Karuna Chanana (1988), *Socialisation, Education and Women- Explorations in Gender Identity*, Nehru Memorial Museum Library, New Delhi.

N. L. Gupta (2000), *Women's Education Through Ages*, Concept Publications Co,New Delhi.

R. K. Rao (2000), *Women and Education*, Kalpaz Publications, Delhi.

Raj Kumar (ed), (2000), *Women and Education*, Anmol Publications Private Limited, New Delhi.

Rekha Wazir (ed) (2000), *The Gender Gap In Basic Education- NGOs as Change Agents*, Sage Publications, Delhi.

S.P. Agarwal (2001), *Women's Education in India, 1995-98, Present Status, Perspective Plan, Statistical Indicators with Global View- Vol III*, Concept Publications Co. , New Delhi.

Sinith Sittirak (1998), *The Daughters of Development - Women in Changing Environment*, Zed Books, London and Newyork.

Footnotes

1. Roger Jeffery and Alaka M. Basu (ed.) *Girls' Schooling, Women's Autonomy and Fertility Change in South Asia*, Sage Publications, New Delhi, 1996.

2. Power dynamics operating at the levels of state politics, police- bootleggers-underworld nexus, rural-urban networking for promotion of country liquor are succinctly portrayed in a film by Shabnam Virmani- *Anti Arrek Movement*, copy of video-cassette available with Vacha Women's Library, Bombay. Trafficking of narcotic drugs is patronised by more powerful lobbies.
3. Verbal presentations of the activists of Dalit Panther (Ahmedabad), Gangaben Baria of Forum Against Oppression of Women (Bombay), Gabrielbhai Gandabhai of Sangharsh Sahitya Parishad (Gujarat) during Gujarat Human Rights Conference in Baroda, 1990. Dalit Voice, a mouth-piece of Dalit Literary Academy has also published reports of covert and overt violence faced by students of marginalised sections in the mainstream educational institutions. One need not wait for anti-reservation violence (in the form of massacre or self-immolation) to bring educational reforms. Victimisation of students and teachers from religious minority, tribal and dalit community must be dealt with.
4. World Development Report, World Bank, 1997, p. 226
5. Reports of Self Employed Women's Association (SEWA) and SEWA Newsletter "Anasuya" 1985 to 1991.
6. Punalekar, S.P., Women Workers in Jari Industry, Centre for Social Studies, Surat, 1987.
7. Fatima Burnad: Teen-age Pregnancy and Unsafe Abortion in Rural Taminnadu, Women and Health Camp, Rural Women's Liberation Organisation, Arkonam, 1986.

   Manisha Gupte, Sunita Bandewar and Hemlata Pisal: Abortion Needs of Women in India- A case Study of Rural Maharashtra, Reproductive Health Matters, *Abortion: Unfinished Business*, No. 9, May, 1997, pp77-86.

   Verbal presentations of women delegates from Bihar, Madhya Pradesh, Uttar Pradesh, Rajasthan, Tamilnadu, Karnataka and muslim women from Ahmedabad (Gujarat) in the IV National Conference of *Women's Movement in India* in Calicut, Dec. 1990.

   Sunita Bandewar: A Note on ABORTION: CAUSE FOR CONCERN IN INDIA-EVEN 25 YEARS AFTER ITS LEGISLATION, Paper presented at Sixth National Conference on **Women's Movements** at Ranchi, Dec. 1997.
8. Gender and Poverty in India, a World Bank country study, The World Bank, Washington, 1992, p. 106.
9. For more details on these programmes, see Maitreyi Das: The Women's Development Programme in Rajasthan-A Case Study in Group Formation for Women's Development, Chapter-X- **Mahila Samakhya and Group Formation for Education**, Policy Research Working Papers- Women in Development, The World Bank, 1992.
10. I arrived at this understanding after listening to verbal presentations of women employees of the WDP (Rajasthan) during **National Conferences of Women's Movement in India,** in Patna (1988) and Calicut, 1990. Discussions with women animators of Mahila Samakhya in Karnataka, Gujarat and Uttar Pradesh in Calicut, Surat and Ahmedabad between 1990 and 1994 corroborated the same.
11. Annual Report, Ministry of Human Resource Development, Government of India, 1992-93.

12. Anita Rampal: "Education for a Possible Structural Change", in N. Rao, L. Kurup, R. Sudarshan: *Sites of Change, The Structural Context for Empowering Women in India*, FES and UNDP, 1996, pp. 270-298
13. Report (1994) of Women's Research and Action Group, Bombay which highlighted Muslim women's problems based on their survey research of muslim communities in Ahmedabad, Baroda, Surat, Delhi, Hyderabad, etc.
14. Shahida Lateef: *Muslim Women in India, Political and Private Realities, 1890s-1980s*, Kali for Women, New Delhi, 1990.
15. Ila Pathak, Ila Joshi and others: Sexist Biases in the School Textbooks, Ahmedabad Women's Action Group (AWAG), 1982.
16. UGC affiliated institutions are using *Women and Society in India* by Neera Desai and Maithreyi Krishnaraj, Ajanta Publications, Bombay, 1988. 4 Indian Institute of Technology (IIT)-s are using *Women in Indian Society* edited by Rehana Ghadiali, Sage Publications, Delhi, 1988.
17. Amar Jesani: From Philanthropy to Human Right: A perspective for Activism in the Field of Health Care, A Perspective paper for discussion at the Conference for celebration of the Diamond Jubilee of the Tata Institute of Social Sciences, Mumbai, Nov. 1-4, 1996.
18. Read newsletters of Snehasadan, Jeevan Nirvah Niketan, St. Catherine's home and Justice and Peace Commission, Bombay, 1994 onwards.
19. Sweta Mishra, "Women and 73rd Constitutional Amendment Act- A Critical Appraisal, Social Action, Jan-March, 1997, Vol. 47, No. 1, pp. 16-30.

Eight

Women and Health – An Indian Scenario

World Health Organisation has defined health as "a state of complete physical, mental and social well-being" which is necessary for leading a productive and fruitful life. Health is a basic human right/ women's right. Attainment and maintenance of good health depends on women's access to nutritious food, appropriate medicine to treat illnesses, clean water, safe housing, pollution free environment and health services. Thus, women's health is determined by the forces working at homes, work places, society and the state. According to Dr. Amartya Kumar Sen, "Burden of hardship falls disproportionately on women" due to seven types of inequality- mortality (due to gender bias in health care and nutrition), natality (sex selective abortion and female infanticide)), basic facility (education and skill development), special opportunity (higher education and professional training), employment (promotion) and ownership (home, land and property).[1]

Nutrition

Balanced diet containing carbohydrate, protein, vitamins and minerals make a healthy body and healthy mind. Only 10 per cent of women are fortunate to have the privilege of nutritious diet. Majority of women in our country work more than men and for longer period but eat less, the last and the left over of poor quality of food. Their energy expenditure is not compensated by intake of diet as it is inadequate and lacks in nutrition. India has the highest prevalence of iron deficiency anaemia in the world. 87 per cent of pregnant women, about 68 per cent in the reproductive age group and about 60-70 per cent of adolescent girls in our country are anaemic.[2] This is the major reason for high level of morbidity among Indian women. The Government Organisations (GOs) and Non government Organisations (NGOs) need to make a concerted effort to provide iron rich and vitamin C rich low-cost and locally available foods to women through active nutrition education and change in dietary habits.

Common Illnesses

Women specific common illnesses are aches/pains (back, head, stomach, uterine), weakness, fevers, respiratory problems, gastro-intestinal problems, skin, eye, ear problems and reproductive problems such as reproductive tract infection, white discharge, endometriosis. CEHAT[3] study reveals that morbidity is much higher among women than men. Middle-aged women have arthritis, menopause related hot flushes and uneasiness[4], osteoporosis, migraine and swelling of legs. In both, rural as well as urban areas, proportion of physical immobility is higher among elderly women than among elderly men.[5]

Women are last one to be taken to a doctor and they have the least access to rest, healthy recreation, exercise and sports. All these combined together aggravate the situation and further deteriorate women's health.

Availability of Health-Care

Women avail four types of health services. First of all, the majority of women try home remedies, failing which they approach either a homeopath, ayurvedic doctor, unani healer or the allopath.

TABLE - 1
DEMOGRAPHIC PROFILE

Population of India	102.7 crores
Males	53.1 crores
Females	49.6 crores
Deficit of women in 2001	3.5 crores
Sex ratio (no. of women per 1000 men)	933

Source: Census of India, 2001.

Those who can't afford private practitioner's fees go to a trust run clinics/hospitals, government hospitals or Primary health care centres (PHCs) or the health care facilities provided by the non-government organisations. During the last decade, yoga, meditation.[6], reiki, aerobics have become extremely popular among the middle and upper class educated women [7], while the poor women approach witch doctors.

Attitude Towards Women's Health

Social discrimination against women results into systematic neglect of women's health, from womb to tomb. Female infanticide and female foeticide are widely practiced in BIMARU (Bihar, Madhya Pradesh, Rajasthan and Uttar Pradesh) and DEMARU (Punjab, Haryana, Himachal Pradesh and Gujarat) states.[8] As per 2001 census, there were only 933 women per 1000 men and there was a deficit of 3.5 crore women . Sex ratio is the most favourable to women is Kerala. But , in Kerala also, in the 0-6 age group , the sex ratio was 963, as per 2001 census. Total 0-6 age-group population of Kerala was 36.5 lakhs. Out of this 18.6 lakhs were male babies and infants and 17.9 lakhs were female babies and infants. Thus, 79760 female babies and infants were missing in 2001 in Kerala. This masculanisation of sex ratio is as a result of selective abortion of female foetuses after the use of ultra-sound techniques to determine sex of the foetus.[9]

TABLE - 2

SEX RATIO OF DIFFERENT STATES OF INDIA

State	*Sex Ratio* *Females per 1000 males*
India	933
Andaman & Nicobar Islands	846
Andhra Pradesh	978
Arunachal Pradesh	901
Assam	932
Bihar	921
Chandigarh	773

State	*Sex Ratio Females per 1000 males*
Chhatisgarh	990
Dadra & Nagar Haveli	811
Daman & Diu	709
Delhi	821
Goa	960
Gujarat	921
Haryana	861
Himachal Pradesh	970
Jammu & Kashmir	900
Jharkhand	941
Karnataka	964
Kerala	1058
Lakshadweep	947
Madyapradesh	920
Maharashtra	922
Manipur	978
Meghalaya	975
Mizoram	938
Nagaland	909
Orissa	972
Pondicherry	1001
Punjab	857
Rajasthan	922
Sikim	875
Tamil Nadu	986
Tripura	950
Uttarpradesh	898
Uttaranchal	964
West Bengal	934

Source: Census of India, 2001.

As a result of sex-determination and sex-preselection tests, sex ratio of the child population has declined to 927 girls for 1000 boys. Sixty lakh female infants and girls are "missing" due to sex-selective abortion of female foetuses and pre-conception rejection of daughters.

TABLE - 3

POPULATION IN THE AGE GROUP 0 TO 6 YEARS IN 2001, INDIA

Infants and Children — All	15.8 CRORES
Male Infants and Children	8.2 CRORES
Female Infants and Children	7.6 CRORES
Deficit of Female Infants and Girls	6 LAKHS
Sex Ratio of Child Population	927

Source: Census of India, 2001.

Sex ratio (number of women per 1000 men) of Greater Bombay has reduced from 791 in 1991 to 774 in 2001 inspite of rise in its literacy rate.

TABLE - 4

POPULATION OF GREATER BOMBAY- 2001

Year	*1991*	*2001*
Population	99 Lakhs	1 Crore 19 Lakhs
Sex-Ratio	791	774
Literacy Rate	84	87

Source: Census of India, 2001.

To stop female infanticide, the Tamilnadu government introduced 'Cradle Baby Scheme' urging parents to leave their unwanted baby girls at cradles provided in hospitals, primary health centres and orphanages and encouraging them to take them back if they changed their minds.[10]

Negative attitude towards women's health is the major reason for high levels of perinatal mortality and morbidity including low birth weight babies.[11]

Vicious Cycles and Poor Women

The vicious cycles of poverty generates the vicious cycle of ill health. For mother, poverty leads to low intake of food and nutrients, which results in under-nutrition and repeated insults from nutrition related diseases and infections, which affect them in terms of stunted development and growth faltering, hence they have small body size as adults, which impairs productivity; as a result they have low earning capacity. The end result is POVERTY. For a girl child, poverty gives only three options- child labour, child marriage and child prostitution. Poverty coupled with control over women's sexuality, fertility and labour is manifested in neglect and discrimination of a girl child, she remains a malnourished girl, early marriage makes her pregnant, she is an impoverished mother who produces low birth weight baby,[12] if the baby is female, she faces discrimination, repeated pregnancies/ deliveries to get son results in maternal mortality i.e. DEATH.[13] Miserable profile of reproductive health of Indian women is due to octopus clutches of early marriage and pregnancy, high prevalence of reproductive tract infection, ignorance, high infant mortality rate, no control over fertility and sexuality, anaemia, no control over contraception and repeated pregnancies. As per UNICEF, in 1995, there were 453 maternal deaths per 100000 births in India. Nutritional needs of lactating mothers demand urgent attention.

Violence and Health Issues of Women Over the Life Cycle

As unborn children, they face covert violence in terms of sex-selection and overt violence in terms of female foeticide after the use of amniocentesis, chorion villai biopsy, sonography, ultrasound, imaging techniques.[14] IVF (In Vitro Fertilization) clinics for assisted reproduction are approached by infertile couples to produce sons. Doctors are advertising aggressively, "Invest Rs. 500 now, save Rs. 50000 later", i.e., if you get rid of your daughter now, you will not have to spend money on dowry.

As girls under 5 years of age, women face neglect of medical care and education, sexual abuse and physical violence. As adolescent and adult women in the reproductive age-group,.they face early marriage, early pregnancy, sexual violence, domestic violence, dowry harassment, infertility, if they fail to produce son, then face desertion, witch hunt. The end result is a high maternal mortality. Causes of maternal deaths in our country are haemorrhage, abortion, infection, obstructed labour, eclampsia (blood pressure during pregnancy), sepsis, and anaemia.

TABLE - 5
CAUSES OF MATERNAL DEATHS IN 1993 IN RURAL INDIA

Direct Obstetric Cause	*Percentage*
Haemorrhage	22.6
Abortion	11.7
Infection	12.5
Obstructed Labour	5.5
Eclampsia (blood pressure)	12.8
Other Direct Causes	14.6
Indirect Obstetric Causes	
Anaemia	20.3

Source: Registrar General, India

TABLE - 6
MATERNAL MORTALITY RATE (MMR)

States	*Maternal Deaths per 100000 Births*
Andhra Pradesh	436
Assam	534
Bihar	470
Gujarat	389
Haryana	436
Himachal Pradesh	456
Karnataka	450
Kerala	87
Madhya Pradesh	711
Maharashtra	336
Orissa	738
Punjab	369
Rajasthan	550
Tamil Nadu	376
Uttar Pradesh	624
West Bengal	389
All India	453

Source: UNICEF, 1995.

Escalating number of cases of domestic violence, dowry deaths and bride burning has motivated Bombay Municipal Corporation (BMC) run K.B. Bhabha Municipal General Hospital to collaborate with an NGO, CEHAT to launch a project Dilaasa (means reassurance) to provide social and psychological support to women facing domestic violence. On March 8, 2002, the process will begin to replicate this model in all BMC run hospitals in the Greater Bombay.

Sexual harassment at work place should be treated as an occupational health hazard as it causes damage to both physical and mental health of women. Even women in the medical profession- right from medical students to other women health workers face this problem.[15]

Home and Work Conditions Affecting Women's Health

Pollution of air and water, noise pollution and chemicalisation of environment affect everybody. Scarcity of fuel-wood, fodder, water and herbs as a result of deforestation has taken heavy toll of women's health. Rural and tribal women have to walk for miles for these basic survival needs of human beings and domestic animals. Floods create deaths, destruction and epidemics. Desertification in the western India has accentuated women's survival struggles, as they have to depend on adhoc public works programmes. Global warming has resulted in resurgence of older epidemics such as cholera, typhoid, malaria, dengue, and haemorrhagic fever. Burgeoning sex-trade have made 2 million sex-workers potential carriers of HIV, STD, AIDS. Moreover, women in prostitution may suffer from T.B., other STDs, malnutrition, malaria and skin diseases.[16] At present, there is an evidence of rising HIV rates among young married women who are infected by their husbands. Data from 7 cities in India of ante-natal clinics reveals that HIV-AIDS prevalence rates among pregnant women are 2 per cent to 3.5 per cent in Mumbai and 1 per cent in Hyderabad, Banglore and Chennai.[17]

Modern lifestyle and environment has increased breast and uterine[18] cancer among Indian women. Techniques meant for detecting cancer (e.g. self-examination of breast and pap- smere) are rarely used by women. As a result, detection of cancer and its treatment at earlier stage becomes impossible.

All types of fruits are cornered by liquor industry and alcoholism is aggressively promoted among the toiling poor. As a result, men don't contribute for daily necessity of the households. Women have to shoulder major burden of household expenditure. Use of bio-fuels- wood, dung, crop residue resulting into indoor air-pollution takes away the lives of 5 lakh women annually.[19]

Women and Mental Health

The most neglected area concerning women has been her mental health. Stress generated due to major life events such as break up of marriage, widowhood, illness in the family, financial hardship and substance abuse destroy an individual's ability to cope with and function effectively.[20] Suppression of the extremities of an abusive relationship results in acute mental stress and trauma. In countries like India, economic dependency along with social and financial pressures trap women in abusive relationships, both physical and mental, forcing them to hide their anguish. Social workers and psychiatrists are approached by husbands to issue "mentally unfit" certificates so that they can flash them in a court of law to demand divorce. Relatives do not want to keep mentally ill women in the family.[21] Even after their recovery, they have to languish in the mental asylum. There is a need for **half- way-homes** where mentally ill women can work for few hours under the supervision of couple of professionals and then go home in the evening. Psychotherapy, mutual and group counselling should be promoted. Shock therapy and chemical treatment should be avoided as it cabbagifies women in distress.

Percentage of Institutional Deliveries in India - 1994

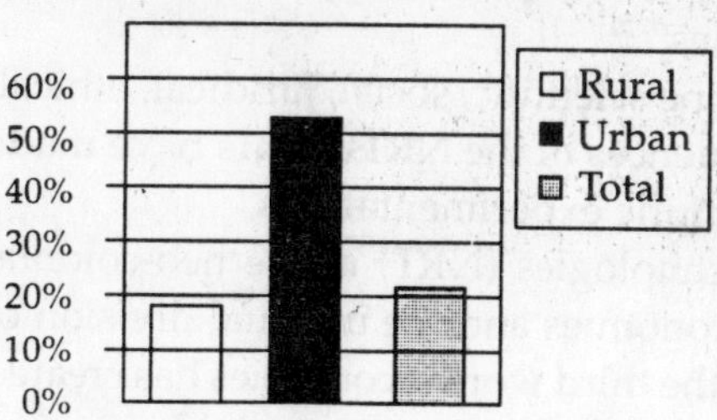

RGI 1997

per cent of women who received

- antenatal check-up by health professionals, Nurses-49.2
- Home Visit by health worker during pregnancy-21%
- Tetanus Toxoid coverage of Pregnant women-53.8%
- Anaemia Prophylaxis coverage among Pregnant women-50.5%

Source: IIPS, 1995.

Health-care Facilities for Women

As women are perceived as mothers, not as individuals in their own right, they are covered under MCH (mother and child programme). Even MCH does not cover majority of Indian women. Only 49.2 per cent of total pregnant women received antenatal check-up by health professionals. Health workers visited only 21 per cent of pregnant women. Tetanus toxoid coverage of pregnant women was 53.8 per cent and Anaemia prophylaxis coverage among pregnant women was 50.5%. [22] Majority of Indian women are left with no choice than to deliver at home.[23] Every 5000 population has an auxiliary nurse midwife (ANM) with responsibility to attend childbirth. Only negligible parts of home-births are attended by ANMs. [24] Institutional deliveries constituted only 22 per cent of total deliveries at the national level. Urban areas were better covered: 55 percent as against a very megre 18 per cent in rural areas.[25]

New Reproductive Technologies (NRTs) and Women

NRTs perform 4 types of functions. In Vitro Fertilisation and subsequent embryo transfer, GIFT (Gamete Intra Fallopian Transfer), ZIFT and cloning assist reproduction.[26] Contraceptive Technologies prevent conception and birth. Amniocentesis, chorion villai Biopsy, niddling, ultrasound are used for prenatal diagnosis.[27] Foetal cells are collected by the technique of amniocentesis and CVB. Gene technologies play crucial role through genetic manipulation of animal and plant kingdoms.[28] Genomics is " the science of improving the human population through controlled breeding, encompasses the elimination of disease, disorder, or undesirable traits, on the one hand, and genetic enhancement on the other. It is pursued by nations through state policies and programmes".[29]

It is important to examine scientific, social, juridical, ethical, economic and health consequences of the NRTs. NRTs have made women's bodies site for scientific experimentations.

New Reproductive Technologies (NRT) in the neo-colonial context of the third world economies and the unequal division of labour between the first and the third world economies has created a bizarre scenario and cut throat competition among body chasers, clone chasers, intellect chasers and supporters of femicide. There are mainly three aspects to NRT -assisted reproduction, genetic or pre-natal diagnosis and prevention of conception and birth. It is important to understand the interaction among NRT developers, providers, users, non-users, potential users, policy makers, and representatives of international organisations.

Assisted Reproduction

The focus of assisted reproduction experts is on the healthy girls who are forced to menstruate at the age of 8 and prolong it upto the age of 80 backed by hazardous hormones and steroids. The processual dimentions involve- Use of counsellors, technodocs and researchers to know the details of personal life of women to delegitimise victim's experience. Utter disregard for woman's pain, carcinogenic and mutogenic implications, vaginal warts, extreme back pain, arthritis, sclerosis, heavy bleeding, growth of hair on face, nose, chin, cheeks, joint pain associated with uterine contractions for production of egg-cells are dismissed as Mood-Swings. Network between stake groups had only one goal-impregnating women for embryo production which in the technodocs' language is *assisted reproduction*. After the mission was accomplished, they wanted these women to either die or disappear form the scene. Those who protested were witch-hunted, blackmailed, raped and photographed in a "compromising" position by clever use of camera.

Western Oriented Gentlemen (WOGs) were hired on a contract basis per PROJECT, ASSIGNMENT and WAR-STRATEGIES. Social and natural disasters were used as sight of experimentation of NRT. Hollywood and Bollywood ruthlessly derived maximum advantage from NRT. Embriyos and foetuses are used for cure of Parkinson's disease among influential and wealthy aging patriarchs. Side- effects on women's health were totally ignored. Growth of moustache, deformation of teeth, dietary requirements are totally ignored.

Political Economy of Assisted Reproduction

By using phallocentric and misogynist psychologists, psychiatrists, state and the politicians (ever ready for plastic smile and neat presentation) have found a ruthless weapon to cretinise, dehumanise, degrade, humiliate, terrorise, intimidate, cabbagify "fortunate (i.e. those who are allowed to live on the junk and leftover)" women to produce 1000 babies per scientist, doctor, engineer, politician and military dictator without any concern for women's future. It is reality not science fiction.

To delegitimise Women's experiences, inexperienced women were hired at high salaries in the so called non government organisations specialising on abortion research and reproductive rights research and these women were constantly reminded not to have female bonding. Those who did not accept forced heterosexual sex were hounded. "Deviants" i.e. same sex partners were severely punished. To create confusion and enmity, the Cold war strategy of the use of Human clones was used for power-struggle. Professional men from minority community and their saviours have been targets for ethnic cleansing. Total female population is classified into four categories- **cats-** who are not able to perform, **bitches-** who are loyal to their husbands or lovers, **cows-** who are obedient but don't have to do housework, **mad-cows-** verbally articulate women who knew too much, **buffalo** - who are doing housework and reproduction. Those who have managed to get livelihood in the industrialised world and those with proper connection to get hysterectomised have been able to manage their career, shapely body and intellectual prowess. Those who are perpetually bleeding are devoid of any charm, lustre and are classified as HOLES/GUTTERS. In spite of highly labour intensive, physically and psychologically damaging male onslaught, women breeders are called lazy, sleepy, cats, non-performers and are kept in the privacy of homes, hospitals, shelter-homes, street children's homes, prisons, mental asylums. Home-based women workers, and men workers in the community are dumped on the voluntary organisations so that the state, corporate world, defence machinery, media, multinational corporations can get a healthy labour force at the minimum cost. Each and every human gesture has a price tag. Young, healthy and bright boys are supposed to masturbate 3 times a day by consuming highly fatty diet mixed with performance enhancing drugs for massive sperm production. Here too, the REPRODUCTIVE BROTHELS have been using the concept of conventional peasant hospitality to sacrifice innocent and uninformed healthy girls for intensive embryo production. Their kidnap, murder, disappearance, social boycott, repeated reproduction is related to NRT. Ideology of homophobia used by their fathers / employers to dissociate them from their biological mothers is most barbaric. I wonder, whether these women will ever be able to trust any human being in their lives.

Sole concentration on supply of rich diet and perpetual lust at the altar of aging patriarchy has taken away human essence, verbal skills and intellectual provess from the educated women. 8 years (1992-2000) of non-stop embryo production has made women involved in assisted reproduction programme virtually useless. Meanwhile new breeds of women have been trained to become managers of world patriarchy on male terms and conditions. Men-Women sexual relations are classified into 4 categories- Those men and women who are raped (African model), rape of a sleeping women- KAR-GILL Model, those who are heavily drugged, forced to have alcohol (PREPARING THEM FOR RAPE- routine catch phrase- Bangkok model), forced child prostitution- Nepal model, "Use my baby" - Philippine model, consensual sex- European model, Kinky sex- American model, Sex- with pornography and code-language for cheating - Japanese model. The common denominator is an abuse of TRUST. Action replay of two world wars aided, abated and magnified by technological onslaught-multimedia after liquidating the feminist activists who knew ins-& outs of NRT. Patriarchs of all hues and variety on this planet cheered in unison.

Third world's professionals were first made addicted to drunkenness, debauchery and drug- addiction and then hired for pimping by the nation-states to earn foreign funding. International mafia openly boasted that all NGOs and disaster managers were in their pockets. Insecurity generated by the xenophobic and socially engineered disasters backed by cunning use of media selectively benefited the comprador bourgeoisie competing with the bored and destructive billionaire of the industrialised world. Most of the resources were appropriated through cheating, fraud and lie. The academic institutions and intelligentsia enjoyed elimination of women from the public life. They were not worried about declining sex ratio as a result of sex-selective abortion of female foetuses because they expected to get wives from the first world, which would ensure their upward mobility.

Selective Elimination of Female Foetuses and Selection of Male at a Preconception Stage

Human Development Report in South Asia 2000: The Gender Question recorded 3178 cases of female infanticide in six districts of Tamilnadu in 1995. In Mumbai only, in 1984, 84 per cent of gynaecologists admitted that they were performing amniocentesis and there were 40000 known cases of female foeticide. Supporters of sex-selection tests for selective elimination of girls/female foetuses, apply law of demand i.e., reduction in the supply of girls will enhance their status but historical evidences don't support this argument. There had been a continuous decline in the sex ratio since 1901 to1971, from 972 per 1000 men to 930 per 1000 men respectively. In 1981 the sex ratio was 933 women per 1000 men, slight increase but in 1991 is became the lowest in the history of the Census, 929 women per 1000 men. In 2001, the sex ratio for the total population is again 933 women per 1000 men. Haryana had the most depressive scenario as a result of misuse of these tests. The current sex ratio in Haryana is 861 men for thousand women, the lowest among the major states in India. The current slogan is " Sons are rising and daughters are setting." As per the UNFPA study female foeticide has been the main cause of widening sex ratio in Haryana. As per The Hindu, 19-10-2001."In the last six years, number of sex-selective abortions have increased from 62000 to 69000in Haryana and from 51000 to 57000 in Punjab. This reckless scale has pushed the fertility rate down from 3.2 to 2.9 in Haryana and from 2.9 to 2.2 in Punjab. "Reduction of birth rate, at what cost?

A study was conducted in 9 provinces viz. Andhra Pradesh,

Bihar, Gujarat, Haryana, Madhya Pradesh, Punjab, Rajasthan, Tamilnadu and Uttar Pradesh which were known for high rates of abortion. This study revealed that the impact of sex-selective abortion is seen in terms of widening gender gap among (O-6) age group, in Punjab and Haryana, two of the most economically prosperous states.

TABLE - 7
SEX RATIO AMONG THE STATES WITH WIDESPREAD USE OF SEX DETERMINATION TESTS (O-6 YEAR AGE GROUP)

States	*1991*	*2001*
Punjab	875	793
Haryana	879	820
Gujarat	928	878
Maharashtra	946	917

Source: Census of India, 2001.

Another argument that prenatal diagnostic tests give women a choice to select a child of desired sex is also unacceptable as women's "Choices" are made within the patriarchal compulsions to produce sons. Women are not taking decision autonomously. Threat of desertion, divorce and ill treatment force them to opt for sex-determination and sex-preselection tests.

Between 1975 and 2001, there was gross violation of The medical Termination of Pregnancy Act (1972) and Prenatal Diagnostic Techniques Regulation and Prevention of Misuse Act (1994). Amniocentesis, chorion villai biopsy and pre-conception sex-selection tests were provided by the technodocs on the door-to-door service basis in some states. Several towns and cities in Maharashtra, Punjab, Gujarat, Uttar Pradesh, Tamilnadu provided these tests by charging fees. As a result there is decline in sex-ratio in (o-6) years age-group i.e. there are 927 girls per 1000 boys in our country as per 2001 census. In Greater Bombay the overall sex ratio is 774 women per 1000 men as per 2001 census. Overall sex ratio for India has also drastically declined in the states where these tests are easily available in the medical market.

The question to ask is: Can we allow Indian women to become an endangered species? We need to counter those who believe that it is better to kill a female foetus than to give birth to an unwanted female child. Their logic is not only short sighted but fatalistic. The technodocs don't challenge anti-women practices such as dowry, instead display an advertisement, "Better Rs.5000 now than Rs.5 lakhs later" i.e. Better spend Rs.5ooo for female foeticide than Rs. 5 lakhs as dowry for a grown up daughter. By this logic, it is better to kill poor people or third world masses rather than let them suffer in poverty and deprivation. This logic also presumes that social evils like dowry are God-given and that we cannot do anything about them. Hence victimise the victim. Investing in daughter's education, health and dignified life to make her self dependent are far more humane and realistic ways than brutalising pregnant mother and her would be daughter.

Population Control Policies

There is a serious need to examine Population policies and Global funding from the perspective of statisation of Medical Market and marketisation of the nation states in the context of newly emerging culture of daily changes of sponsors. Financial economists have reigned supreme to generate moment-to-moment existence among population so that they can get an unending supply of cannon fodder for the NRT experimentation. Budgetary provision on health has a hidden agenda of NRT. The victims are not given scientific details and by labelling them as parasites and beneficiaries, their consent is not sought. So many families have been broken. It has burdened women with backbreaking miseries. The nation states have been coached to implement the use of NRT in Secrecy -in line with the programmes executed by G8 in Thailand, Indonesia and Bangladesh. To achieve population stabilisation, 2.1 per cent growth rate of population and NRR -net reproduction rate of 1(i.e. mother should be replaced by 1 daughter only) are envisaged. These have inherent sexist bias because it desires birth of 1 daughter and 1.1 sons. Those who support sex-determination (SD) and sex-preselection (SP) view these tests as helpful to achieve NRR1.This will further widen the gap between number of girls and number of boys in the country .As it is 100 million women have been missing due to femicide (female infanticide, ill treatment and discrimination leading to higher mortality rate among women/girls in the first three quarters of 19th century, and in the last quarter of 19th century due to misuse of SD and SP) over a period of 1901 to 2001.

Contraceptive Research Treating Women's Bodies as Testing Ground

Invasive birth control techniques entered India along with PL 48O wheat in the late sixties supported by USAID. During the emergency rule (1975-1977) forced male sterilisation programmes created political crisis for the ruling Congress. In the post emergency period to this date, women have been targeted for population control programmes. Hormonal pills (Estrogen - Projestone combinations), injectible contraceptives (Depo-provera-Depot Medroxy Progesterone Acetate, Net En- Nortesteeone Enenthate) and anti fertility vaccine have been foisted on Indian women's bodies without any concern for collateral damage in terms of thyroid, migraine, chest pain, giddiness, upsetting of regular cycle of woman's body. Research by the scientists and doctors of women's groups have shown 78 side effects of these hormone-based contraceptives. Though there was extreme secrecy surrounding their clinical trials, women's groups struggled to gather data and highlighted instances of abuse of health hazardous contraceptives. Pressure from women's groups prevented Depo Provera and Net En from being included in the family planning programme for more than a decade. It also forced IDRC-International Development Research Council, Canada to stop funding the anti fertility vaccine being developed by the National Institute of Immunology, India.

Latest in the list and still more harmful is Quinacrine as a contraceptive, which is being supplied through private routes without the permission of the drug controller or the approval of the Indian Council of Medical Research. To impart knowledge about its side effects, women's groups have to reach out to the public through posters, pamphlets and leaflets.

Racist Biases of the NRT

The Indian feminists have alleged that the NRTs have created reproductive brothels in the name of assisted reproduction- in vitro fertilisation. The white professionals from the G 8 provided BLUE PRINT to get comfort women and concubines. Menu cards were prepared as per the age, look, colour of skin, educational attainment, social-economic and political status of women. The economists called it BROTHEL model of economic development. Images, symbols, cultural programmes, films on electronic and print media were geared to suit the interest of NRT. Improving the quality of population with the help of genetic engineering has an inherent racist bias. They sidetrack the issues such as the need for better quality of life- balanced diet, clean and safe housing, sanitation, full employment and mass education for healthy and superior quality of life.

Action Reply of a neo-colonialist agenda in the 1970s has come out with full vengeance as the so called castration complex felt by the colonial masters of the industrialised world and their compradors in the developing countries find the onslaught on the native man who is sperm-producing machine and native women who is an incarnation of human lust. Dictators and megalomaniacs want to use NRT to retain eternal youth by using women as cannon fodder. It reminds one of an emergency rule of 18 months in 1975-1977.

Modus Operandi of NRT

Scientific papers were presented during 1970- 1980 in small groups under supervision of doctors and scientists from army medical colleges. Utter secrecy is maintained. Forcible separation of adolescent girls from their mothers by their alcoholic and drug addict fathers make them perpetually vulnerable to the unknown men who have total control over transport. Public transport is deliberately withdrawn from NRT operated areas. Girls and boys are picked up and dropped as per the requirements of NRT. Easy money through trafficking of girls for reproductive brothels and use of middle-aged and old women for organ transplant and embryo production is mediated by caste and kinship network under the supervision of the state apparatus.

Global show pieces-4 ASIAN TIGERS with 65 per cent work participation rate of women and high growth rate are touted as most effective policy by the richest foundations of the world.

Singapore model- Educated women should produce more babies and uneducated peasant women should be forcibly sterilised. Selection of good looking (white and yellow) girls for education. "Education is no good for black and brown population."

Korean and Taiwanese model- Use of NRT for production of boys and selective elimination of female embryos which can be used by the cosmetics and food processing industry. For upward mobility, systematic encouragement for marriage of local boys/ men with women from the industrialised world.

Hong Kong model- Hiring unmarried and educated adolescent girls for baby minding for career women. Power of patriarchy is exercised by the family, kinship network, religion, media especially the film industry and the nation states vying with each other to establish racial superiority as per the standards laid by the Hollywood film industry. Telephone calls and home-visits were used to keep some girls on a starvation diet so that the rest can overeat to procreate more. Principle of selection of beautiful and rejection/elimination of ugly has made the business of body hunting, embryo hunting, foetus hunting extremely ferocious. Patriarchs and matriarchs have become Chengiskhans chasing potential ovulators and breeders in their quest for eternal youth. There is no spontaneity left in the human relations, as FEAR IS THE KEY. NRT has changed the sight of war- from soil to human body. Dissenters of NRT are treated with snobbery by the techno-docs. Their pet responses are "We have paid her" or "We don't have any commercial interest" or " It is our social work". Antenatal sex determination tests for selective abortion of female foetuses is considered to be one of the methods of population stabilisation, the equation being, less women means less reproduction.

NRT and Plant Kingdom: Biotechnology and tissue culture in the food processing industry have a positive potential if Processual Dimensions don't involve the use of injectible contraceptives with Carcinogenic implications.

Power-relations and NRT

Search for "perfect' baby through genetic screening, ante natal sex determination tests, pre-implantation diagnosis, commercialisation of sperm and /or egg donation, commercialisation of motherhood and hormonal contraceptives raise many socio-legal and ethical questions.

Division of labour among women to control women's sexuality, fertility and labour by utilising homophobia and pitting women of different race, religions, age and looks to suit the interest of NRT will serve the interest of patriarchy, medical mafia, pharmaceutical industries, scientists, technodocs at the cost of vulnerable human beings as raw material. If the NGOs don't want to get criminalised, they must dissociate from NRTs and divert the funding for public health, library, education, skill building, employment generation as a long-term investment, formation of self-help groups. It is important to understand that reproduction has an individual and a social dimension. While examining birth control practices, an individual is a unit of analysis. While examining the population control policies we have to analyse pros & cons of NRTs, national governments, population control organisations, multinational pharmaceutical industries, public and private funded bodies, medical researchers and health workers who shape women's "choices"- women's autonomy or control at micro and macro levels. Thus choices are not made in vacuum. NRT as a choice for some women (educated career women) can become coercion for others (powerless and less articulate women) as we have seen in this chapter. Hence it is important to be vigilant about power relations determined by race, age, class and gender while examining implications of NRT on different stake groups.

Informed consent and medical malpractice- Power relations in the medical market favour the technodocs and the clients are not given full details of the line of treatment and its consequences. Political use of NRT to settle the score with competitors has been reported on a daily basis. Human beings are classified as hard wares who should be kept in captivity and soft wares which are mobile. Respect for diversity, adoption of child/children is a far simpler and more humane solution than subjecting women to undergo infertility treatment. We need dance, music, painting, skill development classes in the context of baby boom generated by the so-called infertility treatment. Obsession about creation of designer baby boys has made development agenda subsidiary.

Philosophical and medical details of NRT need public debate without iron wall of secrecy, in all Indian languages as NRT is penetrating even in those areas where you don't get even safe drinking water or food. Technologies for population control are primarily concerned about efficiency of techniques to avert births rather than safety of women. Women have to put up with the side effects of barrier or permanent methods of contraception. New reproductive technologies are provider/doctor controlled, not women controlled. Hence the women's groups repeatedly state that NRTs have inherently anti women bias.

Current Use of Contraceptive Methods: Majority of population in our country is not using any contraceptive methods for birth control. Female sterilisation is most widely prevalent method of contraception. Usage of Pill, Intra Uterine Device (IUD) and male sterilisation is 2 per cent for each of the three. Condom use constitutes only 3 per cent of the total.[30]

TABLE - 8
CURRENT USE OF CONTRACEPTIVE METHODS

Pill	2 %
Intra Uterine Device	2 %
Condom	3 %
Male Sterilisation	2 %
Female Sterilisation	34 %
Any Traditional Method/Other method	5 %
Not Using Any Method	52 %

Source: National Family Health Survey, 1998-99.

Contraceptives targeted at women, with serious side effects are quinacrine, Net-en, Norplant, Depo-Provera, anti fertility vaccine, RU 486. Side effects of long acting hormonal contraceptives are menstrual disturbance, circulatory and cardio-vascular problems, thyroid, chest-pain, giddiness, migraine, increased risk of cancer and infertility.[31] Aggressively promoted HRT (Hormone Replacement Therapy) i.e. oestrogen therapy for menopausal women has generated opposition as several studies have shown that HRT has carcinogenic implications for women.[32] Modus operandi of contraceptive research in the Asian countries treats coloured women as raw material for experimentation for eugenics.

Women resort to abortion when faced with unwanted pregnancy due to failure of contraceptives or due to non-utilisation of contraceptive methods. As per UNICEF, 1993, about 50 lakh abortions are performed under the health services network while 45 lakh by the illegal practitioners/quacks. 10 per cent of all maternal deaths are due to unsafe abortion, which result into haemorrhage, infection, incomplete evacuation, cervical lacerations, uterine perforations, thromboembolism[33] and anaesthetic complications. "A spontaneous abortion often results in severe blood loss and is therefore considered very harmful as it can cause anaemia and weakness. It is ironical however, that though spontaneous abortions are considered serious, they are so much a part of women's lives that nothing much is done about them."[34]

Population Policy

The focus of health programme should change from a population control approach of reducing numbers to an approach that is gender sensitive and responsive to the reproductive health needs of women/ men. Women groups have raised hue and cry against sexist, racist and class biases of the population control policy, which perceives uterus of coloured women as a danger zone. They have opposed genetic and reproductive engineering, which reduce women to reproductive organs and allow women being used as experimental subjects by science, industry and the state.[35] They believe that instead of abusing reproductive biology, responsible reproduction is an answer to overpopulation and infertility. Any coercion, be it through force, incentives or disincentives in the name of population stabilisation should be rejected. Instead enabling women to have access to education, resources, employment, income, social security and safe environment at work and at home are precondition to small family norm. Reproductive Rights of Women which guarantee women healthy life, safe motherhood, autonomy in decision-making about when, how many and at what interval to have children are a central axis around which a discourse on population policy should revolve. Several groups have prepared manuals to assist women leaders to reach out to poor illiterate women and teach them about fertility and infertility, giving them knowledge of their anatomy, to teach women to use fertility awareness as a means of family planning and to use natural family planning as an entry point to women's health and development.[36]

Scientifically accurate books for sex-education and fertility awareness are now available.[37] Sex education for women becomes meaningful only when it is linked with assertiveness training. Girls and women who are unable to handle gender based power relations end up as victims even after receiving thorough physiological, anatomical, scientific and medical details of sex-education.[38]

Women, Health and Law

Medical Termination of Pregnancy (MTP) Act (1972) stipulates that only trained doctors are eligible to conduct abortion in registered abortion clinics.

Prenatal diagnostic Techniques Act (1994) prevents the use of antenatal sex determination tests for selective abortion of female foetuses. CEHAT has filed a petition in the Supreme Court of India for effective implementation of the Act as well as to expand the scope of the Act to cover sex-preselection (pre-conception) techniques in its purview.

Women's groups in Delhi and Hyderabad have jointly filed a petition in the Supreme Court of India against human trails of injectible contraceptives.[39]

The Lawyers Collective HIV/AIDS Unit helps many infected women who are abandoned by their families after the death of AIDS afflicted spouse, denied rights to marital home and custody of their children.[40]

For sensitive handling of medico legal dimensions of sexual violence- rape, molestation, assault, dying declaration of the women victims of poisoning, burns and attempted suicide, the doctors, nurses, other health care workers and special executive magistrates need to be trained, as evidences of medical examination play important role during the court proceedings and the final judgement. Women's organisations have prepared an exhaustive code of conduct for the doctors, police, lawyers, special executive magistrates and social workers for recording of dying declaration.[41] Medical kit for examination of victims of sexual violence has been prepared by CEHAT.[42] There is a need for medical kit for examination of women under-trials whose death occurs in police custody or jail to ascertain the nature of torture.

Conclusion

There is a need to situate women's health in the overall macro parameters.[43] Gender divide in the access of health care and health cost is so sharp that women have to access informal providers and informal care. Gender audit in health should be done on the basis of identifying issues for reorientation at each stage of women's life cycle and focussing on the problems of each age group of women. Dr. Veena Shatrughna states, " While writing a book on *Women and Health*, we found that almost every illness could be ripped apart from the point of view of being woman. The medical system is premised on the assumption that there is a family which is caring. Women really struggle to fit into this framework. Women never have that kind of support . Every illness has specific implications and consequences of being women. Looking at gender is seeing how women negotiate in this hostile environment."[44]

To address the problems concerning women's health, a holistic life span approach is needed.[45] Women as growing human beings, homemakers, workers, mothers and elderly citizens face different types of health related issues. Women's health is determined by the material reality generated by socio-economic, cultural forces as well as gender relations based on subordination of women. It is important to make men aware about women specific health needs. Improvement in women's health is a precondition for development of her family. For an effective public education on the above-mentioned issues, charismatic personalities should teach the "Women and health" module. How to engender medical education? This question needs to be addressed. There is also, a need for gender sensitive books for the health practitioners.

Women and health movement in India has come of an age. Women's groups are examining health issues of women from political economy perspective. With the worsening economic crisis, nutritional needs of women are not fulfilled. Structural adjustment programme has affected budgetary allocation for women's overall health needs. Heavy funding is available only for the population control policy. People's Health Movement is highlighting the issues of public distribution system, public health and sanitation. The National Nutrition Policy of the Government of India examines undernutrition as a part of a larger set of interlinked processes in the sectors of agriculture, food production processes and distribution. National Health Policy has become a rallying point for heated debates on socio-psycological health needs of Indian Women. Demystification of medical knowledge and campaign against over-medicalisation of women's health needs have been the top-most priority of women's health movement in India. Campaign for people's right to health has criticized Draft National Health Policy as "The Health needs of women, children, the aged and the handicapped are hardly addressed in the draft. (Advocacy Update, 2001).Women policy makers are demanding that the health plan should be designed in such a way that interventions in health foster gender equality.

References

Bhupendra Yadav (2001), "Haryana's Setting Daughters", Economic and Political weekly, Vol. XXXVI, NO. 45, pp. 4257-4259.

Centre for Enquiry into Health and Allied Themes (CEHAT) and Mahila Sarvangeen Utkarsh Mandal (MASUM), Women and Violence, Bombay and Pune, 2000.

Chayanika Shah, Swatija Paranjape and Kamakshi Bhate 1992), We and Our Fertility, Research Centre for Women's Studies, SNDT Women's University, Bombay, 1992.

G, A, Siddiqui (2001), *Fertility Status of Women*, Mohit Publications, New Delhi.

Heidi Bart Johnson (2002), Abortion Practices in India- A Review of Literature, Abortion Assessment Project, India, Centre for Enquiry into Health and Allied Themes, Mumbai.

Jyotsana Agnihotri Gupta (2000), *New Reproductive Technologies, Women's Health and Autonomy: Freedom or Dependency?, Sage Publications,* New Delhi, .

Mahbub ul Haq (2000), Human Development Centre, *Human Development in South Asia 2000: The Gender Question,* Oxford University Press.

Medico Friend Circle (2002), "How Gender Sensitive is the National Nutrition Policy of India?-A View of the Policy Through The Gender Lens", Numbers-292-293, Bombay, January-February, 2002.

Mohan Rao: Female "Foeticide: Where Do we Go?" Issues in Medical Ethics, October-December, 2001

N.B. Sarojini: "A Woman's Body is not a Testing Ground", Humanscape, October, 2001.

National Campaign for Advocacy Studies (2001), Campaign for People's Right to Health, Advocacy Update, Pune, No. 16, October- December.

Neha Madhiwala: "Sex Selection: Ethics in the Context of Development", Issues in Medical Ethics, October-December, 2001.

Pamela Harrington (2001), "Gender and Health", Advocacy Internet, Vol.3, Issue No. 5, September-October.

Radhika Ramsubban and Shireen J. Jejeebhoy (2000), *Women's Reproductive Health in India,* Rawat Publications, Jaipur.

Sunita Bandewar and Shelley Saha (2000), Studies in Reproductive Health Services in India (1900-1999), Selected Annotated Bibliography, Centre for Enquiry into Health and Allied Themes, Bombay.

Veena Shatrughna (2001), "Body Weight- Role of Nutrition", Medico Friends Circle, Numbers- 290-291,Mumbai.

Vibhuti Patel: "Sex Determination and Sex Preselection Tests: Abuse of Advanced Technologies" in Rehana Ghadially (ed.), *Women and Society in India,* Sage Publications. 1988.

Vibhuti Patel: "Girl Child: An Endangered Species" in Viney Kirpal (ed.) *The Girl Child in 20th Century Indian Literature,* Sterling Publishers Private Limited, New Delhi, 1992

Vibhuti Patel (2002), "Women and Health in India", Health Action, Vol.15, No. 1, March, Hyderrabad, 2002.

Footnotes

1. Amartya Sen : "Many Faces of Gender Inequality", an inauguration Lecture for New Redcliff Institute at Harward University, 24-4-2001.
2. Institute of Health Management- Prevent Anaemia Now, Pachod, Maharashtra, 2002.
3. Sunil Nandaraj, Neha Madhiwalla, Roopashree Sinha and Amar Jesani : Women and Health Care in Mumbai- A Study of morbidity, utilisation and expenditure on healthcare by the households of the metropolis, CEHAT, Mumbai, 2001.
4. Iqbal Grewal and Manju Purohit: *Women's Health- A Complete Guide,* Gyan Sagar Publications, Delhi, 1999.
5. Uday Shankar Mishra: "Health Implications of Ageing", **Medico Friends Circle**, Pune, Nov.-Dec. 1999.

6. Prabha Krishnan: *Health Care, Earth Care, Interrogating* Health and Health *Policy in India,* Earthcare Books, Mumbai and Calcutta, 1998. p. 42.
7. Family Medicine in India, Official publication of IMA College of General Practitioners, New Delhi, April-June, 1999.
8. Ashish Bose; "Without My Daughter- Killing Fields of the Mind", The Times of India, 25-4-2001.
9. Mridul Eapen and Praveena Kodoth: Demystifying the "High Status" of Women in Kerala, An Attempt to Understand the Contradictions in Social Development, Centre for Development Studies, Kerala, 2001.
10. Lalitha Sridhar (Women's Feature Service) : India: Killing in Cradle, POPULI- The UNFPA magazine, Vol. 28, No. 2, September, 2001, pp. 10-12.
11. S. Wal and Ruchi Mishra: *Encyclopaedia of Health, Nutrition and Family Welfare,* Volume 1, Health and Family Welfare in Developing Countries, Sarup and Sons, New Delhi, 2000. pp. 254-255.
12. K. Rameshwar Sharma : When the Baby Weighs Low- On Low Birth Weight and How to Remedy it', **Health Action,** Vol. 14, No. 12, December 2001. pp. 18-19.
13. ARROW for Change, Women's Gender Perspectives in Health Policies and Programmes, Malaysia, Kuala Lumpur, Vol. 7, No 1, 2001.
14. Vibhuti Patel "Girl Child: An Endangered Species?", in Viney Kripal (ed) *The Girl Child in 20th Century Indian Literature,* Sterling Publications Pvt. Ltd., New Delhi, 1992. p. 9.
15. Thelma Narayan: "Gender and Power Issues in Medical Education", **Consultation on Gender and Medical Education,** Understanding Needs for Gender Sensitisation, Critiquing Content and Method of Medical Education- Developing Long Term Strategies for Intervention, organised by Achutha Menon Centre for Health Science Studies in collaboration with CEHAT, at SNDT Women's University, Bombay, on 31-1-2002.
16. Gracy Fernandes and Cecily Stewart Ray: *Raids, Rescue, Rehabilitation, The Story of Mumbai Brothel Raids –of 1996-2000,* The College of Social Work, Nirmala Niketan, Mumbai, 1991. p. 75.
17. Sameera Khan: "The Indian Women: Confronting HIV/AIDS", SANKALP, The Newsletter of the International AIDS Vaccine Initiative in India, Nov.-Dec. 2001. p. 7.
18. S. Wal and Ruchi Mishra; op. cit., pp. 27-30.
19. Sarla Gopalan and Mira Shiva: *National Profile on Women's Health and Development,* Voluntary Health Association of India and World Health Organisation, Delhi, 2000, p. 213.
20. Jayashree Ramkrishna Nair and Hema Nair "Engendering Health: A Brief History of Women's Involvement in Health Issues", SAMYUKTA, A Journal of Women's Studies, Women's Initiatives, Vol. II, No. 1, January, 2002, pp. 13-44.
21. The Times of India, 26-1-2002.
22. International Institute of Population Sciences, Bombay, 1995.
23. Kalyani Menon Sen and A.K. Shivakumar: *Women in India- How Free? How Equal?* Report Commissioned by the United Nations Resident Coordinator in India, New Delhi, 2001. p. 37.

24. Shyam Ashtekar: *Health and Health Care Systems- Observations From China, Philippines and Thailand & Reflections on India*, Bharat Vaidyak Sanstha, Nasik, p. 128.
25. Registrar General of India, 1997.
26. Tarala D. Nandedkar and Medha S. Rajadhyaksha: *Brave New Generation*, Vistas in Biotechnology, CSIR, Department of Biotechnology, Government of India, 1995.
27. Vibhuti Patel: Sex Selection, in *Routledge International Encyclopedia of Women-Global Women's Issues and Knowledge*, Vol. 4, 2000. pp. 1818-1819.
28. Jyotsana Agnihotri Gupta: *New Reproductive Technologies- Women's Health and Autonomy, Freedom* or *Dependency*? Indo Dutch Studies in Development Alternatives-25, Sage Publications, New Delhi, 2000.
29. Chee Heng Leng "Genomics and Health: Ethical, Legal and Social Implications for Developing Countries", Issues in Medical Ethics, Bombay, Vol.X, No. 1, Jan.- March, 2002, pp. 146-149.
30. National Family Health Survey, 1998-99.
31. Chayanika, Kamakshi, Swatija: We and Our Fertility, Research Centre for Women's Studies, SNDT Women's University, Bombay, 1990.
32. Sherril Sellman: "Osteoporosis- the bone of contention", Drug Disease Doctor, Quarterly Journal on Rational Drug and Therapy, Drug Action Forum, Kolkata, Vol. 14, No. 2, April, 2001.
33. IPPF Medical Bulletin, International Planned Parenthood Federation, London, Vol. 35, No. 5, October 2001.
34. Anu Gupta Choudhury, Bharati Roy and Indira Balachandran *Touch Me, Touch Me Not: Women, Plants and Healing- Women's Beliefs About Disease and Health*, Kali for Women, 1997, pp. 66-91.
35. Feminist International Network of Resistance to Reproductive and Genetic Engineering (FINRRAGE)- UBINIG-Policy Research for Development Alternative- DECLARATION OF COMILLA, Bangladesh, 1989.
36. Mahila Samooh: Fertility Awareness, published by Jagori, Delhi, 1995.
37. Tarala D. Nandedkar and Medha Rajadhyaksha: *Reaching Womanhood*, National Book Trust, India, 1999.
38. Sabala and Kranti: Na Shariram Nadhi- *My Body is Mine*, edited by Dr. Mira Sadgopal, Bombay, 1995.
39. Documentation on Women and Health, Section on Contraceptives, Streevani Documentation Centre, Pune, 1991-1994.
40. Lawyers Collective: Study of Cases Involving 130 Clients From May 1998-May 2001", Bombay, September, 2001.
41. Sakhya, College of Social Work, Nirmala Niketan, Bombay, February, 2002.
42. Lalita D'souza: Medical Kit for examination of Sexual Violence, CEHAT, 1997.
43. Laxmi Lingam *Understanding Women's Health Issues- A Reader*, Kali for Women, New Delhi, 1998.
44. Veena Shatrughna: **Consultation on Gender and Medical Education**, *op. cit*. 2001.
45. Nisha Gupta: Social and Gender Perspectives in Women's Health, **Health for the Millions**, Vol. 27, No. 3, May- June 2001, pp. 11-12.

Section II

Social Change and Gender Relations

Nine

Women's Movement in India

Introduction

In the 19th century, the male social reformers with the blessing of the British administrators, influenced by western liberal democratic values initiated the process of fight against female infanticide, widow-burning, segregation of women from the public life, prostitution and begging by the destitute women. They also organised public functions for widow-remarriages. As a result, their relatives, neighbours, community leaders and the organised religion boycotted them. In a way, it was a blessing in disguise because their isolation from petty politics gave them ample time and resources to interact with the power-structures to bring about legal reforms and establish educational institutions, shelter homes, training centres for women from where the first generation of teachers, nurses, skilled workers came out. Enormous amount of literature of that time, produced by the Indian social reformers in Marathi, Hindi, Gujarati, Malayalam, Tamil, Bengali bears witness to their path-breaking efforts. The first generation of English educated empowered women became pioneers of the women's movement in the pre-independence period. Most of them channelised their energies in building pioneer women's organisations such as All India Women's Conference (AIWC), Young Women Christian Association (YWCA) and Anjuman-e-Islam. The political agenda of AIWC was to fight against child marriage, mobilise public opinion in favour of voting rights for women, impart basic skills (such as tailoring, embroidery, cookery, hair-style, childcare, folk and classical music and dance, letter-writing etc) to women to become efficient home -makers. Cultural ambiance of AIWC suited the needs and aspirations of the high caste Hindu women. For all practical purpose, YWCA was multi-religious in terms of its areas of activities and beneficiaries, though its decision-makers happened to be the Christian wives of politicians, bureaucrats, professionals and managerial cadre who were in the close proximity of the British rulers. YWCA provided vocational training courses to groom nurses, typists, secretaries and teachers, classes in bakery products, flower arrangements, Western and Indian classical dance and music. Anjuman Trust was committed to the cause of women's education and skill formation, which would enable them to be home-based workers. They had to work within the matrix of purdah. YWCA women had to face outside world with nominal male protection. AIWC women had their male family members as facilitators. Women leaders from Anjuman Trust interacted only with the Muslim community. Differences in eating habits, dress-code and language barriers prevented them from collaborative ventures though their leadership was from the economically better-off sections.

Non-violent means of protest actions under the leadership of Gandhiji, ensured massive participation of women in the national liberation movement. Women family members of the Congress leaders gave up purdah, participated in public functions, rallies, demonstrations and experienced prison-life. Families, which allowed women to take political risks, emerged as powerful politicians. Some of the highly educated women joined educational institutions, diplomatic crew, public service boards, public and private sector industries. The rest became enlightened home-makers with a strong commitment for their daughters' education.

Women's Liberation Movement of the Seventies

Genesis of the new women's liberation movement lay in the radicalisation of Indian politics in the late sixties. Rebellious mood of the youth, poor peasants, marginal farmers, educated dalit and tribal men and women, industrial working classes found its expression in the formation of innumerable special interest groups addressing themselves to the needs and demands of the local masses. Macro political processes were also finding major shifts in their rhetorics as the protest movements of the subaltern masses had taken militant paths guided by different political ideologies. The official communist parties faced major political challenge in the form of the Naxalbari movememt in Kerala, West Bengal, Andhra Pradesh, Bihar and Punjab. Middle class mass upheaval in Gujarat (popularly known as Navnirman movement) against corruption, price rise, unemployment, speculation, hoarding and black-marketing in 1974 was replicated in Bihar in the name of Sampoorna Kranti Movement under the leadership of a Gandhian leader, Jay Prakash Narayan. Unprecedented strike of the railway workers gave a proof of the political power of collective strength of the working class. Tribal people's struggles against destructive development which served the interests of the kulaks, moneylenders, contractors, bootleggers and indigenous industrialists thriving on the barbaric means of surplus extraction developed in Chhatisgarh, Singhbhoom, Bhojpur, Srikakulam, Chandrapur, Dhulia and in the pockets of the North Eastern states. In response to the 1974 drought paralysing normal agricultural activities, the tribal masses in Dhule region of Maharashtra demanded Employment Guarantee Scheme (Vibhuti Patel, 1987). This historic demand has revolutionised the thinking of the development workers about responsibility of the state at the time of economic crisis.

In the Himalayan valleys, under the leadership of Gandhian community workers the struggle against arbitrary felling of the trees which led to deforestation and massive scarcity of fuel, fodder, water and seasonal fruits, landslides devastating villages after villages began. Women evolved creative method to protect the trees from the axes of contractors' henchmen. This movement was popularly known as Chipko because women hugged the trees when their adversaries made ferocious efforts at felling the trees. In Maharashtra, women activists and women intellectuals involved in progressive movements took initiative in forming a united front called Anti-price rise Women's Committee and organised direct action against the culprits who created man-made scarcity of essential goods (Vibhuti Patel, 1988). Thousands of poor and lower middle class women joined the struggle under the leadership of seasoned and able women from the left and socialist background. Mrinal Gore, Ahalya Ranganekar, Manju Gandhi and Tara Reddy made their special mark in the eyes of the masses as a result of their unique ability to reach out to the women of different class backgrounds. Their intellectual self-sufficiency, ability to relate micro issues to macro political reality, simple lifestyle and non-bossy nature provided role models to the younger generation of women's liberation activists of all political hues. Around the same time a conference of Women's Liberation Movement Coordination Committee was organised in Pune. This had even larger socio-political and cultural base, as right from young educated women, professionals, writers, teachers, industrial working class women, unorganised sector women workers, temple prostitutes and tribal women participated in the deliberations and highlighted their demands. Stree Mukti Sangathana in Bombay and Progressive Organisation of Women in Hyderabad were formed in 1974. In Delhi, new leadership among women evolved from the radical students' movement and the democratic rights movement. Individual women in different political groupings all over India were feeling discontented about patriarchal biases in their organisations but they came out openly against it only after the emergency rule got over. These were independent, self-determining and democratic movements, which questioned all hierarchical structures. In India, young people of that period had not participated in the dreams of the nationalist movement. Faced with multiple crises: - economic, social and political, along with corruption, drought, inflation, unemployment, pauperization of the rural poor - the disenchanted youth responded with protest. Widespread, open discontent was expressed in action and consolidation of the action developed into powerful organisations throughout the country. These movements raised a number of diverse issues-land-rights, wages, employment, security at work-place, water availability, destruction of nature, oppression and exploitation of the Dalits (the untouchables) and the working masses. Many women participated in these struggles with enthusiasm, responsibility and creativity.

The UN Declaration of 1975 as an International Women's Year, coincided with the Emergency Rule in India. By the time the Emergency was lifted in 1977, several women's groups had developed around democratic rights issues. The press swung into "action" after the imposed silence of nearly two years. Atrocities committed against women during the Emergency were openly documented and reported in the press. These atrocities struck a chord in most women's own experience of life in the family, in the streets, in the workplace and in political groups. The culmination of this process was reached in 1980 when many women's groups took to the street to protest. During the 1980s, the issue of women's oppression was depicted not only in discussion forums, seminars and `serious' articles but also in the popular media. Women who had on their own identified the sources of their problems and indignity, began to acquire a language, an organisational platform, a collective identity and legitimacy they did not have earlier.

The Status of Women's Committee appointed by GOI released a voluminous report in 1974. This report called Towards Equality was prepared by the scholars with an interdisciplinary perspective and was presented in the Parliament of India, where it received a tremendous response from the decision-making bodies, the state apparatus and the print media. Shocking description of Indian women's reality, which manifested in declining sex ratio, very high rate of female mortality and morbidity, marginalisation of women in the economy and discriminatory personal laws were some of the major highlights of the report. But the report failed to throw any light on violence against women in the civil society and by the custodians of law and order. Major achievement of the report lay in the policy decision taken by the principal research body like the Indian Council of Social Science Research (ICSSR) i.e. to provide financial support to scholars committed to the women's cause, to conduct research into problems faced by women in poverty groups.

Between 1977 and 1979 new women's groups emerged in the cities like Delhi, Banglore, Hyderabad, Bombay, Ahmedabad, Patna, Madras. They organised protest actions against dowry murders, beauty contests, sexist portrayal of women in media, pornographic films and literature imported from abroad, introduction of virginity tests by the U.K. immigration authorities, custodial rape and pitiable condition of women in prison. These groups were multicultural in their composition and worldview. As a result, their political agenda reflected the contemporaneous handling of the complex reality of women constructed by interplay of class, caste, religion, ethnicity and globalisation. The spokesperson of these groups had an advantage of high level of ideological investment and the experience of the radical movements of the late sixties. Their collective wisdom provided main backbone to the movement (Vibhuti Patel, 1985). Their newsletters, magazines and booklets in regional languages as well as in English provided creative way of handling Indian women's problems. Launching of MANUSHI in January 1979 was a qualitative leap in this direction. The need to study women's issues in academic institutions and to conduct research based on experiential material and affirmative action was beginning to be discussed among Indian women's studies scholars by the early eighties. The discourse on this subject has proved to be a fruitful exercise for activists, academics, researchers, policy planners and the UN system. The apex body of higher learning, University Grants Commission defined WOMEN'S STUDIES as a discipline that involved research, documentation, teaching, training and action. It is understood that women have subordinate status in our society so the knowledge base created by WS should be used for empowerment of women.

Methods of Functioning of the New Women's Groups

Most of the women who took initiative in formation of the new women's groups were extremely averse to authoritarian structures within the family, educational and religious institutions and society at large as all of them did not allow women critical thinking and a space to grow as independent, cerebral and politically conscious human beings. Hence they were very clear in their approach that they would encourage each and every member of the group to articulate her thoughts and establish intimate working relationship based on the collective decision-making processes. Initially this method proved very effective in creating new cadre of women who were intellectually enlightened, politically articulate, well informed and supportive to each other within their small groups as there were no male political bosses to curb their initiative and make them rot only in routine activities of fund-raising, translating, typing, posting, cleaning and cooking for the members of their political groups. Such groups in Madras, Banglore, Hyderabad, Bombay, Pune and Delhi brought out documents, position papers, manifestoes, pamphlets and reproduced whole lot of documents of the women's liberation movements in the other countries containing debates which had direct bearing on our situation. They had tremendous urge to reach out to more and more like-minded women. Their meetings were throbbing with new ideas, powerful polemics on epistemological issues, at the same time they reflected deep concern for immediate problems of women. As they believed that women's issues needed to be taken up on a day-to-day basis and patriarchal power needed to be challenged in both 'personal' and 'political' spheres of life. They simultaneously started support work to individual women, solidarity work for the mass movements and united front work on an issue to issue basis. But, at the same time, they maintained their political autonomy and organisational identity. These groups kept in touch with each other by circulating their leaflets in English and regional languages, mimeographed documents and letters. They functioned purely on an informal basis and organised meetings in the homes of one of the members or sympathizers. Between 1977and 1980, only in Maharashtra, a new culture of exclusively women's workshops, women's conferences and women's gatherings, in which women of politically diverse views were invited, was found. As these gatherings were multi-class and multi-caste (within the matrix of Brahminical Hinduism), women pursuing different occupations- right from agricultural labourers, beedi workers, industrial working class women, students, teachers, journalists, writers, researchers, white collar employees shared their experiences and put forward their demands.

Proliferation of the Autonomous Women's Groups

Nationwide anti-rape campaign in 1980 resulted into emergence and proliferation of the autonomous women's organisations in several cities and towns of India. These groups managed to get tremendous publicity in the print as well as the audio-visual media because at that time 'violence against women' was the most sensational and the newest issue. Family members, especially fathers and brothers of the women victims of violence flooded the women's groups. Later on, the women victims started approaching these groups on their own. While doing agitational and propaganda work against series of rape cases in custodial situation, domestic violence and dowry harassment, these groups realised that to work on a sustained basis and to take care of the rehabilitative aspects of violence against women, it was important to evolve institutional structures for support to the women victims of violence based on feminist principles of solidarity (mutual counselling) and sisterhood. Criminal legal system in India made it inevitable for these groups to establish rapport with the police for an immediate redressal to the women victims of violence. Condition of women in the remand homes and the Nari Niketans were so repugnant and barbaric that they could not be trusted for women's rehabilitatior.. In fact, many women who suffered at their hands approached the new women's groups. The women activists had to deal with the attitude of victim baiting and double standards of sexual morality, sexist remarks, sick humour from the staff of the police, the legal apparatus and the public hospitals. At each and every step, they encountered class, caste and communal biases. These resulted into confrontation between the women's groups and the established institutions. But in course of time, they realised that it was necessary to suggest concrete alternatives in terms of legal reforms, method of interventions and the staff-training for attitudinal changes. For public education, literature written in convincing style was a must. Audio-visual material for reaching out to more and more people was necessary. Professional bodies and educational institutions were approaching these groups for understanding the women's question. In these context SPECIAL INTEREST GROUPS focusing on agitation and propaganda, media-monitoring, resource material for consciousness raising, creation of cultural alternatives, publications, research and documentation, bookstalls, legal aid work came into existence during the eighties and got consolidated in the 1990s. These groups played complementary roles in each other's development, though the process was not so smooth.

Issues Taken up by the New Women's Groups

The movement got momentum with the campaign against the Supreme Court of India's judgement against Mathura, a teenage tribal girl who was gang-raped by the policemen at the dead of night, in the police station in Chandrapur district of Maharashtra in 1972. After 8 years of legal battle in the Session's Court, the High Court and the Supreme Court by her sympathetic lawyer Ad. Vasudha Dhagamwar, Mathura lost everything - her status, her self-esteem and her credibility, the Court declared that Mathura was not raped by the men in uniform but Mathura being a woman of 'an easy virtue' gave a willful consent for sexual intercourse. Vasudha and her three colleagues in the legal profession wrote an open letter challenging the Supreme Court's verdict in an extremely poignant and logically convincing style. This letter was widely publicized in the print media. Two major points concerning this issue were:

Reopening of the Mathura Rape Case and amendments in the Rape Laws that put burden of proof on women and had a narrow definition of rape. Around these demands, the women's groups were formed. They collected signatures on their petitions, conducted study-circles where experienced lawyers spoke, organised rallies, sit-ins, demonstrations in front of the offices of the concerned authorities, prepared poster exhibitions, plays, skits, songs, slogans against violence against women, wrote letters to the editors of different news-papers, wrote articles in newspapers and magazines for the first time on women's problems.

Initially they concentrated on the women- specific issues such as wife-battery and dowry-murders, rape and eve-teasing, pornographic films, plays and literature on harassment of women at the work place. Militant actions, social boycott, *gherao* of tormentors, raiding of the matrimonial homes for retrieval of dowry had to be resorted to because of antipathy/lethargy of the state apparatus. From these experiences of direct action the activists of the women's groups got to know the power relations operating within modern families (working class, middle class and upper class), different religious communities and various caste organisations.

Domestic Violence

Sakhya, a women's guidance cell was initiated by the college of social work in the mid eighties to render counselling services to clients with pre-marital , marital and family problems, to provide legal guidance and rehabilitate women in distress, to conduct sensitization and awareness programmes in schools, colleges, institutions and communities on issues affecting relationships between women and men. To coordinate with women's organisations and others, on micro and macro issues such as unjust laws and policies of the government.[1]

Campaign for Legal Reforms

While providing support to women facing problems concerning marriage, divorce, maintenance, alimony, property rights, custody of child/children and guardianship rights, the activists realised that the existing personal laws and most of the customary laws were discriminating against women. Hindu daughters were deprived of coparcenary rights in parental property as per the codes of *Mitakshara.* Christian women could not get divorce on the ground of husband's adultery; it had to be coupled with cruelty, bestiality and sodomy; while Christian husband can just declare his wife as an adulteress and divorce her. This antiquated law was enacted in the colonial period to serve the interests of the British bureaucrats who had their legally wedded wives in England and were cohabiting with the Indian (in their language 'native') women. Parsee daughters who married non-Parsee men lost their property rights and non-Parsee wives of Parsee husbands got only half the shares in husband's property as per the Parsee Personal Law. Shariat Law subjugated Muslim women by imposing *purdah,* allowing polygamy and unilateral divorce by men to his wife/wives and by depriving divorced Muslim women of maintenance rights. Underlying philosophy of all these personal laws was that: women are not equal to men. They are governed by the patriarchal ideology. Irrespective of their religious backgrounds, these personal laws perpetuate patrilineage, patrilocality, double standard of sexual morality for men and women and perceive women as dependent on men. Individual women from different communities have challenged the constitutional validity of discriminatory aspects of the personal laws in the Supreme Court of India. Increasing number of educated working women and housewives from all religious backgrounds have been approaching secular women's organisations. Main problems faced by them from their natal families have been forcible marriage, murderous attacks in cases of inter-caste, inter-class and inter-religious marriages, property disputes, incest and from their husbands and in-laws have been adultery, bigamy, polygamy, divorce, custody of child/children, property, incest etc. As the issue of personal laws is intertwined with the religious identities, the secular women's movement had to face tremendous hostility from the elite of the different communities, mass organisations, patriarchal secular lobby and the parliamentary parties cashing on block-votes. Individual women (divorced, deserted, single and married under duress) are questioning discrimination in the customary laws. Tribal women in Maharashtra and Bihar have filed petitions demanding land rights in the Supreme Court of India. Several women's groups (*Saheli*, Delhi, *Vimochana*, Banglore and Forum against Oppression of Women, Mumbai) and human rights lawyers team (The Lawyers Collective, Mumbai and Indian Social Institute, Delhi) have prepared drafts containing technical detail of gender just and secular family laws. In 1996, Ahmedabad Women's Action Group (AWAG) filed writ petition to declare Muslim Personal Law which allows polygamy as void as offending Articles 14 and 15 of the Constitution.[2] " The issue of women's rights and family law reform has been increasingly entangled within the polemics of identity politics and minority rights"[3], says a feminist lawyer, Ad, Flavia Agnes.

On April 23, 1985, the Supreme Court of India awarded lifelong maintenance to an old divorced Muslim woman, Shah Bano. The communal tone of the judgement – which, instead of highlighting the right to maintenance of a divorced woman, spoke of ' Muslim woman" and 'muslim husband'-created unnecessary and harmful polarisation on religious grounds. Lawyers, women's groups, progressive and conservative people reacted sharply. Demonstrations, rallies, petitioning, signature campaigns, media war, public meeting, both for and against the Muslim Personal Law- all totally communalised the issue of gender justice (Vibhuti Patel, 1995).

Human Rights Law Network, YUVA and College of Social Work, Mumbai have prepared domestic workers' bill to regularise terms and conditions concerning work condition and wages of the domestic workers who happen to be women from the depressed classes. Deepalaya, Justice and Peace Commission of St. Pius College has published a manual focusing on practical and operational aspects of legal battles, law and order machinery and community's initiatives such as people's courts, out of court settlement in presence of an impartial individual or a body.

Women's Movement and Population Policy

When it comes to reproductive rights of women, most of the efforts of the women's groups in India have been directed against excesses committed in the name of family planning programmes. Now, Indian Council of Medical Research, All India Institute of Medical Sciences and Institute of Research in Reproduction (IRR) have shown readiness to discuss scientific, medico-legal and operational dimensions of bio-medical researches conducted on human subjects. UNFPA and WHO have drawn guidelines about population policies so that its focus shifts from targeting women for population control to women's reproductive rights. Ethical guidelines for bio-medical research are drawn.(Mastroianni, Faden and Federman, 1994). Still in the interior parts of India, poor women have been the main targets of the abusive sterilization operations and unsafe injectable and oral contraceptives (UNFPA, 1998).

Recent researches on adolescent girls and abortion have highlighted the problem of teenage pregnancies, trafficking of young girls for sex trades and complicity of the criminal justice system. Campaign against sex determination resulted into central legislation banning amniocentesis, chrion-villai-biopsy and sex pre-selection techniques for femicide. But, much needs to be done to make the legislation effective in the real life. CEHAT and the Lawyers Collective have jointly supported a petition (Public interest Litigation in the Supreme Court of India) filed by Dr. Sabu George for effective implementation of the Act: In 1998, All India Democratic Women's Association challenged the use of the drug quinacrine as a method of female sterilization by filing a Public Interest Litigation case against Quinacrine.[4] Women's groups are demanding that the population policy should focus on women's reproductive rights (Vibhuti Patel, 2001).

Prostitution

Series of raids by the Bombay police in the red light areas " generated public opinion that strongly called for joint cooperation of the Government and non-government agencies in the matter of rehabilitation."[5] Several women's rights groups and health groups are working in collaboration with refuge homes for rehabilitation of the ex-prostitutes in a humane manner.

Child Sexual Abuse

Women's groups have taken up the cases of child sexual abuse within childcare institutions. [6] In response to sexual assault of a deaf-mute juvenile in the observation home, Forum Against Child Sexual Exploitation (FACSI) came into existence. Juvenile Welfare Board situated in the premises of the observation home took 10 days to respond to the event and that too after massive pressure exerted by FACSE which conduced thorough inquiry and submitted its report to the National Commission of Women. In its recommendations it demanded formulations of code of conduct for the child care institutions. Transparency in its functioning, regular inspection, social audit by the citizens groups were some of the crucial measures for checking and controlling abuse. In case of child sexual abuse, FACSAE suggested that the institution must launch a public inquiry or constitute a truth and reconciliation commission.

Two Decades of Advocacy for Legal Reforms

Many progressive laws have been enacted in the last 25 years. In response to the demand raised by the women's movement, series of legal reforms were made. Some of them are:

- Equal Remuneration Act (1976),
- Family Courts Act (1984),
- The Indecent Representation of Women Act (1986),
- Immoral Traffic (Prevention) Act, 1986
- Juvenile Justice Act, 1986
- The Act on Women's Commission, 1993
- Pre-Natal Diagnostic Act, 1994
- Domestic Violence Act, 2002

The most visible campaigns of the women's movements have been the efforts made for legal amendments. Print and electronic media responded to the campaigns for reforms in the rape laws, amendments in the Dowry Prohibition Act, introduction of a clause, section 498 A in the Indian Penal Code, From SITA to PITA to deal with prostitution, The Commission of SATI (Prevention) Bill, 1987, the Maharashtra Regulation of Use of Pre-natal Diagnostic Technique Act, 1988 (Vibhuti Patel, 1988) .

"Judicial reforms require many things. The transformation of statutes, the assertion of its spirit and intent through judgements, the recruitment of women judges determined to do justice and care as to the minutest detail regarding enforcement, which must be swift and merciless. India did reasonably well in the first part and failed miserably in the second."[7]

Some groups are focussing on out of court solutions for solving legal issues with the help of Lok Adalat and negotiated settlements.(Jaya Menon and Jean Saldanha, 1998).

Women's Movement and the Development Agenda

During 1970s and 1980s, the women's movement highlighted marginalisation of women from the economy. The efforts of women activists were directed in agitation and propaganda for women's rights, street-fighting against escalating violence against assertive women and team-building to counter sexual harassment at work-place. In the 1990, the women's movement is demanding its legitimate place within the mainstream with its own agenda of empowerment of women with partnership with men (Martha Nussbaum and Jonathan Glover, 1995). It has been able to identify its allies in all sections of society. Its horizontal and vertical networking has created congenial atmosphere to execute development agenda with the help of effective use of information technology, communication channels, modern managerial practices and efficient law and order machinery. The most difficult areas have been providing educational opportunities for the poverty groups, low -cost housing, environmental and occupational safety and human rights concerns. Development thinkers and workers need safety nets to operate without pressure from the local bullies and vested interests (Vibhuti Patel, 2001). Dadas of each and every communities are increasingly taking advantage of development workers/teachers/academicians because they are non-hierarchical in their functioning and also because they are not commercial minded in their day-to-day affairs. When individual women activists sense threat/pressure in advance, they do change their accommodation and jobs. This is another form of sati. The state, political parties and beneficiaries of women's groups too have duty to ensure democratic and multicultural atmosphere within which the women activists can take judicious and gender-just decisions about allocation of developmental resources and development funding for construction of schools, community centres, sports-clubs, libraries and reading rooms, low cost hospitals and low cost housing for the poverty groups leading **settled life** (Hemlata Dandekar , 1993).

Women's Movement and Peace Initiatives

The most important contribution of the women's movement has been its commitment for peace-initiatives in the disturbed areas torn by communal conflicts, ethnic tensions and mob violence. Its work in the refugee camps has been acknowledged by the state. Media publicity on this issue is extremely important so that such work can be replicated in the places where such groups don't exist. Indian women's movement has played a crucial role in the global peace initiative (Women for Peace, 1994).

Women's Movement in INDIA and Decision Makers in the Educational Institutions

To incorporate a gender perspective in the academic curricula, our decision-makers will have to be prepared for numerous reforms in the existing syllabi and teaching methods. Conceptual issues regarding gender perspective will have to be integrated in all subjects within humanities, social sciences, technical training institutes, Academies on essential services such as railways, road transport, police, military and paramilitary forces, health-care, school of architects, engineering and science colleges so that we can get gender-aware human resource for area development, town planning, travel and tourism, public health projects, industrial growth and disaster management. Fine arts faculties, communication schools, sports department, music colleges and libraries should integrate relevant research findings generated by the women's movement in their course content. The most difficult task in this direction is - identification of motivated teachers who are ready to evolve course- content on women, which can be integrated in the mainstream discipline. This exercise will have to be supplemented with textbook writing, translations and funding. Vice-chancellors of our universities need to be convinced about foundation course on women and Development. Educated women (with specialization to deal with technical aspects) of the women's movement can be invited as resource persons to provide inputs in curriculum development (Margot Duley and Mary Edwards, 1986). Sexual harassment of women employees, contract labour, Ph.D. students, women field workers and women teachers should be handled with utmost sensitivity, by the heads of the institutions and academic council. Witch-hunting of women academicians fighting for women's rights must stop.

Ideological debates Among Autonomous Women's Group in India

The autonomous women's groups (AWG) are marked by their 'untraditional' approach towards women's question. They emerged as an alternative to traditional women's organizations and women's wings of political parties. Right from the beginning they have generated ideological debates on many issues concerning women.

The first and foremost feature of AWG is their way of looking at women's oppression, exploitation, injustice and degradations as an outcome of complex mix of patriarchal class society that has caste, religious and ethnic dimensions too. They believe in fighting against all types of domination relationships between men and women in both "personal" as well as "political" sphere of life. They believe that it has much important to fight against individual cases of violence against women-rape, wife beating, discrimination and harassment at workplace etc. As fighting for amendments in the rape laws, trade union rights for women. AWG also believe that to achieve women's liberation, it is important to fight for women's right on day to day level. Belief of the traditional left that once there is social revolution, all problems of women will be automatically solved, has been challenged by AWG. They believe that if consistent efforts are not made by women to assert and preserve their own rights even after revolution there will not be women's liberation.

Feminists consider that economic independence of women is a minimum necessary condition for women's liberation. It is not sufficient because if the patriarchal value persists in the society, women's wage work alone does not enhance their social status, because it creates 'double burden' of wage work and housework. As regards the moralistic, puritanical view of rape (Kotwal, 1979), for liberals and democratic minded people, rape is a question of "violation of sanctity of an individual'. Political parties see it as a "Law and Order Problem" (Farooqui, 1976). Most of the leftists are concerned only with incidences of mass rape or individual rape during class struggle, communal and caste riots (Report, Manushi, 1980), While feminist believe that rape is the worst manifestation of patriarchal power to humiliate, subjugate and intimidate women, and every woman irrespective of her class and cultural background is its potential rape victim.(Gotoskar, 1982). Cases of police rape have been tackled by women's groups (Lalitha, 1980)

Violence in the family is generally looked at as 'personal problem' by most of the institutions in our society (Rebello, 1982). Many women's organizations provide 'protection' to women victims of violence in the family, destitute and deserted women, unwed mothers, and divorcees. They look at this work in a traditional social work framework where expert counsellors help, guide, do charity for 'poor', 'harassed', 'unfortunate' women. Feminists have criticized this approach of 'we up here help you' and 'you down there should be helped'. They see taking up individual cases of harassment of women and providing support structure in term of medical aid, etc. as a part of women's right movement. Instead of taking help from expert counsellors, they believe in 'mutual counselling' i.e. women who have undergone similar experiences share their problems, emotionally support each other (d'mello, 1982)

Women's groups have taken up issues such as temple-prostitution (Hankare, 1981) and exposed patriarchal values underlying prostitution. Moralist and puritanical concern towards prostitution has met with severe criticism from the feminists

(FAOW, 1980). Women's groups in Pune, Nasik, Nagpur have tried to organise maidservants by forming their union. This has generated debate about 'exploitation of poor women by middle class women' (Pawar, 1982). Power relationship between the management and working women in hostels has been challenged by AWGs in Goa, Hyderabad, Banglore etc. (Malkote and Tharu, 1980). Many AWGs are facing dilemma whether to concentrate on only women specific issues or work for other issues involving men, women and children and highlight specific problems that women face as it happens during tragedies like drought, floods, earthquakes, Bhopal gas carnage, caste and communal riots etc.

Structure and Method of Functioning of AWGs

Most of the AWGs have informal style of functioning. There is no hierarchy of President, Secretary, Treasurer, and Executive Committee Members at the top and general members at the bottom (Patel, 1982). There is a collective decision making process. (Desai, 1982). Some AWGs that provide various types services have to have legal structure so they have nominal trustees. Working Women's Organisations have trade union structure (SEA, 1985) . Most of the agitational organisations have two types of memberships; those who come for all its activities are the activists and the rest are sympathisers (Introduction – FAOW, 1980 and Saheli, 1982). Mass organisations of tribal, agricultural labourers, workers have their women's wings, but decisions are taken by the main body.

Need for Autonomy

It is very important for women's organisations to be autonomous from the political parties and other organisations such as co-operatives, mass organisations, trade unions, religious groups or their decision making process because the experience of past have shown that if the organisation does not remain for women, by women and of women, in the true sense of the terms, the thrust gets diluted. While for a general cause women are used when specific demands for women are raised, men show indifference. (Gotoskar and Savara, 1980). Lessons of Bodh Gaya and Chipko struggles have also proved that women's group have to face strong resistance from the male members of the mass organisations, whenever they raise issues such as equal pay for equal work, land-rights for women, wife beating, alcoholism (Manimala,1985 and Joshi, 1989). In many tribal areas when a tribal women is molested or raped or dubbed as witch by the landlord or police official, the mass organisation would protest against it but when such things happen within the community, no one would stand by that woman. In Singhhoom, Gua, Santhal and Dahanu, there were many examples of this sort. Hence it is of utmost importance to have autonomous organisations of women even if the mixed mass organisation is very militant. The women's groups must establish its linkages with the mass organisations, they need not be separatist or divisive but should strengthen the general struggle also by making women more confident, vocal and assertive and by evolving leadership qualities among them, since in the mixed group, women remain merely followers and in the background. Further, they do not feel confident to discuss issues like wife-beating , rape and molestation, harassment by the in-laws. Women's organisations such as Mahila Mukti Morcha (Sen, 1984) and Shramik Stree Mukti Sangathana , Dhulia bear witness to the positive role of such organisations. Hence the need for separate mass organisations of poor women which may collaborate with organisations of poor men at higher levels to promote common interests. (Rahman, 1985).

Types of Linkages

It is very important for rural women's organisations to establish linkages with different types of organisations. They must try to evolve the organisations working for women' s development. For maintaining the dynamism as well as freshness of approach, it is crucial for the rural women's organisations to exchange ideas, share experiences with other organisations. If they are in touch with trade unions, democratic rights groups, legal groups etc, they can organise camps in collaboration with them so that its members can get better education on social problems.

On general issues like land rights, equal wages, state repression, the legal aid can be provided to them. Urban women's organisations can assist rural groups in providing audio-visuals, films, exhibitions, camps and workshops for their rights, issues, national policies, international problems. At the time of repression, they can intervene and also raise public awareness through petitioning, writing articles and sending investigating teams in the area o atrocities. (Lokshahi Hakk Sangathana, 1983). Professional organisations such as medical groups, health groups, lawyers, trained social workers and specialists such as scientists, geologist, botanist can also be used for rural women's cause. For this, women's groups in the cities should make arrangements to fulfil the specific needs of the rural women's group. It becomes very difficult to sustain rural women's organisations in isolation because as it is they have to face lot of societal resistance. Linkages with other special interest groups can enhance enthusiasm, strengthen struggle and help in evolving overall perspective for long-term functioning of rural women's organisations.

Time and again, fear is expressed that the state is co-opting women's organisations. There are debates going on among women activists on the issue such as:

1. If strength of women police is increased, will the condition of women in custody, lock-ups and police station be safer? Are not women police also part of the same oppressive, coercive state force? To what extent, is it justifiable to think that by virtue of being women, women police will be more humane to women in general?
2. Can we put together a demand like ban on pornographic literature, sexist obscene films and magazines ? When the state represents the interest of patriarchal ruling class, what help can they give to enhance women's image? Will the state not ban the activities of progressive forces who are trying to combat existing obscurantist values being perpetuated in the name of 'national ethos' and 'Indian culture'? Instead, won't it be more appropriate to mobilise public opinion for social boycott of such films, magazines, posters, hoardings, etc.?
3. That demands like special tribunal to conduct rape-trial or family courts to look into cause of violence in the family or of dowry harassment create the illusion that the existing state machinery can give justice to women. " If

women's liberation movement restricts itself or emphasises the demands made to the state, the effects would be a limitation of the movement, to forms of struggles like demonstration, solidarity actions, etc. It would also mean strengthening of certain illusion that police, the protector of law and order , is neutral, and therefore, the state is above classes etc. The entire emphasis of building strong women's groups to fight their own oppression is thus diluted. It prevents women from standing on their own feet, makes them dependent on the state and makes such organisations adequate only for making petitions or taking out morchas, etc."(Feminist Network, February, 1979).

Hence, it is emphasised again and again that only the grass roots women's movement can change the status of women. And to increase their strength, the women's rights organisations will have to establish linkages with the organisations of other exploited and oppressed strata like toilers, tribals, dalits, slum dwellers, etc.

Defying degradation
Tossing aside tradition
We have come!
Battered women, worker, farmer
In the army together.
To end dowry, rape, misused authority,
To stop wife-beating and cruelty,
We have come!
From mill and mine, field and shed
Inspite of owners' threat and dread
We have come!
Look! Look! You blind tyrant
Our army has come!
To destroy injustice, our army has come!

(Originally written in Hindi by Vibhuti Patel in March 1982, translated into English by Joy Deshmukh).

Conclusion

There have been various ideological shades in the women's movement. Old women's organisations have an elitist bias. To them, privileged 'women from good families' do some philanthropic, social work activities for common, poor, miserable women. They do not believe in transcending the existing social order. In their personal lives, they abide by the rules of caste system and generally believe in maintaining the status-quo.

Women from the traditional left parties believe that after the social revolution, automatically all problems of women will be solved. They highlight mainly economic exploitation of women.

The members of new women's groups believe in fight against all forms of sexual oppression and consider women as an oppressed sex. They believe, like casteism and communalism, sexism is also one of the most effective weapons utilised by the ruling class to divide masses. Hence, they believe in fighting against caste system, religious chauvinism and sexism simultaneously. In their personal lives also they practise non-discriminatory attitudes towards people of different religions, castes and classes. They consider that economic independence of women is a minimum necessary condition for women's liberation but it is not enough. One has to fight for women's rights in socio-cultural, educational, political fields to achieve total liberation. Many of those members of women's rights groups call themselves feminists. They do not like the term 'social worker' for themselves. Those who believe that legal reforms can change women's position are known as liberal feminists. Those who consider men as responsible for the plight of women are known as radical feminists. And those who situate women's oppression in the overall socio-economic and cultural reality are known as socialist feminists. Socialist feminists believe in establishing linkages between women's movement and broader socio-political movement by working in collaboration with various types of mass organisations like trade unions, democratic rights organisations and issue-based united fronts. They think that women's demands have to be fought on a day to day basis. Then only new ethos, new ideologies, new morality and new egalitarian relations between men and women can be evolved.

References

Amarja Pawar, "The Pune Domestic Servants Revolt; Background and Causes", Institute of Social Research and Education, Bombay, 1982.

Anna Mastroianni, Ruth Faden and Daniel Federman (Eds.) *Women and Health Research- Ethical and Legal Issues of Including Women in Clinical Research*, National Academy Press, Washington, D.C., 1994.

Forum Against Oppression of Women, Report of the National Conference on Perspective for Women's Liberation Movement in India, 1985.

Flavia D'mello, "Our Fight Against Wife-beating", HOW, Vol. 5, No. 9&10, November, 1982, pp. 19-22.

Goa Tourism Development Corporation, Government of Goa.

Hankare, P.D. "Maharashtra Devdasi Organise", Manushi, Vol. 2, No. 1, 1982, pp. 28-30.

Hemlata Dandekar (ed.), *Shelter, Women and Development- First and Third World Perspectives*, George Wahr Publishing Co., Michigan, 1993.

Jaya Menon and Jean Saldanha (Compilers) from Deepalaya, Documentation, Research and Training Centre, TOWARDS A PEOPLE"S COURT, Justice and Peace Commission, St. Pius College, Goregaon (W) Bombay, 1998.

Lalitha, K, "Rape- A Case Study of Rameeza Bee" Stree Shakti Sangathana, Paper presented at the National Conference on Perspective for women's liberation Movement in India, hosted by Forum Against Oppression of Women, Bombay, 1980.

Medha Kotwal, " Pune- Don't Sell Our Bodies To Sell Your Products ", Manushi, Vol. 1, No. 1, pp. 17-18, 1979.

Margot I. Duley and Mary I. Edwards (Eds.), *The Cross- Cultural Study of Women- A Comprehensive Guide*, The Feminist Press, New York, 1986.

Martha Nussbaum and Jonathan Glover, *Women, Culture and Development- A study of Human Capabilities*, Clarendon Press, Oxford, 1995.

Rama Melkote and Suzie Tharu, "Patriarchal Relations in Working Women's Hostels: Implications for Women's Movement", Paper presented at the National Conference on Perspective for Women's Liberation Movement in India, hosted by Forum Against Oppression of Women, Bombay, November, 1980.

Sangeeta Purushottam *(1998), The Empowerment of Women in India- Grassroots Women's Network and The State*, Sage Publications, Delhi.

Shaila Rebello, " A Survey of Wife-beating in Kanara", Institute of Social Research and Education, Bombay, 1982.

Shakuntala Narasingha (1999), *Empowering Women- An Alternative Strategy From Rural India*, Sage Publications, Delhi.

Sujata Gotoskar, "Grassroots Experiences of Organising Working Class Women", HOW, Vol.5, No. 1, pp. 11-14, January-February, 1982.

Sujata Gotoskar and Meera Savara, "Organising Tribal Women in Maharashtra", Asia Pacific Centre for Women's Development, Malaysia.

Sukanya Nihal Singh (2001), *Prospectus for Women Empowerment- Dynamics of Enablement*, Commonwealth, New Delhi.

UNFPA, Summary Report of Consultations to Assess Implementation of the International Conference on Population and Development Programme of Action, National Consultation, 27th to 29th October 1998, Goa.

Vibhuti Patel, "Women's Liberation in India", **New Left Review**, No. 153, August 1985, London, pp. 75-86.

Vibhuti Patel, "Adivasi Women on Warpath", in Miranda Davies (compiled by), *Third World- Second Sex,* Zed Press, London, 1987. pp.249-252.

Vibhuti Patel, "Emergence and Proliferation of Autonomous Women's Movement in India", in Neera Desai(ed*), A Decade of Women's Movement in India,* Himalaya Publishing House, Bombay, 1988, pp.117-127.

Vibhuti Patel, "Sex Determination and Sex Preselection Tests: Abuse of Advanced Technologies", in Rehana Ghadiali (ed), *Women and Society in India*, Sage Publications, Bombay, 1988. pp.178-185.

Vibhuti Patel, " Shah Bano Controversy and the Challenges Faced by Women's Movement in India", in Asghar Ali Engineer (ed*), Problems of Muslim Women in India,* Orient Longman, India, 1995, pp.140- 148.

Vibhuti Patel, "Gender Issues in New Social Movements in India", Perspectives-AVEHI- Audio Visual Education Resource Centre, March, 2001pp.2-3.

Vibhuti Patel, "Vision 2010 A Gender Analysis", **People's Reporter**, Bombay, July 10-25,2001.

Vimla Farooqui," Women, Special Victims of Police and Landlord Atrocities", National Federation of Indian Women, Bombay, 1978.

Women For Peace, Published by Women in Black, Belgrade, 1994.

Footnotes

1. Sakhya, Anti Dowry- women's Guidance Cell, College of Social Work, Mumbai, 2002.
2. Christine Chorine, Mihir Desai and Colin Gonsalves **Women and the Law-Volume 2** , socio-legal (Information Centre, Bombay, 2000, p. 861.
3. Flavia Agnes *Law and Gender Inequality- The Politics of Women's Rights in India*, Oxford University Press, New Delhi, 2001, p. 1.
4. Christine Chorine, Mihir Desai and Colin Gonsalves *Women and Law, Vol. II*, Socio- Legal Information Centre, Mumbai, 1999, p. 850.
5. Gracy Fernandes and Cecily Stewart Ray *Raids Rescue Rehabilitation*, Research Unit, The College of Social Work, Nirmala Niketan, Mumbai, 2002.
6. Maharukh Adenwalla *Child Sexual Abuse*, India Centre for Human Rights and Law, Mumbai, 2000, p. 17.
7. Christine Chorine, Mihir Desai, Colin Gonsalves Women and Law, Vol. I, Socio-legal Information Centre, Bombay, 1999, p. 1.

Ten

Challenges of the New Millennium for the Voluntary Organisations

Introduction

The last quarter of the 20th century treated NGOs and women's organisations as donkeys to do the drudgery prone tasks of the economy to facilitate the lifestyles of the upwardly mobile sections of the educated middle and upper classes of the society in its quest for the primitive accumulation of the capital and wealth. Weapons of dowry- murders, female feticide, witch-hunting of women challenging family laws and honour killing were used to drive out women from this quest. Poverty groups and the marginalised sections of the society for whom, the NGOs were supposed to work got in return- awareness of the worsening material reality and demoralisation, functional literacy through non-formal educational channels and micro-credit facilities. Development sector thrived on the cheap or unpaid labour of women and children. Female heads of the household (widows, divorcees and deserted women) were projected as leaders for execution of new development experiments as they were supposed to be more "accommodating" and "flexible". In the name of women's rights, old fashioned concern (Chivalry- respect for women) was replaced by total hostility and indifference towards 'Successful' women. Self-pity became fashionable among men in the voluntary sector because they were less cutthroat and merciless as compared to the men and women in the mainstream. De-skilling of the NGO sector's professionals reduced its bargaining power in the economy even though their visibility and credibility enhanced. This is the period, when the highest level of cornering of all life sustaining resources- safe drinking water, housing, healthcare facilities and road transport took place. The Panchayati

Raj institutions used NGOs and women's groups to do the activities, which can be classified as "extension of housework". Any plan to deal with the challenges of the new millenium has to keep this background in mind.

Professionalisation of the NGOs

To deal with the complex market forces, it is extremely important for the NGOs to professionalise its functioning and dissociate its agenda from that of the charitable organisations. Workshops, seminars, conferences in which studied presentations are made and field experiences are discussed in a non-threatening atmosphere, should become regular feature of their functioning. Details of the programme should be given well in advance so that the participants get enough opportunity to do homework. Skills of rapid analysis of the situation, report writing, preparation of executive summary and statement of accounts should be a MUST for all NGOs.

IMPACT OF OFFICE AUTOMATION on THE FUNCTIONING OF THE NGOs has been double edged. On the one hand, it has facilitated their communication and generated employment for an army of tele-workers. They have enabled the NGOs to establish rapport with the GOs at the time of natural or man-made disasters. On the other, the spokes-persons of NGOs are losing their skills of verbal expression, extempore presentations, debates and discussions due to their dependence on technology. CONFLICTING INTERESTS OF TELEWORKERS AND FIELD-WORKERS create war-like situation in the office. Tele-workers have an overload of information and mental stress, while the field workers are both, physically and psychologically stressed out. Tele-workers are working with the known people in a safer surrounding and field-workers are exposed to hazardous and uncertain circumstances.

INTERACTION BETWEEN THE NGOs and GOs has been full of tension because of differences in their sub-cultures. NGOs in India consolidated their base from the social movements. Hence, they have internalised values of informal functioning, non-hierarchical way of team-work and less fear of the 'unknown'. GOs are used to blue-prints and order from above. Moreover, their reference group comes from 6 per cent of the labour force, namely the organised sector. GOs attitudes and preferences-likes and dislikes are shaped by this factor. Field-reports, area studies and eye-witness accounts of investigative journalists are their major sources for policy planning. Now, NGOs and GOs, both have global connections. Competition between GOs and NGOs has ensured transparency, accountability and efficient functioning.

Induction of Scientists and Technocrates in the NGOs

Before launching any new campaign, advocacy programme or policy intervention the NGOs have to undertake research in the specialized fields. This effort makes them work with professionals-doctors, scientists, engineers, architects, media persons and management experts. This interaction has changed the character of Indian NGOs as the workers in the organisation are forced to work beyond slogan mongering and giving fiery speeches. Importance of technical competency and scientific thinking is accepted by everyone in the organisation. Use of transparencies, video films, slides projectors and exhibitions have become organic part of the NGO study circles. Sometimes, they are more equipped than the mainstream bodies working on the same issues.

NGO Professionals Working as Consultants of the Mainstream Bodies

NGO professionals who are up-to-date in their database and effective in verbal conversation are accepted by the mainstream bodies as consultants. This gives intellectual freedom and scope for experimentation to the professionals and at the same time the mainstream bodies get ready-made pool of knowledge from the experts for their think tank. NGO professionals are more democratic in sharing their skills, know how and intellectual output with the non commercial sector of the economy. Ethical guidelines are evolved by NGOs about research methods, right to information, informed consent and accountability.

Civil Societies and the NGOs

In western and southern states of India, NGOs are legitimised by the civil societies. Development media and regional language television channels, print media have played a major role in enhancing credibility of NGOs in the eyes of the masses. Visibility of NGOs' activities have had mixed responses in the BIMARU (Bihar, Madhya Pradesh, Rajhasthan, Uttar Pradesh) states. Programmes concerning public health, education and employment generation are accepted by the community while social reform agenda (fight against child marriage, domestic violence, anti-dowry campaign, plight of child labour and prostitution) meets with resistance form the vested interests. NGOs in such situations have to depend on moral and material support from long distance friends. Day to day survival struggle in the midst of social boycott created by the bullies make NGO functioning quite challenging. In several pockets in the northern and north-eastern states retired civil servants and religious persons have started NGOs addressing specific issues such as anti-alcoholic movement and reforestation programmes.

State Machinery and the NGOs

NGOs functioning for more than two decades have established their equilibrium with the state machinery. NGOs collaborating with the government apparatus are dealing with major policy issues and using their credibility for area development. Some NGO activists have become politicians, academicians and decision makers with the government bodies and international organisations.

Task Force of the Crorepati NGOs

This has been very tough as each section of society wants to use its good office for sectional interests. When the NGOs were poor the upper section of the society either ignored them or gave them awards. Now they are perceived as competing entrepreneurs. Hence, it is increasingly difficult for them to take up development agenda that would ensure better quality of life to the have-nots. Moreover, due to high stakes of such organisations, fund-raising becomes 'be all and end all' of their existence.

Task Force of the Lakh Pati NGOs

Its relatively straight forward for these category of NGOs to function as the stakes are not so high and goals are limited and boundaries are well defined. They face comparatively less competition. Their agenda is flexible and they don't face any threat from the vested interests which are economically more powerful than them. They also get easy legitimacy from the local self government bodies, Panchayati Raj institutions and the state secretariat. But in the absence of self-sustaining income-generating activities either from production of goods or services such as training programmes or certificate courses, many of them have to be on the continuous lookout of project funds, endowment funds and corpus funds.

Political Parties and Safety for Community Workers

There has been much hue and cry from the NGOs and Human rights organisations about safety of community workers, investigative journalists, documentary film makers, street theatre actors in response to harassment by the political parties.

Financial Institutions and NGOs

In response to development debate over the last decade most of the financial institutions have started supporting projects of the NGOs. Guidelines of the major financial institutions include development-oriented programmes in their list of priorities.

Conclusion

The millenium era will see more fruitful interaction between NGOs and the GOs. The voluntary organisations working with the perspective of human resource development are found to be recruiting bodies for the decision-making apparatus. NGOs are taking major advantage of communication revolution, information technology and modern managerial practices with the perspective of social justice, distributive justice and gender justice. Human rights will be the major concern of NGOs as economic differentiation and the gap in the standard of living of different sections of society will accentuate as a result of market forces.

References

CURRENT SCIENCE (2000) Volume 78, Number 11, 10 June.

From the Lawyers Collective (20000, "LAW FOR THE PEOPLE- Intellectual Property Rights: Challenges for India", Vol. 15, No. 5, May.

Humanscape (2000), "Principles and Profit- The Search for Ethical Business", July, Bombay.

Indira Hiraway & S. Mahendra Dev (2000), "Eliminating Poverty in India: Exploring Possibilities", NGO- Academics Paper on Poverty in India, Centre for Development Alternatives , Ahmedabad and Centre for Economic and Social Studies, Hyderabad, May .

The Indian Journal of Labour Economics (2000), Volume 42, Number 3, July- Sept.

T.M. Thomas Issac (2000) "Democratic Decentralisation- Empowering Women", Frontline, June 24- July 7.

Eleven

Effective Governance: Importance of Women's Leadership in Local Bodies

COLOURS

I glanced at the various shades of blue,
in the temporary morning sky,
And all the types of red and orange,
when the burning sun went by.
And when the ball of fire set in the sea,
I peered at the green waters turn violet
while the shining star lost itself in the night,
I saw the blues and indigos at the deepest.
As the light left without a hint of its presence,
I felt the aura emitted by the silver moon.
And in the dizziness caused by the blacks,
I sensed the glittering of twilight soon.
As I felt the darkness would swallow me up,
And the night would pull the world down;
I saw the magical transformation of colours
from scary black to brooding brown.
Just as this change took away my breath,
the dying night was replaced by dawn,
And the enticing colours of nature thus fell,
As they went forever on and on.

—*by Lara Jesani*

Rainbow Politics and Democratic Decentralisation

Slowly and gradually we are moving towards rainbow politics. The mainstram political bodies as well as the social movements are faced with their leaders and rank-n-file adhering to different political and religious moorings. Managing work of the constituency with peace and harmony is the most challenging task of the elected representatives. Democratic Decentralisation in governance means more responsibility for elected representatives who can't get away by saying, "we are waiting for an order from the high command".

"Maharashtra has 28000 gram panchayats, 298 panchayat samitis and 29 zilla parishads. Total number of elected women in these bodies is almost 94000." (Thakkar & Gawankar). 73rd and 74th amendments to the constitution of India ensured 1/3 reservation of seats for women among elected membership and functionaries of the panchayat system. As a result, there are about 1 million women elected representatives in Panchayats. This move has provided legitimacy to women's non-traditional role in Panchayats. As a result we find increasing confidence, change in lifestyle, awareness about critical need for education, increased concern about village development among women representatives. (D. Bandyopadhyay). A massive churning is taking place. When the 81st constitution Amendment Bill (Women's reservation Bill) was tabled in the parliament in 1996, there was serious opposition to 1/3 reservation of seats for women in the state assemblies and the parliament.

These women as elected representatives are faced with the private and government supported commercial sector which is using education (ability to handle cash nexus) as a weapon to sustain super-exploitation of the toiling poor. Seventies in Maharashtra's women's liberation movement emphasised *prabodhan (consciousness raising)*, eighties and nineties represented actions for survival and self-defense. Now, we are faced with a problem of fulfilling the demands of women's development after scrupulous examination of our allies in the power structure.

In today's era, it is next to impossible to make a major economic intervention without prior research. Let me illustrate this with some examples from Maharashtra where I have done extensive fieldwork.

Specificities of Development Agenda in Pimpri Chinchwad (modern Industrial belt), Alandi & Dound (predominantly agrarian activities), Shirur (small scale industrial belt), Talegaon (inhabited by educated Senior citizens and retired employees) and Lonawala (tourist resort and sweet-meat and fruit processing industry). To execute the area development projects with higher and higher success rate and to avoid repetition of the past mistakes, it is important to evaluate existing body of research material produced by Pune-based institutions and individual workers.

Need for Area Studies for Effective Administration

Area studies done by CEHAT (Pune), Foundation for Research in Community Health (FRCH), Gokhale Institute's Labour Studies Department (Pune), Sane Guruji Trust (Pune), Sarva Shramik Sangh (Pune) and Masum (Pune) should be considered before implementing development programmes by the elected representatives.

Pattern of Economic Growth and its Implications on Work-life and the Civil Society

Rapid industrial development, export oriented commercial agriculture, expanding network of public distribution system of essential items and uprooting of the urban poor has enhanced the role of elected representatives- from supervisors and chief guests to crisis managers and visionaries with expertise to handle macro-policy issues and day-to-day ground reality.

"The National Forest Policy,1988 talks about actively involving the people in programmes designed for the protection , conservation and management of forests. The National Housing and Habitat Policy, 1998 speaks of correcting the imbalance caused by the excessive dependence on public agencies and seeks to foster an environment conducive to forging strong public- private partnership for talking habitat issues." (Videh Upadhyaya) Planning , capacity building and development of slums as per the National Slum Policy have not ensured better quality of life. Too much glorification of mud-houses and grass houses (without cross ventilation for air-circulation and smokeless chullas- stoves) by the Hindi and Marathi film industry and travel journalism has brought indifferent attitude towards rural housing projects by the government. Not a single voluntary organisation or the central trade unions, peasant organisation has built housing societies with proper amenities for the industrial and the agrarian proletariat.

Housing colonies for the toiling masses should be constructed on the principles of public- private mix model. In the Maharashtra state policy for women, there is a mention of 'right to shelter for female headed households', but in reality, not a single construction site has been ear-marked for FHH, though there are enough women engineers, architects and technicians who are ready to work for such projects if safe environment is provided. To achieve this goal, we need more **Vocational Training Institutes**- where healthy and food-secure youth (both man and women) are groomed to be turners, fitters, plumbers, electricians, drivers, mason, carpenters. Tailoring, painting, screen-printing, computer literacy and weaving can be taken care of by the private sector. Sweetmeat industry should aim at global market, especially in Africa (as the Africans have strong teeth) using existing network of cultural centres such as Maharastra Samaj and Marathi Vangmaya Sabha.

Agrarian Development in the Region

The eco-technology is entering the agrarian market. India's green man, Dr. M. S. Swaminathan has rightly stated, "Eco-technologies are knowledge intensive. Fortunately, modern information technology provides opportunities for reaching the unreached. Computer aided and internet connected virtual colleges linking scientists and women and men living in poverty can be established at local, national and global levels to disseminate knowledge of the benefits and risks associated with genetically manufactured objects, so that both farmers and consumers will get better insights into the processes leading to the creation of novel genetic combinations." NDDB's model involving 10 million farmers located in over 97000 villages (Amrita Patel) of replacing liquor dens with milk bars and Haryana model of replacing hooch with fruit juice shops need to be replicated in Maharashtra, especially in the areas where shakersheti (sugar cultivation) is predominant. Children who are earning and learning need special facilities such as **reading room** near the place of work and free time to watch educational programmes for distance learners by UGC (university Grants Commission) and EMRC (Education Media Research Centre) on television. All work-sites should be encouraged to use radio. Women working for Bhakhar centres should be, fed first and then made to work. *"Amchya baya upashi rahun bhakkhar banavite"* (Our women fast and make bread for buyers) is a shameful approach to manage employment generation programme for destitute women.

In **the Street food enterprises** in Pune district, 13 per cent are women and 33 per cent (i.e. 1/3) enterprises have women as assistants. Women economists should organise training programmes for them to handle factor, labour and product markets and various saving and insurance schemes. In the larger units, refrigerators and mixers should be provided from the funds collected for festival celebration or core fund.

Tourism

This region is experiencing rape of mother earth as a result of weekend tourists of the urban Maharashtra, national tourists during vacations, international tourists (includes NRIs) during winter. Commercial interest of the supply side and the consumerist motive of the demand side are responsible for this crisis. Down to Earth approach demands sustainable tourism. "Mountaineers, walkers, skiers, surfers, artists, pantheists can all have their pleasure without humiliating the dignity of ecology." (Tirtho Banerjee) .

Professionals attending educational workshops in the holiday homes of the educational and research institutions and central trade unions should give benefit of their knowledge for development of this region. Near privately owned holiday homes and farm houses of the urban rich, temples, madrasaa, libraries, cultural centres and parishes should be constructed to protect the honour and life of innocent young girls and boys. Girls in the constituency should be encouraged to move in a group. It is encouraging to note that between Pune- Bombay highway, there is no prostitution among the native girls as a result of strong work ethics created by Marathi medium schools.

Public Health Issues

Preventive and curative health care should be responsive to seasonal variations in work, income and food (Health Watch). Provision of iodised salt for Iodine deficient population (Drug, disease, Doctor), equal importance to HIV and T.B. based on

SELF-HELP intervention strategy, policy in favour of safe abortion and RTI services as back-up service in Maharashtra Health System Development Project, 2000 to strengthen the secondary health care system. Primary Health Centre should have all medicines listed in the Essential Drugs list prepared by LVS -Lok Vignan Sangathana (Anant Phadake).

Land rights for Women have been ensured in some pockets of Nasik district due to two decades of political education by Shetkari Sangathana by ex- World Bank economist, Dr. Sharad Joshi. SS had been able to neutralise loompan elements by organising *karyashalas* (workshops). Two public interest litigation cases from Dhulia (Maharashtra) and Singhbhum (Bihar) concerning landrights of tribal women are pending in the Supreme Court of India.

Dealing With Local Vested Interests

Film festivals of socially oriented docu-drama can be most effective way to bring attitudinal changes among local vested interests. At the same time at an implementation level, the following steps can be taken to neutralise the vested interest.

a. Money lenders- their skills of accounting can be utilised by Grameen bank in exchange for education and vocational training for their family members. Facilities of recurring account for daily wage earners in the bank.
b. Bootleggers- their ability to deal with chemicals can be channelised in the pharmaceutical industry. Low-cost manufacturing of essential drugs can be established in consultation with MFC.(Shreedhar Srinivasan)
c. Paid killers- their ability to handle weapons should be employed in the food and fruit production and (cutting and chopping) processing industry.
d. Education of domestic workers to convey that their job is only of cooking and cleaning, they should not provide sexual services. They should be encouraged to join Molkarin Union. (Amarja Pawar and Leelatai Bhonsale) *Malak ni je sangitla, ti karaych (Whatever the master says should be done)* syndrom should be out. Standaradisation of molkarin-malkin(master-domestic-worker) relation

should be done after going through the labour laws in the Southern and East African countries. (Iqbal-South Africa, Joe Beal- London University)

e. Caretakers of SOS villages where orphan children and unwed mothers from poverty groups are looked after should be in touch with women's rights organisations in Pune and Bombay. Refuge homes for *parityaktas (deserted, divorced, destitutes) need modernisation in management and capacity building.*

f. Pimps and procurers of virgin girls (mostly Muslim and dalit *parityaktas*) can be reformed only by the caste and kinship network. NGOs can provide moral and material support in collaboration with doctors working in the red light areas of Pune. Direct intervention by the voluntary organisation can be , at times, counter-productive.

g. Estate Agents- Standard for land/ building evaluation and meticulous paper work should safeguard women's and senior citizens' interests.

h. Landlords should be invited for area development meetings where agrarian and other community development issues are discussed.

i. Employment Agents should be enlightened about labour laws, occupational health and safety and women's rights.

j. Head-loaders, coolies- Demands of Hamaal Panchayat (Pune) should be implemented. De-addiction centres for coolies and truckers should be opened and instead of young M.S.W.s, retired military officers and administrators should manage them with adequate police protection.

k. Dalits, tribals, religious minorities, artisans and the toiling poor who are facing tremendous social hostility and/or super-exploitation should be helped to out-migrate in favour of greener pastures without social discrimination.

l. Non-formal education should include vocation oriented scientific and technical details along with computer education.

m. Labour studies of this region have revealed that 65 per cent of men's income is utilised for liquor, tobacco, narcotic drugs and female companionship. Hence, so far as possible, the wages should be given to women or part of wages should be given in kind (soap, towel, food, tooth-brush, tooth paste, medicine) to their family members.

Women Specific Issues

Campaign against domestic violence should be coupled with formation of shelter homes, grameen banks and employment bureau. Campaign against social evils have to be combined with attractive alternatives- fight against liquor dens, gambling dens, narcotic drugs and brothels should go hand in hand with efforts to provide more playgrounds, jogging parks, bhajan mandalis, cultural centres. Female-headed households should be given preferential treatment in jobs, shelter and training for skill development.

Quality assurance of reproductive care in private hospital to reduce female morbidity and mortality should be given top priority. (Alex and Srilata). Micro-finance and working capital requirements of vendors should be taken care of after consulting development-oriented economists (ARROW). Bride-price (among tribals) and dowry (among almost all communities), both brutalise husband-wife relationship. Hence, both should be opposed.

Budget Analysis

So far as possible, Women Economists should be consulted for budget analysis. Corporators should have thorough knowledge of budget. Corporators should be aware of hundreds of schemes of the government of Maharashtra with an objective of social upliftment. For example, 3.55 crores for village sanitation campaign budgeted by the government of Maharashtra should be used to lessen the workload of the dalit community and to enhance environmental sustainability.

Decisions about water reservoirs, genetically modified food, mechanisation should be taken jointly by the tripartite body with representatives of workers associations (kisan sabhas-udyog senas-workers panchayats. Local level self-sufficiency in the fodder market is important to reduce uncertainty of supply and reduction of transport cost.

Public Life and Women's Predicament

Induction of Women Decision-makers in different levels of hierarchy needs fresh approach. Instead of cost considerations and male comfort, the criteria for selection should be gender justice and social justice. Conventional understanding of grooming of weak, frail, delicate girls as tele-workers and office administrators- interns who are allowed to go out in group, does not allow women to take up leadership roles. Now technology has changed this equation. Safe transport (two-wheelers, three wheelers, four wheelers and bus-train), changing dress-code, cellular mobile phones, pre-planned programme, press coverage allow even physically weak and short women to successfully handle their functioning in public life.

Need for Office Automation

For effective governance, it is important to equip the office with computers, fax-machines and mobile phones. Local self government bodies turn the information highway towards villages to promote education of rural children, to make available village maps and land-records, to reduce red-tape and to ensure quick movements of papers and files, as the M.P. government has done. (Down to Earth,15-11-2000). Use of internet and website are important for information dissemination and establishing long-distance and speedy communication for efficient governance.

Conclusion

Non-sectarian outlook, eagerness to learn and concern for the welfare of each and every community, caste and religious group can make women's leadership in local self-government bodies effective.

A Little Inspiration by Marsha Forest

Inclusion is a future
Inclusion is belonging to one race, the human race.
Inclusion is a basic human right.
Inclusion is struggling to figure out,
How to live with one-another.
Inclusion is not something we do a little of

It either is or is not.
Not a bandwagon.
It is a trend, similar to democracy.
" With liberty and justice for all."
All means all. No buts about it.
Inclusion is a battle cry, a patient's cry,
A child's cry to be welcomed, embraced, cherished, prized.
Inclusion is a kaleidoscope of diversity-
Bits of colours, sounds, shapes, sizes...
Inclusion is future.

References

Amar Jesani, Manisha Gupte, Ravi Duggal (1995), *NGOs in Health Care*, **FRCH,** Bombay- Pune, 1995.

Amrita Patel (2000), "There Must Be Limits To Growth", **Humanscape,** Bombay, July, 2000.

Anant Phadake, **Lok Vignan Sangathana,** 50 - LIC Colony, University Road, Pune-16.

Anjali and Gunum Pattanayak(2000), Child Labourer: An Economic Supplementation, ***Ancient Science of Life,*** A Quarterly Journal of International Institute of Ayurveda, Coimbatore, October.

D. Bandyopadhyay, "Gender and Governance in India", Economic and Political weekly, Vol. Xxxv, No. 31, pp.2696-2699.

Down to Earth and GOBER TIMES (2000), Centrere for Science and Environment, Delhi, October,31.

Drug, Disease Doctor- Quarterly Journal on Rational Drug and Therapy, 10/a Parshibagan Lane, Calcutta- 700009.

Ajoy Mitra (2000), "To Iodise or not to Iodise-That is the question", No. 3.

Lalitha D'sousa (1999), "Sexual Assault- Role of Examining Doctor", **Issues in Medical Ethics,** Bombay, no.3, July .

Duggal Ravi(2000), Country Presentation- India, The Gender and Reproductive Health Impacts of Health Sector Reform in Asia, Kunming Medical College, Ford Foundation, China, March, .

Health for the Millions (2000), VHAI, New Delhi.

Health Watch (2000), National Population Policy, 2000, Contact address: Prof. Gita Sen, IIM, Banglore Issue 9-10.

M.S. Swaminathan (2000) "The Ecotechnology Revolution", in Special number on THE EVERGREEN REVOLUTION, **Humanscape,** p.o. Box 26922, Santacruz (W), Mumbai- 400054.,Sept., p. 8.

ICMR Bulletin (1999), **AIIMS,** October- November, New Delhi.

Iqbal (2000), Doctors Against Torture, ANC, COSATU, Physicians for Human Rights, South Africa.

Joe Bael (2000), Department of Urban Governance, University of London, The United Kingdom.

Leelatai Bhonsale, Medha Joshi, Mukta Manohar and Amarja Pawar: Pune Molkarin Sangathana, Pune Nurses' Union, Sarva Stramik Sangh, Parvati, Pune, 1986.

Loriette Bernjamin and Nayana Kulkarni(1982), Experiences as workers in Maharashtra Employment Guarantee Scheme in Kamshet, **Workshop by Maitrini** in Lonawala.

Medico Friends Circle, 11- Archana Apartments, 163 Solapur Rd, Hadapsar, Pune-411028,2000.

Monique Cohen with Mihir Bhatt and Pat Horn (2000), *Women Street Vendors: The Road to Recognition*, SEEDs, **Population Council,** New York, 10017.

Sarala Gopalan and Mira Shiva (Editors)(2000), *National Profile on Women, Health and Development*, Voluntary Health Association of India and World Health Organisation, April, 2000.

Shelley Saha(2000), "Safe Abortions Are Still a Diastant Dream in Maharashtra", **Humanscape,** September.

Shreedhar Srinivasan(2000), "Drug Price Reduction: The Low Cost Experience", ACASH News. No, 3, **Association for Consumer Action on Safety and Health (ACASH),** Bombay.

Subhashini Mahapatra (2001), *Women and Politics*, Rajat Publications, Delhi.

Tara Kanitkar(2000)," The Changing Health Scenario of Maharahtra- Problems and Prospects", **Health for the Millions**, May- June.

Tirtho Banerjee(2000), "Towards Green Tourism", **One India One People**, November, p. 50.

The Indian Journal of Social Work (1990), Focus Issue on Personnel Management and Industrial Relations, Tate Institute of Social Sciences, Deodar, Bombay, April.

Dr. Usha Thakkar and Dr. Rohini Gawankar(2000), "Panchayati Raj and Women", ***One India, One People***, Mumbai,October, p. 16

Videh Upadhyay(2000), People's Participation in Policy Formation, **From the Lawyers' Collective,** October.

Twelve

Rape Laws: Travesty of Justice

Introduction

Women's rights movement in India gained a national character with an anti-rape movement in 1980. Its genesis lay in the excesses committed by the state repressive machinery during the Emergency Rule in India from 1975 to 1977. For many middle class women it came as a major shock. In the post emergency period, civil liberties organisations also highlighted rape of women in the police custody, mass rape of poor, untouchable and Muslim women during caste and communal riots and sexual molestation of tribal women by Central Reserve Police (CRP), State Reserve Police (SRP) and other para-military forces. The print media gave an enormous coverage to the testimonies of women victims of sexual violence. Many began to question the powers given to the police and State authorities in the control of people's lives. In 1980, when the Supreme Court of India gave its verdict on the Mathura Rape Case, there was a national outcry.[1]

Mathura, a teenage tribal girl was raped by two policemen, in the police station at dead of night while her relatives were weeping and wailing outside the police-station. The legal battle began when a woman lawyer took up her case immediately after the event in 1972. The Sessions Court blamed Mathura for being a woman of "an easy virtue", and the two policemen were released. In the High Court Judgement, the accused were given seven and half years imprisonment which was reverted by the judgement of the highest legal authority-The Supreme Court of India. It held that Mathura had given a wilful consent, as she did not raise any alarm.[2] The resulting nation-wide anti-rape campaign in 1980 demanded reopening of the Mathura Rape Case and amendments in the Rape Law.[3] Prominent lawyers took up the issue, as did the national and regional language press. New groups of women were formed around this campaign. They organised public meetings and poster-campaigns, performed skits and street-theatre, collected thousands of signatures in support of their demands, staged rallies and demonstrations, submitted petitions to MLAs and the Prime Minister, and generally alerted the public to the treatment meted out to the rape victims. The initiative came from the middle class, educated and urban women. Later on, the political parties and the mass organisations also joined the bandwagon.[4]

Debates on Reforms in the Rape Laws

The demand of the amendments in the Rape Law touched wide variety of issues concerning social construction of sexuality that reflected in the assumptions in the law and in the civil society about women, past sexual history of the rape victim, procedures of the criminal justice system-First Investigation report (FIR), inquest, medical examination, rights of women in custody-in India. Two booklets represented the debates and discussions amongst the feminists and the democratic rights activists on gang-rape, custodial rape, rape in the family, burden of proof, etc. [5] When the national conference on 'Perspective for Women's Liberation Movement in India' was held in Bombay in November 1980, the proposed rape bill was the most controversial issue. As a result of rigorous debate amongst the feminists, it was resolved that demands of the women's organisations should be as follows:

1. A woman should be interrogated only at her dwelling place.
2. During interrogation by a police officer, a woman should be allowed to have a male relative or friend or women social workers present with her.
3. Women who are detained in custody should be kept in a separate lock-up meant for women only. If there is no such lock-up available then the women should be kept in a children's or women's home meant for the protection and welfare of women.
4. The medical report of a rape victim should state the reasons for arriving at the conclusions and should be forwarded without delay to the magistrate to avoid possibility of tempering.

5. During a trial of rape, the past sexual history of the rape victim should be excluded from the evidence.
6. A police officer who refuses to record a complaint should be guilty of an offence.
7. Section 375 of the Indian Penal Code which clarifies that the consent of the woman in order to be considered as consent must be absolutely free and voluntary must be amended in view of the Mathura case.
8. The provision about 'burden of proof' in Section 111a of the Indian Evidence Act must be changed and it should be added that in cases where the accused in a rape trial is a public servant, police officer, superintendent or manager of a jail or hospital or remand home, where sexual intercourse is proved and the woman makes a statement on oath that she did not consent to the sexual intercourse, then the court shall presume that she did not consent.[6]

The last point raised a major controversy as many feminists felt that in all cases of rape the burden of proof should be on the accused and not on the victim, given the nature of the offence, the dominant position of men over women and the impossibility of proving lack of consent except by stating that she did not consent. While women activists from the background of the mass movements felt that such provision could be abused to victimise the male members of the trade-unions by the management and the male activists of the dalit, tribal and peasant organisations by the local vested interests.

The Criminal Law Amendment Act (1983)

After three years of heated debates in the women's groups, media and the Law Commission of India, the parliament passed the Criminal Law Amendment Act (1983). This Act amended the Indian Penal Code, The Code of Criminal Procedure and the Indian Evidence Act with respect to the law relating to rape. As per this Act, revealing the identity of a rape-victim is an offence. Though this Act maintains more or less the same definition of rape, it introduces many new categories of offence of sexual intercourse by persons in custodial situation-such as superintendents of hospitals, remand homes, prison and police officials-with women in their custody. In cases of custodial rape, burden of proof lies with men and if a woman victim makes a statement that she did not consent, the court would believe that she did not consent. Feminists had demanded that marital rape should also be considered a punishable offence, but this demand was rejected and thus the government supported the popular social belief that a married man has the right to have sexual intercourse with his wife, with or without consent. The rejection certainly meant that the Act did not meet the aspirations of the women's movement. Inspite of this limitation, popular debate on the subject enhanced self-confidence and sense of solidarity within the women's movement. [7]

Definition of Rape

The Act defines rape as being sexual intercourse with a woman under either of the following Descriptions:

A. Against her will.
B. Without her consent.
C. When her consent is obtained by putting her or any person in whom she is interested in fear of death or of hurt.
D. With her consent, when the man knows that he is not her husband and her consent is given because she is under an impression that he is her husband.
E. With her consent when she is incapable of giving consent because of unsoundness of mind or intoxication.
F. With or without her consent when she is under sixteen years of age.

The Act makes it clear that "Penetration is sufficient to constitute the sexual intercourse necessary to the offence of rape."[8] The only change made by the amended Act, is in provision that sexual intercourse with consent, when it is obtained by putting any person in whom she is interested in fear of death or hurt is rape.

Punishment for Rape

As per section 376 of the Act, the minimum punishment for rape is seven years and the maximum life imprisonment. If the judge finds valid reasons he/she can impose a sentence of less than seven years. In the cases of 'custodial rape' or 'gang rape' the minimum sentence is of ten years and the offence is cognisable and nonbailable. Sexual intercourse by a man with his wife, who is living separately from him under a decree of separation or under any custom or usage without her consent is punishable with imprisonment which, may extend to two years. This offence is cognisable and bailable. This definition of rape makes it clear that the husband has a right to have sexual intercourse with his wife with or without her consent. The underlying notion in this provision that does not see a man guilty of raping his wife is, that a woman is the private property of her husband and he can use/abuse her the way he wants.

Many women's rights organisations had demanded that forcible sexual intercourse by a man with his wife should also be defined as an offence of rape. But the Law Commission of India refused this demand. At the same time it introduced a new section, which makes forcible intercourse by a man with his judicially separated wife an offence. Commenting on this, a progressive legal activists' organisation Lawyers Collective commented; "This new section is a small step forward in the direction of recognising the rights of the wife not to be raped by her husband."[9]

Rape Victim and the State Enforcement Machinery

According to the criminal justice system in India, rape is an offence against the state not a crime against an individual. The matter has to be reported by the rape-victim to the police and First Investigation Report (FIR) prepared by the police, inquest and identification parade conducted by the police and medical examination report prepared by the recognised government hospital have major bearing on the judgement. After the police file a charge sheet, the trial is conducted in a Sessions Court. During the trial the victim has no choice to select a lawyer to defend her case. The state appointed public prosecutor represents her. The rape-victim is merely the prosecution witness. Hence during investigation and rape trial she is completely at the mercy of the state.

How Does a Woman Experience the System of Law?

In a book by a retired Inspector General of Police, Mr. S. K. Ghosh there is an admission to the fact of police involvement and connivance in the cases of rape as a generalized phenomenon.[10] In cases of custodial rape such as rape of prisoners by the jailer and other staff of the prison or of a patient by her doctor or of a woman employee by her employer or of the women hostilities or inmates of remand homes by the members of the management; the state apparatus in most of the cases chooses either to maintain a conspiracy of silence or to hush up the case. [11] In many parts of the country where remand homes for minor girls do not exist, minor victims of rape are kept either in police custody or in prison, sometimes for 8 to 12 years without any legal redress. In such cases the rapists lead free, 'respectable' lives and the victims stay confined in institutions. In West Bengal, the Association for Protection of Democratic Rights has taken up the cases of such victims.[12]

When an individual woman accompanied by her relatives or neighbours approaches the police stations she has to meet with either hostile or indifferent attitude of the custodians of law and order. Lewd remarks, jokes, double-meaning sentences, weird smiles and cynical laughter are used by the police force to generate fear and uneasiness in the minds of the victim seeking legal redress. Comments on her dress, hairstyle, looks, figure, sex appeal and overall physical attributes are considered to be a part of normal behaviour by the police officials. National Conference of Rape in 1990 declared that "A woman victim of rape is raped twice-first by the culprit and then by the criminal justice system."[13]

Experiences of Women Activists while Dealing with Rape Cases

As a member of Forum against Oppression of Women (FAOW) since 1980 one has been experiencing the biases and misogyny of the criminal justice system that sees rape-victim as an offender.

In response to a news item about the rape of a teenage construction worker by the three policemen and a bootlegger in 1980, FAOW (at that time known as Forum against Rape) decided to follow up the case. To get the case filed in the FIR we had to organise a demonstration in front of the police station. The police charged the women activists and the local social workers with 'riot, trespass and dacoity'.[14] This event happened before the amendments in the Rape Laws were made, the situation has not changed even after the enactment of the legal reforms.

In 1983, when a six-year-old girl was raped by her neighbour, her uterus was ruptured and she had to be hospitalised. Inspite of repeated plea by the victim's mother, the police refused to register a case because there was no penis penetration. As the rapist did not succeed in penetration, he had inserted an iron rod and his fingers.[15] Penis penetration remains the only and exclusive concern of the authority while deciding the rape case.

Police Attitude

- "Do you know the definition of Rape?"
- In 1992, as a member of an investigation team concerning the gang-rape of a middle-aged woman worker living in one of the slums of Bombay, we had several meetings with the police officer in charge of the case. We had found out from the victim and the community that the police did not help them in any way. The rape victim accompanied by her neighbour and social workers approached the policemen to file an FIR; the police were not only indifferent but also very hostile. It was past midnight. The police station was busy making accounts of drugs they had captured in their raid. First of all the police did not believe that rape had taken place. When the victim kept on repeating that she was raped and other witnesses also supported her statement, the police officers and constables had a hearty laugh. They then cynically asked the victim, "Do you know the definition of rape?" The victim was totally dazed. She showed her injuries on the forehead, head, neck, hand, chest, etc. Without doing any paperwork, they just told the victim and her friends to go to the government hospital without any note or accompanying constable. In the hospital she was just given first aid, diazepam and pain-killer tablets. In the morning she approached a woman activist. Once again they went to the police-station and after a great deal of verbal exchanges between middle-class women activists and the police officer, finally the FIR was filed but in the meantime all important evidence was lost.

"If you pursue this case, no one will marry your daughter." Every police officer has an obsession with the crime record in his area. He has to see that it does not exceed certain 'limits' or else his chances of promotion will be jeopardised. Hence many a time he shows a reluctance to file cases of crimes against women. In 1982 we were involved in support work of a minor girl who was raped by a teenage boy. The victim's mother was in a state of shock and deep anguish and wanted to see that the culprit was punished. In a slum where all communities live, the victim's community who are migrant 'untouchable sweepers' from Haryana, face the most discrimination. The police officer who conducted the inquiry was humane while dealing with the victim and her mother. But he kept on insisting that the case should not be filed as it would involve a long drawn, tiring and humiliating legal battle. Moreover the girl would get defamed no one would marry her etc. The victim would be kept in the government remand home, as she was a minor, till the case ended. But the mother wanted us to take up the case as it would teach all other miscreants in the slum a lesson. We argued endlessly with the police to convince him of the necessity to file a case. Finally he confided to us that if the crime record in his jurisdiction increased, it would reflect on his career.

- "After all she is a petty thief. "

  When a 16-year old poor girl was taken into custody, unlawfully confined, repeatedly gang-raped by the Bombay Suburban Railway Police, she became pregnant. The policemen quietly arranged her abortion in the government hospital. When this girl managed to reach her home after some weeks she was bleeding profusely. Her relatives approached a feminist group. While conducting an inquiry we had verbal exchanges with the bosses of the rapist policemen. When we alleged the higher authorities of collusion with rapists they retorted back by saying " Why are you so worried about this girl? After all she is a petty thief, a pick-pocket. It is good that our men taught her a lesson."

- "There can not be smoke without fire. "
  In the urban as well as rural India as a result of lumpanisation of socio-cultural life; in college and school campuses, on lonely roads, in buses and trains, in middle class neighbourhoods and in slums, incidences of eve-teasing have increased. Earlier the law enforcement machinery was not taking any cognisance of it. Women's groups in Delhi played a very important role in making this issue officially recognised. Eve-teasing and ragging during certain festivals (like Holi, the kite-flying festival of Gujarat or balloon throwing during the month of Shravan) have provoked many individual women as well as women's groups to protest against the law enforcement machinery. Eve-teasing of women by bus conductors and bus drivers, railway police, road traffic police are still not paid attention to, inspite of the legal provision. Most often women or girls do not report incidents of harassment such as obscene phone calls or lewd remarks by miscreants for fear of getting into trouble. When the protectors of 'law and order' have a reputation of themselves being eve-teasers in the public eye, how can we expect women to approach them? Class, caste and communal biases along with gender bias of the police and other bodies of the state are responsible for apathy, inertia, indifference and hostility faced by women when they seek support in the cases of eve-teasing.

Molestation of Madhushree Dutta

Two years back, a noted film and stage director Madhushree Dutta was badly molested by two railway policemen who were in plain clothes in the railway station at the midnight. At the time of molestation she was not alone. Ms. Flavia, a feminist lawyer was with her. Both of them being involved in the women's rights movement for over a decade and fully aware of the legal provisions immediately prepared a notice against the molesters. When they went to submit their write-up at the appropriate police station, the police officer in-charge refused to co-operate. Madhushree being well-known in media circles, the news of the incident appeared the very next day on the front page of the leading newspapers of the country. In response to the news reports a strong protest demonstration was organised by women's groups to demand suspension of the police officer as well as the molesters. To make her withdraw the case, the policemen kept on making anonymous and threatening phone calls to her lawyer's office. The court trail was an extremely humiliating experience as the defence counsel hired by the policemen kept on shooting questions after questions implying that for a budding artiste like Madhushree it was a cheap publicity gimmick to get a lime light. If a woman, so articulate, visible and well connected with the media world, aided by an equally strong and articulate feminist lawyer, has to face such terror-tactics by the police. One can imagine what must be happening to "ordinary" and "helpless" women victims of sexual violence? This incident happened in Bombay anti-rape campaigns have been consistently taken up since 1978. Inspite of wide media coverage on the issue of sexual violence, the attitude of both the state as well as the civil society, as reflected in readers' reaction in the newspapers, was not sympathetic to the victim. Many asked, why was Madhushree there at such a late hour?

An analysis of the judgements of the Sessions Courts, The High Courts and the Supreme Courts since 1980 done by Ad. Flavia reveals an extremely negative view of the judiciary of women's sexuality. She gives several examples of rape-cases were stereotypical arguments of victim-baiting were used liberally to reduce punishment to the culprits. Supposedly pro-women judgements in cases of rape of minors were also coloured by a conservative concern for 'chastity' and 'purity'. Flavia states, "The positive judgements which are reported involve rape of minor girls resulting in multiple injury where the question of consent does not arise. But even these judgements have a conservative reasoning for the conviction. Here is an example of how the judiciary looks at the issue: 'Virginity is the most priced possession of an unmarried girl. She would never willingly part away with this proud and precious possession'."[16]

Mass Rape of Women During Caste and Communal Riots

The human rights organisations and the women's groups have provided detailed testimonies of mass rape of Dalit women during caste riots in Marathawad (1978), Ahmedabad (1983), Bhojpur (1985), Nagpur (1988) and communal riots in Delhi and Bombay (1984), Bhagalpur (1988), (1993), Bhopal and Surat (1993) to the government. In most of the above mentioned cases, the state enforcement machinery was either indifferent to the plight of the victim or directly involved in perpetrating violence against the victim in collaboration with the anti-social elements. But, in none of the above mentioned cases the criminal justice system has brought the culprits to book. Raising an issue about the role of Indian military and para-military forces in torture and rape of women in Assam, Tripura and Nagaland, Punjab and Kashmir, tribal regions of India and in Srilanka generates great deal of hostility in the government circles.

Efforts to Activise the State Apparatus

During the decade of eighties, the women's movement in India was concerned mainly with fighting against sexist behaviour of the state enforcement machinery but now its efforts are more in direction of creating pro-women environment so that the victims of sexual violence can get legal redress and societal attitude towards women's sexuality can change. Articulate women journalists, researchers, academicians, independent consultants and activists attend the government sponsored training programmes and act as resource-persons for 'gender-sensitisation' of police officers, administrators, judges, etc. Initially the women activists were reluctant to have a dialogue with them as, while dealing with day-to-day practical issues, the government bureaucrats, forest officials and police officials were not found helpful to women's cause.

In the beginning of the anti-rape movement, many women's groups had put forward the demand to the state that it should increase its number of women judges to ensure gender-justice and more police-women to ensure sympathetic treatment to women victims. But the last one decade has given ample evidence that just by virtue of being women, they are not going to be more sensitive or judicious about women's issues. Women judges and women police being representatives of the state do not behave differently from the male judges when it comes to taking sides. After all Maya Tyagi was inhumanly tortured by a woman police constable who also encouraged her male colleagues to rape her. Women officials in jails and remand-homes behave as inhumanly with women in their custody as their male counterparts behave. The government had set up several judicial inquiries to contain public fury after an individual case of rape or cases of mass rape were reported. Reports of the inquiry Commissions gather dust in the government offices, not circulated or discussed widely. None of their recommendations are implemented. To the government, this exercise is a safety valve tactics to contain public fury.

Public Interest Litigation (PIL) by the Women's Groups

Women's groups have filed PILs to activise the state enforcement machinery and to sensitise the masses. Manushi, a women's magazine files a PIL in the Supreme Court of India after the Delhi riots in 1984 in which hundreds of Sikh women were raped and who are still languishing in the refugee camps. So far, none of the culprits have been charged. When a tribal woman, Guntaben was raped by eight policemen, paraded naked, brutally beaten and verbally abused; the concerned police station, district magistrate and the hospital staff got together to hush up the matter. There was an atmosphere of terror in the community. In this situation, two women's groups and democratic rights organisations filed public interest litigation and also continued their campaign. The government responded by setting up a tribunal which, declared that the rapists must be punished. Amnesty International also took up this case. Finally, the culprits were punished.

Role of Media Publicity in Activising the State Apparatus

Media publicity has proved to be the most effective tool in activising the state apparatus. In the post-emergency period, investigative journalism got pride of place in the mainstream media. On the one hand plethora of sensational articles trivialised the issue but on the other hand several sensitive portrayals of the issue were also given space in the media. Many protest actions by the women's groups and mass organisations against rape of poor, dalit, tribal or minority women without media coverage would have been ruthlessly crushed. Thus media publicity can be double edged. Gender sensitisation programmes for journalists and other mass communication personnel are viewed seriously by the women's groups.

Conclusion

The existing rape laws do not recognise the unequal power relations between the rape victim and the rapist. The victim is not given a choice to get her voice heard by her own lawyer. She faces sexist biases and hostility at every step- inside the family, within the community, at the police station, at the time of medical examination in the government hospital and in the court-rooms. The criminal justice system expects the victim not only to get over the trauma and be calm and composed at the time of prosecution but also shed all her inhibitions and give a vivid description of the event in the court-room. After the act of rape, if the victim washes herself (but naturally), important evidence will be lost. In this situation, the women's movement and the concerned authorities need to direct their energies to amend the procedures so that the case can be handled speedily and the victim does not face humiliation at the hands of the administration that is known for its inertia, indifference and antipathy towards women. Attitude of the judges in cases of rape is another deplorable area. Some feminist lawyers have put forward a demand of special courts for rape trials to ensure speedy dispensing of justice. Majority of judgements in rape cases are coloured by the preoccupation of the judges with 'past sexual history' of the victim and their notions of 'virginity', 'purity' and 'chastity' of women. Gender-sensitisation programmes for judges must be given top priority by the state.

About redefinition of rape there is a consensus among the women's rights groups that 'rape', 'attempt to rape' and 'violating women's modesty' as they are defined at present must be clubbed together under a heading of 'sexual offence'. It is also suggested that the redefinition of rape must be brought out of the patriarchal confines where 'penetration of penis' only is taken into consideration while defining rape. [17]

The most controversial issues for which there is no consensus amongst the women's groups are marital rape, punishment for rape and demand of monetary compensation to the victim.

Women's groups providing support to women in distress have found that sexual assault by husband is the most common and blatant form of rape. But those who oppose to recognise existence of rape within marriage put forward an argument that when a woman enters a matrimony she knows that it is her duty to fulfil the desire of her husband. Many experienced lawyers have expressed their concern over the fact that stringent punishment codified in the law results in fewer convictions. While the women's groups have always demanded higher punishment in rape-cases. Some women's groups have asked for a compulsory monetary compensation either from the state or the culprit looking at the fact the rape victim faces tremendous social stigma, employers shun her and in most of the cases even her own family disowns her. After decade and half years of struggle against rape, the most of the women activists are feeling that they have reached a square one position so far as changing the situation of rape victims or prevention of rape is concerned.

An international campaign initiated by Centre for Global Issues and Women's Leadership to include ' violence against women as violation of human rights' in the UN Charter on Human Rights has become a rallying point for women's rights organisations in India. In the context of the recent developments in Somalia, Bosnia and India, this campaign is also focusing on the issue of 'Rape as a war-crime'.

Reference

Cheris Kramarae and Dale Spender *(2000), Encyclopedia* of *Women- Global Women's Issues and Knowledge,* Vol. I,II,III,IV, Routledge, New York & London.

Footnotes

1. Vibhuti Patel: *"Women's Liberation in India"*, New Left Review, No. 153, 1985.
2. Tukaram and Ganpat versus State of Maharashtra, 1979, Supreme Court of India, Delhi.
3. Neera Desai and Vibhuti Patel: *Indian Women-Change and Challenge in the International Decade, 1975-85,* Sangam Publications, 1990.
4. See Vibhuti, Sujata, Padma (Forum Against Rape): *"The Anti-Rape Movement and Issues Facing Autonomous Women's Organisations in India"* in Miranda Davies (Compiler): *Third World-Second Sex,* Zed Press, 4th Impression, 1987.

5. See, Lawyers' Collective: "*Rape and the Law*", Bombay, 1980 and Sudesh Vaid, Amia Rao and Monica Juneja: "*Rape, Society and State*", People's Union for Democratic Rights, New Delhi, 1980.
6. Vibhuti Patel: "*Needs and Rights: Experiences of Women's Movement in India*", United Nations University, 1984.
7. Susie Tharu: "*Slow Pan Left: Feminism and the Problematic of Rights*", paper presented at National Seminar on "*Indian Women-Myth and Reality*" on March 9, 10, 11 1989 at School of Women's Studies, Jadavpur University, Calcutta. Also see, Neera Desai and Vibhuti Patel, 1990.
8. Flavia: *Journey to Justice-Procedures to be Followed in a Rape Case*, Majlis, Bombay, 1990.
9. A Lawyers Collective Publication: *Recent Changes in Laws Relating to Women*, Bombay, 1985.
10. S. K. Ghosh: *Women in Policing, Light and Life Publication*, Delhi, 1981.
11. Maithreyi Krishnaraj (ed): *Women and Violence-A Country Report*, A Study sponsored by UNESCO, Research Centre for Women's Studies, SNDT Women's University, Bombay, 1991.
12. Ibid. See, the section on Women's Action Groups and the State Machinery.
13. Report of National Conference on Rape, Forum Against Oppression of Women, *kali for Women*, Delhi, 1990.
14. See an evaluation report of one decade (1980-1990) of Forum Against Oppression of Women: *Moving... But Not Quite Thére*, Bombay, 1990.
15. Ibid., p. 7.
16. Flavia: "*A Critical Review of Enactments on Violence Against Women During the Decade 1980-1989*", Economic and Political Weekly, April 25, 1992, w.s. 19-33.
17. Report, *op. cit.*, 1990.

Section III

Women in Decision Making

Thirteen

Globalisation and Women's Question in India

Women's movement in India has had its global connections right from its beginning in the early seventies due to involvement of its leaders in the global movements against racism, imperialist invasion in Indochina and for solidarity for the national liberation struggles in Africa, Asia and Latin America. In the 1970s, the discourse of the Indian women's rights activists revolved around agitation and propaganda for women's economic and political rights in the national and global fora. In the eighties, several institutions were formed, mostly with the help of global connections to initiate support groups for women victims of violence in the family, neighbourhood and at the work-place, income generation projects, to form self-employed women's cooperatives and banks, to provide shelter to women in distress (divorced, deserted, widowed women), to create R&D base for feminist intervention, to support creative expressions of women. But soon, the realisation came that though these ghettos did give women temporary relief, they did not make women self-sufficient and empowered in the long term. Continuous dependence on individual donors and donor-agencies was reproducing the Brothel Model of Women's development. It was very important to deal with the world market with apt understanding of women's predicaments in the new international division of labour between the white and the coloured (yellow, brown and black) women. Without entering the existing power structures in the local, regional and global systems of governance, it was not possible. Hence, in the nineties, mainstreaming of women leaders got intensified.

Implications on Gender Relations

Women's entry into the decision-making bodies of the industry, financial institutions, government structures, international aid- agencies, electoral bodies, international human rights organisations, electronic media with global coverage has removed several bottlenecks coming in the way of empowerment of mass of women. Women's projects are executed faster, salary scale of women in the government and non-government sectors have risen, remuneration of women beneficiaries and workers of women's projects has enhanced, complaints of sexual harassment at work-place are judiciously examined and the culprits are punished, global travelling of single women has increased multifold, women professionals are ready to work with women's groups, parents with only daughter/ daughters feel more confident in their survival struggles. Chief accountants in several NGOs are women. Feminist economists who were working on a national plane are now working globally with membership of 550 economists working in 31 countries. The first two decades of the women's movement attracted mainly sociologists and English literature experts who gave strong analytical input and new vocabulary respectively, for women's concerns. The third decade legitimised the experiences of women from all walks of life. All over the world, feminism grew side by side of fundamentalism.

Statistical Profile of Women

Globalisation has brought in range of new reproductive technologies, which have potential for making the Indian women, *an endangered species*. As per the 1991 Census, India had 439 million men and 407 million women, i.e. there was **deficit** of 32 m women (See Table 1). As per 2001 census there are 531 million men and 496 million women, i.e., there is deficit of 35 million women. Though there has been a small change in the sex ratio in favour of women from 1991 census, the improvement is not significant because the absolute deficit during the last decade is of about three millions. Moreover, rapidly declining child sex-ratio indicates that the overall sex ratio is headed for further decline.

TABLE - 1
SEX RATIO (FEMALES/1000 MALES)

States	*1991*	*2001*
All India	**927**	**933**
Andhra Pradesh	972	978
Arunachal Pradesh	996	901
Assam	922	932
Bihar	910	921
Goa	966	960
Gujarat	934	921
Haryana	865	861
Himachal Pradesh	975	970
Jammu & Kashmir	N.A.	900
Karnataka	959	964
Kerala	1036	1058
Maharashtra	933	922
Manipur	957	978
Meghalaya	955	975
Mizoram	921	938
Madhya Pradesh	931	920
Nagaland	886	909
Orissa	970	972
Punjab	881	874
Rajasthan	909	922
Sikkim	878	875
Tamil Nadu	973	986
Tripura	944	950
Uttar Pradesh	878	898
West Bengal	917	934

Source: Census of India, 1991 and 2001.

Globalisation has intensified femicide in rural Punjab and Haryana where doctors equipped with the latest medical technologies imported from abroad, pay home visits in their Maruti cars to the pregnant women to collect amniotic fluid to conduct sex-determination tests. As per the 1991 Census, sex ratio in Punjab was 881 and in Haryana it was 865. (See Table 2). According to 2001 Census, the sex-ratios in Punjab and Haryana are 861 and 874 respectively. In both the states, women's movement is virtually non-existent. Himachal Pradesh, Gujarat, Uttaranchal, Maharashtra and Chandigarh are some other states where the sex-determination tests are very popular. Because of consistent whistle blowing by the women's groups, the government bodies are taking stern action against female infanticide, female foeticide and neglect of girl child. But, to deal with the commercially minded private sector and patriarchal forces within different communities, enlightened leadership is needed.

TABLE - 2
TEN DISTRICTS WITH THE LOWEST CHILD SEX-RATIO (0-6 AGE-GROUP)

District	*State*	*Method of femicide*	*Girls per 1000 boys*
Salem	Tamil Nadu	Killing of girls	849
Bhind	Madhya Pradesh	Killing of girls	850
Jaisalmar	Rajasthan	Killing of girls	851
Kaithal	Haryana	Sex selective abortion	854
Jind	Haryana	Sex selective abortion	858
Amritsar	Punjab	Sex selective abortion	861
Faridkot	Punjab	Sex selective abortion	863

Source: UNICEF, 1995.

Recently, the United States (Orangberg, South Carolina) based manufacturers have targeted Indian market for Gen-select, sex selection product with a claim of success rate of 96%. Several national news papers are publishing its advertisement. They are looking out for Indian retailers and distributors for their product.

As this technique does not involve abortion, it is expected to be popular through out the country where ideological hold of son-preference is widely prevalent. At present they have been using electronic media to reach out to their clients and charging Rs. 6000 for Gen Select kit. With increasing popularity of Gen Select, girl child will not be allowed to be born.

Global awareness about reproductive rights of women has reduced coercion in the birth control practices. Introduction of harmful contraceptives by the pharmaceutical industry has been opposed by doctors groups such as Forum for Medical Ethics and Akash. But, at the same time, we must note that proportion of birth attended by trained nurses in India is only 33 per cent. Maternal mortality rate for Indian women is six times higher than that of women in a neighbouring country, Sri Lanka (See Table-3).

TABLE - 3
DEMOGRAPHIC PROFILE OF WOMEN

Country	*Maternal deaths*	*Female life in years*	*Proportion of Births Attended by trained nurse (%)*
India	360	57.9	33
Sri Lanka	60	72.5	87

Source: Ministry of Health & Family Welfare, GOI, New Delhi, 1992.

Women and Education

As per the 2001 census, the literacy rates of women have improved and drop out rates have reduced (See Table 4 and Table 5). Globalisation has increased the opportunities for higher learning for highly educated women who can compete in the global market. But, for majority of girls, commercialisation of educational institutions has proved detrimental. New phenomena of 'earning' and learning' has become a marked feature of the 90s. Teleworking and teletrade is drawing lot of Indian women in this high- salaried sector. Open schools, open universities, correspondence courses and distance education are becoming increasingly popular. Lectures and demonstrations by globally renowned teachers, experts and specialists telecast by various television channels become source of learning for women who are in *purdah* and women who have restricted mobility. This saves them from sexual harassment and transport cost. Still 61 per cent of Indian women are illiterate. As per Economic Survey, GOI, 1995 only 24 per cent of Scheduled Caste women and 18 per cent of the Scheduled Tribe women were literate. (See Table 6) The states with higher percentage of child labour, child marriages and child prostitution (vicious circle of CL-CM- CP) have higher drop our rate of girl-students.

TABLE - 4
LITERACY IN 2001

Literates	*Absolute*	*% of Total population*
Persons	56.7 crores	65
Males	34 crores	76
Females	22.7 crores	54

Source: Census of India, 2001.

TABLE - 5
PERCENTAGE DROPOUT OF GIRLS AT DIFFERENT STAGES OF SCHOOL EDUCATION (1993-94)

Level of education	*Percentage of dropouts*
Primary	39.50
Middle	56.78
High School	74.54

Source: Indian Economy, Statistical Yearbook, 1997.

TABLE - 6
LITERACY RATES AMONG ALL CATEGORIES, S.C. & S.T., 1991.

Caste/Tribe	*Total*	*Male*	*Female*
All	52	64	39
S.C.	37	41	24
S.T.	30	41	18

Source: Economic Survey, 1994-95.

Women in the Workforce

Occupational diversification due to globalisation has increased employment opportunities for women in the food processing, horticulture, floriculture, software, electronic, garment, textile designing, fashion and aviation industry. Highly qualified women are absorbed in the human resource departments of the corporate world. Development projects supported by the Non-resident Indians, government and non-government foundations of the industrialised countries, globally operating religious institutions have opened new avenues for career women. As per the 1991 Census, work participation rate of Indian women was 22.3 per cent, while in 1981, WPR was 18 per cent. We can say that globalisation has increased Work-participation Rate of Women, while sex ratio suggests deplorable status of women. (See Table 7). As compared to several Asian countries , the work participation rate of Indian women is quite low.

TABLE - 7
SEX RATIO AND FEMALE WORK PARTICIPATION RATE

Year	*Sex Ratio*	*Female Work Participation Rate*
1901	972	31.7
1951	946	23.4
1961	941	28.0
1971	930	14.2
1981	934	19.7
1991	927	22.3

Source: Census of India, 1991.

There is increasing acceptance of women in the decision-making bodies. Wherever, women bosses have been generous, kind and respectful towards male colleagues and subordinates, they have met with less resistance. Male hostility towards visibility of women in the high profile jobs has reduced due to mandatory gender-sensitisation programmes organised for over a decade for the decision makers. But, in the field situation, women still face lot of prejudice from the conservative forces.

As per Human Development Report 2000, women professionals and technical workers constitute 20.5 per cent of the total workforce. As per the World Bank estimates, rape and domestic violence account for 5 per cent of the healthy years of life lost among women in 15-44 age group in developing countries. The global health burden from domestic violence against women in the reproductive age group is about 9.5 million disability-adjusted life years (DALYs), compared to fatal diseases like AIDS (10 million DALYs).

Entry of Women in the Development Sector

GOs (Government Organisations) and NGOs (Non-government organisations) have humanised employer-employee relations. Due to pressure generated by the development media and the socialist feminists, new work-ethics is fostered which challenges caste-based division of labour. In the development sector, women's organisations have created their constituency, mass-base, think-tank, pool of professionals, progressive male allies and self-sustaining financial base. To seal corruption and leakage and to stop wastage of institutional resources on leisure-time activities, conscious efforts are being made, both by the funding institutions and the local groups to involve articulate and fearless women in the work with poverty groups.

Women and Prostitution

India has learnt the lessons from several Asian countries about Globalisation and sex-tourism. Hue and cry created by the women's groups made the Ministry of Tourism in India take enough precautions to promote only healthy tourism which would foster ties with different countries through art, culture, literature, music, variety of Indian cuisine, safe transport, visits to archeological sights. Initial attempts by the tourism department to use a woman's body to earn foreign exchange were thwarted by the women's groups. Educational institutions and voluntary organisations are promoting development tourism for meaningful rehabilitation of women victims of prostitution. (See Annexure 1). Still, prostitution has been the most challenging and burning problem faced by the development activists. Girls form the rural and urban poverty groups provide cannon fodder for the flesh trade. Once inducted, it is virtually impossible for an individual victim to break the nexus of procurer, pimp, police and politicians. Cross-border prostitution involving Nepal and Bangladesh are even more complicated to deal with.

Poverty in India

Different estimates of poverty in India reveal that 35 per cent of the population is poor. While the international estimates on poverty in India show that 52.5 per cent of the Indian population gets less than US $1 per day and 88.8 per cent of the Indians get less than $ 2 per day. As revealed in Table 8, it is more than poverty in South Asia. As per Social Watch, 37 per cent of rural, 31 per cent of urban and 35 per cent of total Indian population were classified as poor in 1994. As per UNDP 's Global Survey, in 1998, 36 per cent of Indians were below poverty line. National surveys using income criteria revealed that in 1992, 40.9 per cent and in 1994, 35 per cent of Indians were below poverty line (For global comparison see, Table 8). 19 per cent of the population is without access to safe water. Collection of fuel, fodder and water becomes major concerns for women in poverty groups who are struggling to survive. What solutions does globalisation offer to these women?

TABLE - 8
PERCENTAGE OF POPULATION LIVING ON LESS THAN 1 U.S. $ PER DAY

Region	*1987*	*1993*
Latin America and Caribbean	22.0	23.5
South Asia	45.4	43.1
South East Asia and the Pacific	28.8	26.0
Sub Saharan Africa	38.5	39.0
Europe and Central Asia	0.6	3.5
Near East North Africa	28.8	26.0
Total	30.1	29.4

Source: SOCIAL WATCH, Casilla de Correa,1539, Montevideo 11000, Uruguay.

India in the World Economy

Stark disparity between the rich and the poor countries in terms of global opportunity have created new human insecurities. They are economic vulnerabilities, job and income insecurity, cultural insecurity, environmental insecurity, political insecurity, personal insecurity and health insecurity as per UNDP Human Development Report,(HDR)1999. As per HDR 2000, India's Human Development Index rank was 128. Its military expenditure was 2.1 per cent of the GDP. India has signed and ratified the following key international agreements:

1. International Covenant on Economic, Social and Cultural Rights, 1966.
2. International Covenant on Civil and Political Rights, 1966.
3. International Covenant on Elimination of All Forms of Racial Discrimination, 1969.
4. Convention of the Rights of Children.1989.
5. Convention on Elimination of Discrimination Against Women, 1979.
6. Convention on the Political Rights of Women, 1979.

India has not signed and ratified convention regarding the status of refugees, 1954.

Women and Culture

Globalisation has encouraged cultural exchange, language courses, festival celebration keeping into consideration global media coverage and global market. Careful projection of women singers, dancers, painters, actresses, poets, writers, journalists, art-critiques, film-makers and educationists has a hidden agenda of promoting India's multi-cultural heritage. Their involvement in building new educational institutions and cultural centers and rejuvenation of old educational and cultural centres has been fruitful. These women are self-made, intellectually independent, conversant with foreign languages, life-styles and fit into a norm of "Global citizens". Era of one *cultural zarina* controlling *native monkeys* seems to have gone. This is a major departure from the colonial legacy in which, instead of caricaturing colonial power relations (highly glamourised by the Hindi film industry), ethos of multiculturalism, 'respect for all cultures' find place of prominence.

Well- researched serials like *Discovery of India* about Indian cultural heritage are giving due recognition to women's work and worth.

Women and Media

Construction of new gender relations based on egalitarian principles as portrayed in some of the advertisements must be encouraged. Even the chat-shows projecting new and realistic images of self-confident career women, caring father, efficient male cooks (who are not comic characters), male beauticians, male fashion designers with professional touch are gender-sensitive. Interviews with women entrepreneurs, women industrialists, women managers convey that both, the interviewers and the interviewees know their profession well. In comparison, Hindi film industry's record is quite deplorable with its crude dialogues, male violence and voyeurism. Hindi serials are perpetuating hedonistic and consumerist culture of the upper class which has purchasing power. What Hollywood did in the seventies, Bollywood did in the nineties. Both betrayed the male anxiety towards increasing autonomy and self-confidence of women.

Women and Housework

Globalisation has definitely changed attitude towards housework of 50 per cent of India's population, which has purchasing power. Thousands of home appliances shown in the advertisement and through door-to-door sale have made men interested in housework. Introduction of modern gadgets to ease housework has encouraged male members of the house to share housework. Men's Participation in the food and fashion Industry has challenged patriarchal stereotyping of women's place among the educated middle class. Variety of processed and semi-cooked food has increased men's interest in cooking.

Science, Technology and Women

Globalisation has encouraged induction of women engineers, architects, pilots, scientists, technicians, journalists with super-specialisation into challenging and rewarding assignments. Facilities of safe transport, flexi time, variety of fresh and durable food available in the market, absence of policing, place for night-halt, separate toilets and rest-rooms for women and enlightened management which does not see women employees as burden have provided conducive atmosphere for women to join the fields which are highly demanding. Even the R&D Department of the corporate world, multinational companies, government institutions and autonomous research institutions are providing congenial atmosphere to women employees.

Analytical Shift in Policy Planning

Globalisation had changed the mindset of the Indian elite. Earlier, India was a unit of analysis, and interstate comparisons played an important role in the macro-planning. Now the policy statements are made on the basis of cross-country comparisons. This process was facilitated by the UN system- UNICEF, UNESCO, WHO, UNDP and UNIFEM. International Decade for women (1975-1985) focussed on Equality, Development and Peace as goals and promoted projects for women on education, health and employment. SAARC decade for the girl Child highlighted problems of girl-child labour, girl mothers (married and unwed) and trafficking of girls from Nepal, Bangladesh and rural India. Without scientific understanding of international factor market, labour market and product markets and nature of their segmentation, no policy intervention will be rewarding for women. So far women's development projects have been used to execute the tasks rejected by the economic elite due to its labour intensive nature. Moreover, the labour processes adopted in the women's development programmes depend on the technologies rejected by the mainstream. Feudal labour relations in women's groups are resented by the younger generation, which prefers wage-labour contract system offered by the World capitalism. Home based work is gaining ground among all classes of women due to identity politics and massive restructuring of infrastructure sector, which curb their autonomy and mobility. Globalisation has definitely changed women's agenda- from day-to-day survival issues to quality of life issues. Hundreds of new institutions (for girls and women) with high financial stakes have come up in the current decade. Gender implications of official Indian policy in the global bodies concerning biomedical and agricultural researches, Trade

Related Intellectual Property Rights and human rights issues need serious examination by gender-aware experts. Use of poor women for experimentation of harmful drugs/vaccines and medical technologies banned in the first world must be stopped.

Conclusion

Globalisation has made civil society more inward looking. Caste, religious and kinship networks are activised to bring reforms within the community. All networks with global connections are executing development projects, which would benefit their stake groups. In this situation, women's rights activists with multicultural perspective can play important role as catalysts for women's empowerment. Without ensuring women's rights, globalisation can't have a human face. We should not forget that globalisation has widened income gap between the resource poor and resource rich countries. Female-headed households are the poorest of the poor households. Free play of market forces has made majority of Indian women more vulnerable. NGOs have provided islands of security in some pockets. In this situation, affirmative action by the democratic institutions and the nation state, in secular areas of human governance is the only answer. Ordinary women can be empowered in the context of globalisation only if human rights are considered as a framework for global governance and the marginalisation of poor countries reversed. National policies and actions for human development need to be strengthened. Equitable distribution of benefits of technological progress by tapping the potential of new technologies for human development and poverty eradication must be made a new agenda for technology. Action plan should include review of intellectual property rights and trade related intellectual properties to track the human and economic cause in terms of effects on prices, impact on biodiversity and on access to medical resources. Public investment should be made in technologies for poor people and poor countries, especially in the areas of medical and agricultural research.

Annexure I

Profile of Prostitution

As per the survey of 3000 prostitutes in 6 metropolitan cities of Delhi, Bombay, Calcutta, Hyderabad, Banglore and Madras, conducted by the Central Social Welfare Board of GOI, the following scenario emerged:

(a) 15 per cent of the women were children at the time of entry into the sex-trade.

(b) 25 per cent were minors (between 16-18 at the time of entry).

(c) 36 per cent were scheduled caste women, *devdasis* (temple prostitutes) included.

(d) 24 per cent were backward class women.

(e) 71 per cent were illiterate women.

(f) 54.2 per cent were divorced, deserted or widowed women.

(g) 34.4 5 were unmarried women.

(h) 10.6 per cent were married women.

Causes of Entry Were

(1) Economic distress	44%
(2) Desertion by spouse	24.5%
(3) Deception	11.9%
(4) Social custom and family tradition	10.5%
(5) Abduction and kidnapping	2.25 %

Earnings: 60 per cent of the women earn less than Rs. 3000 per month, average earnings retained by the prostitutes were between Rs. 500-600, after the brothel keepers and pimps had taken away their cuts and after sending money and goodies to the families of the prostitutes. Average indebtedness is Rs. 10000-15000, which keeps the women in bondage for a long period.

Fact-file, Newsletter of India Centre for Human Rights and Law, Mumbai, 1997.

"Study on 'Child Prostitution in India' by the Centre for Concern for Child Labour, a Delhi- based NGO estimates the number of prostitutes in India to be around 9 lakhs. Of these, some 30 per cent are children, numbering 2,70000. The number of children below the age 14 years in commercial prostitution is increasing at the rate of 8 to 10 per cent per annum. Workshop on Child Sex-workers in Gujarat, Annual Report, 1998-99, Centre for Social Studies, South Gujarat University, Surat -390007, p. 21

As per the information given **by Ministry of Planning & Programme Implementation, GoI,** New Delhi, by the end of 1997, a million children under the age of 15 are expected to be living with HIV, over 90 per cent of them in developing countries. In India, over 200 children get infected by HIV everyday.

Orphans in Mattancherry & fort Kochi area are the hapless victims of the 'primitive' muta (temporary) system of marriage prevalent among Muslims of the area. Globalisation has accentuated their misery as these helpless girls are exported to the gulf countries.

References

Annual Report(1998-99), Centre for Social Studies, Surat.

Economic and Political Weekly (2000), Teleworking and tele-trade in India: Diverse Perspectives and Visions, Vol. Xxxv, No . 26, June 24-30,Bombay.

Health Economics and Financing Programme (1999), Research Portfolio, Health Policy Unit, London School of Hygiene and Tropical Medicine, October.

Hakan Bjorkman : "The Message of the 1999 Human Development Report- Globalisation With a Human Face", UNDP,

Implementing the 20/20 Initiative(1998), Achieving Universal Access to Basic Social Services- A Joint Publication of UNDP, UNESCO, UNFPA, UNICEF, WHO and The World Bank, 3- United Nations Plaza, H-9f, New York, NY 10017, USA.

International Ethical Guidelines for Biomedical Research Involving Human Subjects, Council for International Organisations of Medical Sciences, WHO, 1993.

Jagadananda, Sunder N. Mishra (1999), ***India**- Commitments: A Barren Fluency ?* **Social Watch**, Casilla de Correo 1539, Montevideo 11000, Uruguay. An NGO Watchdog System aimed at monitoring the commitments made by governments at the World Summit for Social; Development and the Beijing World Conference on Women.

Jeffrey Sachs, *Sachs on Development*, The Economist, 14-8-99.

Leela Visaria (1999), "Deficit of Women in India- Magnitude, Trends, Regional Variations & Determinants" in Bharati Ray & Aparna Basu (ed.) *From Independence Towards Freedom, Indian Women Since 1947*, Gender Studies, OUP, India, N.Delhi.

Martha C. Nussbaum (2000), Women and Human Development: The Capabilities Approach, Kali for Women, Delhi.

The Indian Journal of Labour Economics (1999), Institute of Applied Manpower Research Building, I. P. Estate, Mahatma Gandhi Marg, New Delhi- 110002, India, Vol. 42, No. 3, July-Sept.

Fourteen

Women in Decision Making

The decade of 90s has witnessed several roundtables on Women in Decision-Making. Round tables in the Eastern parts of India highlighted the need for networking. In the Western India they focused on the achievements of women's movement and need for women's policy. In the Southern states the round tables were concerned about initiatives in women and development. In the Northern states, they were concerned about formation of state sponsored National Commission of women. In the national round table, the need for mainstreaming of the women's agenda was emphasized.

Herstory of Decision Making in India

The first generation of women decision-makers in India was the product of the independence movement. In the post-independence period, they made important contributions in the fields of education, institutions for women's welfare, diplomatic relations, and administration of the state and central government and in politics. They were perceived as super women and enjoyed honorary male status in the society.

Collective Decision-making Processes of the New Social Movements in India

1970 onwards, development of social movements highlighting the problems of the rural and urban poor, industrial working class, tribal masses and minorities threw up a new kind of women decision makers who had strength of street-fighting, formal education and strategic thinking. They had to work under tremendous adversity, as they were a part of politics of protest. In the nineties, other sectors of the society also gave space to competent and highly qualified women to be in the decision-making bodies. At present, gender sensitization of state and central government, management and trade unions, mass organisations, educational institutions is one of the topmost priorities among the development-oriented organisations. In the last two decades, women who have held important positions have had positive experience whenever they have done thorough homework and have played a role of problem shooters diligently and fearlessly. At the same time, in several places they have faced tremendous male hostility and physical violence. Competent women in the public life who have promoted the ethos of distributive justice have managed to get popular support.

Women Getting A Foothold in Politics

.......Let us enter politics,
continue our struggle
and take leadership.
Can't put up with patriarchal power any more,
O, Venubai, why do you remain repressed ?
Come out and join our rally.

This is how the song sung for the first time by "Toiling Women's Liberation Movement" members in the late seventies ended. It represented the gusto of a newly formed mass organization of tribal women of Dhulia district (Vibhuti Patel, 1987). It became popular among the women's groups not only in Maharashtra but also all over India. This song represented the new understanding of 'politic'. Politics as not only electoral politics or membership of political parties, but as collective action of women against oppressive patriarchal power with a long term goal of social transformation that ensured women's liberation from exploitation, degradation, injustice, subjugation and superstition. The slogan ' Personal is Political' is popularized by the western women's liberation movement appealed to many city-based women's groups who realized how individual cases of violence against women were not merely 'personal problems, but an outcome of socio-cultural, historical, political and economic realities in which Indian women had to survive. As a result, the issues which affected women and treated as personal problems such as rape, family violence, dowry-murders, harassment at the workplace were put on the 'public-political agenda' of the women's movement (Vibhuti Patel, 1988). The pressure from the new women's groups forced the mainstream political parties also to show greater concern for women's issues at least in their public speeches, press statements and election manifestos. After the nationwide anti-rape movement in 1980, cases of violence against women became issues for parties to score points against contenders in electoral battles as well as in the local power struggles (Vibhuti Patel, 1994).

Mobilisation of Women by the Political Parties

The parliamentary parties started viewing women as a constituency in the eighties. This changing attitude of the parliamentary parties towards women is reflected in their election manifestoes, their attitude towards women candidates and their overall electoral strategies. In Andhra Pradesh, at the time of the State assembly election, the popular regional party of that time, Telugu Desam, promised land rights for women. Mrs. Indira Gandhi made references to "Stree Shakti" and Bharatiya Janata Party began advocating the revival of ancient Indian culture, eulogizing mythological women characters. They also demanded a uniform civil code but from an anti- Muslim angle rather than women's rights perspective.

In the electoral process, we find two contradictory processes. On the one hand we have powerful, articulate women leaders who are mainly elite and on the other we have women who are mere rubber stamps. However, the elite women's political presence derives from their relations with male politicians- husbands, brothers, fathers, father-in-laws. Between 1962 and 1984, the total number of women who contested the Lok Sabha (Lower House of Parliament) has increased from 65 to 157 and the number of women who were elected was increased from 33 to 42. After 1985, meetings of women members of parliament (M.P.) to discuss important issues of women, became more or less a regular feature. This was achieved at the initiative of the Minister for Women's Development and Social Welfare.

Implications of Increased Political Participation of Women:

Women's visibility in the political scenario can be understood in the following ways:

- Increase in the number of women in the electoral process and their meaningful contribution in highlighting women specific issues.
- Qualitative change in political goals and processes as a result of accommodating of women's perspectives and priorities.

We have seen increasing number of meetings, camps, welfare programmes, weekly meetings, national conventions organized by different political parties of their women cadres. Mahila Congress, BJP Women's front, Communist Party of India, Communist Party of India (Marxist), Republic Party of India, Janata Front and Shetkari Sangathana have all organized conventions to discuss/ highlight women's problems. In terms of rhetorics on women, as all of them are competing with each other to establish their credibility in the eyes of women. If the Congress Government brought National Perspective Plan for Women, the Janata regime came up with Women's Commission. But in this image building exercise, both of them shared the same ideology. A good illustration is their response to the Muslim Women's Protection of Rights (on Divorce) Act that took away the right to maintenance from a divorced Muslim woman. Likewise neither regime did anything to bring the culprits of Deorala Sati episode to book.

Hurdles Faced by Women Candidates

Most of the women face tremendous opposition from family, community and the male political leaders if they decide to enter electoral politics or public life. The present political leadership, in spite of its populist rhetoric, want to keep women out of the political arena. Indian women's lower educational level, inferior social status and lack of autonomy are reflected in their lower participation in poli :s. Increasing criminalisation, corruption and compromises required to sustain one's political career also deter women from entering mainstream politics. Even among the majority of women's rights groups, 'politics' is equated with 'politicking', 'dirty' maneuvering and manipulations and therefore power and politics remain an anathema to them. But at the same time, women activists involved in direct action for past one and a half decade have also realized the limitations of micro level activities.

Women in the Electoral Bodies

With amendments of Constitution in 1993 to decentralize political power as per 73rd and 74th Amendments, a provision has to be made for devolution of power and decision-making in favour of women. One third of all seats in the local self- government bodies have to be reserved for women. Rural India has already elected village panchayats with one third elective seats reserved for women i.e. India has one million elected representatives. Women elected representatives are taking active interest in using budgetary allocations for promotion women's education, safe drinking water and sanitation. But,

> "neither the people's representatives at the center nor at the state level, wish to give up their powers over their constituencies and to share their power at the local level. Similarly the bureaucrats are not geared to play the role of facilitators. Giving up powers to representatives of the Panchayati Raj system is difficult for them. Voluntary organisations can play a major role in developing training programmes for all three groups- The politicians at the center and in the states and the bureaucrats in order to help develop new perspectives on their roles."[1]

Elected representatives are facing innumerable problems. Shetkari Sangathana Mahila Aghadi managed to win election for their all women panels in the last Gram Panchayat elections in spite of stiff opposition from the local vested interests. In spite of threats of rape and witch-hunting by rival political parties, several women in Dhulia district contested elections in Gram Panchayat. In South Gujarat, when a woman activist working for women's rights contested election, the local vested interests tried to divide votes by putting up a 'rubberstamp' woman candidate. When Vijayatai Chowk, a courageous woman's rights activist of Dhule district applied for a Lok Sabha seat, she was refused the seat by the party bosses on the ground that while she would win votes from the brides side, she will not from the bridegroom's side because she had taken up so many cases of dowry-murders in the past 15 years. Ms. Neelam Gore who contested the Lok Sabha election on Republican Party of India ticket resigned her secretary ship of its mahila Aghadi (Women's Front) due to sexist biases she had to face in the party. The political compromises of principles and programmes in the policy resolutions, the increasing importance of 'mafia' politics and exorbitant money power required by the electoral politics act as deterrent for women's participation in the mainstream politics.

Yet Indian women have come on the political agenda of the country through various techniques – collective actions, programmes of consciousness raising, petitioning and lobbying. In addition they have produced well-researched documents and obtained, after great effort, some media visibility for women's issues. This contradictory process must be kept in mind to evolve a proper political understanding of women's political participation in India.

Women as Voters

Indian women have become more aware of their rights but the level of political information of women voters is low. Many women's groups in Ahmedabad, Pune and Bangalore have prepared women's manifesto. They conduct educational campaigns, organise know thy candidate programmes and issue leaflets concerning women's issues. They expose those candidates who had a criminal or unsavoury background such as involvement in murder of wives or daughter –in-law, or sexual molestation of women. Vimochana in Bangalore campaigned against several candidates who had a record of violence against women by organising street –corner meeting, writing in newspapers, issuing leaflets in Kannada and English. As a result of this campaign, all the candidates lost their seats.

In response to the candidates of sexual violence by Mr. Narvekar, Speaker of Legislative Assembly of Goa and CPI (M) cadres, the feminists' organisations demanded 'a code of conduct' for the party cadres. Stree Mukti Andolan Sampark Samiti (Women's Liberation Coordination Committee), a state level United

Front of the progressive and the leftist women's organisations issued a leaflet before the Lok Sabha Election in February, 1990 that expounded the perspective of women's organisations on elections and suggested to voters the principles and programmes around which the choice of candidate should be made. The manifesto considered the issues such as fundamentalism, family laws, as well as development. Development with women and ecological perspective should address fuel-fodder-water issues, implications of electrification, and dams and education, health, employment etc. Political education of the masses on violence against women, sexist media, rural and tribal women's survival struggles, need to be carried out and the candidates should be answerable to constituencies on these issues.

Recent Debate on 33 per cent Reservation of Seats For Women in the Electoral Bodies

In the thirties, the women leaders of India involved in the nationalist struggles were pressing for universal adult franchise and now, sixty years later, the women leaders of the same political parties have agreed to support 33 per cent seats for women. Is this mode one step forward or two steps backward? Those who regard it as one step forward is empowering women to do so because they think" It will broaden the base of women's political participation and will help to strengthen women's faith in the political process which is otherwise dominated by men". (Women and Media Committee, Bombay). Those who are opposed to this move have consistently held this approaches undesirable, right from pre-independence days. Moreover reservation as such is unlikely to solve the main causes of limited political participation of women in furthering women's cause, because given socio-political context where mass illiteracy prevails along with the style of politics that encourages growing violence, mafia politics, character assassination of candidates, prohibitive election expenses and opportunistic/debased politicking pursued to achieve very narrow and short term political goals. Where such influences are operative in the Indian politics in an overwhelming way, more reservation of seats has a limited value.

It is interesting, that same national level male politicians who support 33 per cent reserved seats for women in the Panchayati Raj institutions have expressed their outrage against the reservation of 33 per cent seats for women in the Legislative Assembly and in the Parliament(IAWS, 2002). They are using the same arguments as our colonial masters used against the native then, i.e. women will not be able to govern, as they are inexperienced. Many corporators of Bombay Municipal Corporation have openly expressed their discontentment over this decision of the present government.

During 1990s sharp polarisation of political opinions took place around Women's Reservation Bill. It was first tabled in parliament in 1996, "and was mired in the conflict over the demand for special quotas for women of the other backward classes and minorities"(Mary John, EPW, 2000).

The autonomous women's organisations' doubts about 33 per cent reservations have different reasons. They fear that by participating in the corrupt electoral process women's rights activists will not be able to further the broader interests of women (Vibhuti Patel,1993). They feel that women activists will have to make compromises in their principles, programmes and practices. Moreover, the talented women will be co-opted by the system. The 33 per cent reservation has other dangers. It prepares the ground for opponents of the women's rights movement (the mothers-in-law) to get elected in most of the places. These women will be from the elite sections, mainly the kith and the kin of male politicians. Women politicians in South Asia are not different from their male counterparts (Rounaq Jahan, 1987).

Some scholars and women's organisations do think that the entry of women in the electoral process will help the curbing of violence and corruption, in other words, female presence will moralise the system. Experiences of Karnataka and Kerala have proved the same (Uma Prachar, 2001). This is the argument that women have often advanced as for example in the U.S.A.

National Commission for Women

At present, the National Commission for women has generated a lot of debate among the women's groups. The Committee for the Status of Women (974) had recommended the formation of such a commission to take up women's problems. The Congress (I) government did not pay any attention to this demand. The report of the National Commission on Self-Employed Women ('Shramshakti') gave a comprehensive picture of women's status and recommended many concrete steps for women in the informal sector. This too was not officially discussed in the parliament. In this climate of official apathy to do anything concretely for women, when the bill on the National Commission for Women was tabled in Lok Sabha on May 22, 1990 many welcomed it as a forward step but these early hopes were soon belied. The content was found less than satisfactory and invited a lot of criticism from women's group as it lacks an autonomous status and has an inbuilt structure that provides far too much governmental interference. The Women's Organisations have proposed to the government that it explicitly define the clauses to protect the autonomy and independence of the commission. Moreover, the reports of the commission should go straight to parliament via the president. It should be empowered to conduct enquiries concerning women even when the government officials or agencies themselves are involved in perpetuating violation of women's rights. Alas, inspite of detailed recommendations given by the women's groups, the present government has not included all of them in the Act. Now, State level women's commissions are active in Maharashtra, Karnataka and Kerala. They are executing state policies for women, promoting advocacy work on women's problems, strengthening elected women representatives in the Panchayati Raj institutions and selectively taking up cases of violence against women. They are effective in the social sector of the economy as take up women's problems in the areas of education, employment, welfare and health- public health and reproductive rights.

Professionalisation of Decision Making

Complexities of contemporary reality make it imperative for women decision-makers to be multifaceted in their approach towards the issues at stake. Only professional expertise is not enough, but the understanding of human angle and power dynamics is equally important. The first hand experiences of women who have worked on important committees of the government and non-government bodies are noteworthy for new entrants in the public life. Hence *Vacha* and YWCA, Bombay organised a round table in which four women – Dr. Kalindi Mazumdar, College of Social Work, *Nirmala Niketan*, Ms. Neera Adarkar, Architect from Majlis, Bombay, Ms. Sara Samuel from YWCA, Bombay and Ms. Ulka Mahajan from Samarthan, Bombay shared their experiences. Main issues highlighted by them were as follows:

Dr. Kalindi Mazumdar, Nirmala Niketan, Bombay

Women decision makers working with government institutions such as ICDS (Integrated Child Development Scheme), government remand homes, refuge homes for women in distress, beggars' home can't afford to ignore material reality of women beneficiaries, verbal and physical assaults faced by them at the hands of the supervisory staff and usurpation of financial and other resources. *Nirmala Niketan* (NN) is MITC (Middle Level Training Center) for ICDS and closely interacts with CDPOs (Community Development Project Officers), anganwadi workers, helpers, ANMs and UNICEF officials. In the process, the NN also deals with the problems faced by women at different levels of the hierarchy. E.g. Impersonal and insensitive handling of ICDS programmes, use of ANMs and other women workers as personal servants of the CDPOs, sexual harassment of women employees of the project, distribution of vitamins and other eatables to the beneficiaries, management of accounts.

Women social workers working with police have been able to sensitize them on criminal matters concerning women though initially they had to face lot of prejudices in cases of dowry-harassment, bride-burning, rape and molestation. It is very difficult to get JJ Act (Juvenile Justice Act) implemented. Since last nine years JAPU (Juvenile Aid Police Unit) has been under operation. Condition of women police constables has been deplorable, as they are powerless and marginalised in their own families and within the police force. Many of them are insulted, taunted, molested and harassed by their male colleagues and superiors and hence they fear them. The rescue of commercial sex-workers in the recent past has been under utter chaos. The report submitted by the committee of women social workers on their food, water and toilets was taken seriously for the first time in 1995. The condition of government supported remand homes considerably improved after the public debate on this issue in the print and electronic media. Maharashtra State Women's Commission was able to seal leakage in the distribution of items allocated for women victims in the remand homes as women members of the commission took personal interest in material resources provided to the inmates. Health status and mental condition of inmates improved because women were ensured food-security, clean toilets and proper clothes.

The College of social work is giving Bombay police, the training programmes on a regular basis on family-life education, sex education, communication skills, inter-personal skills and knowledge of the JJ Act through lectures, role-plays and audio-visual aids.

Women's organisations need to be sensitized to take up developmental issues affecting women. Refuge homes like *Baapriu Ghar* and *Sukh Shanti* should allow women to work outside their premises.

We need to work closely with elected members of the local self- government bodies. Work of *Mandalik* Trust in Konkan region in these regards has made a difference. Earlier, women members of *Gramsabha* were diffident. They had to face a backlash of violence. Even a lady sarpanch was told to sit on the floor and also told that the chair was meant only for men. In another village, a lady sarpanch, while cooking in a kitchen, saw a mob outside her house. When she made an inquiry, she found out that the villagers had come to congratulate her husband for her victory. *Mandalik* Trust has been able to include the health component in the *Gram Sabha*'s agenda. To reach out to the local self-government bodies, we need to generate material in simple *Marathi*.

What Actually Needed while Working with the Government?

While working with the government departments, municipal bodies, state supported institutions, police stations and the legal system; the social worker needs to have the following attributes:

1. Good academic background helps the social worker to

articulate the problem in an effective manner. Verbal and writing skills give confidence to face the government officers without losing temper.

2. Command over local language and English is an asset. Most of the government officials happen to be rooted in the local culture. Hence, to reach out to them, command over local language is necessary. At the same time, in today's multicultural reality of Bombay, the knowledge of a link language, namely, English is useful.
3. Middle and advanced years are likely to be respected more. The young social workers feel uneasy with the way officials look at them. In their own words, They undress you from top to bottom'.
4. Broken gramophone record technique
5. Communication skills- while dealing with the government we need to put forward the problem in a condensed and focused form giving full details of technical aspects and accurate information on the problem as a whole, in point form. If executive summary is added at the end of the application/ petition/ memorandum/ resolution, it helps the officials who are dealing with a number of issues at a time.

Ms. Neera Adarkar, an Architect, Majlis, Bombay

Women's Movement has been doing advocacy work about housing rights for women since 1980. In the beginning, I saw myself as an architect. But after being a practicing architect, who was dealing with building construction activities for a number of years, I have started critiquing my profession. Housing and other environments with which we worked have to follow certain norms as they affect our lives on a daily basis. We take our built environment (house-community-city) for granted. We think that this environment exists, but actually it is built by men. We have to ask ourselves questions such as, 'Do we as women, use space differently?' 'Can we create environments which are more gender sensitive?' 'Can we make policy makers and planners who are working at the state level understand the politics of built environment and gender rules?' 'What are our alternatives to the existing approach adopted by Sight and Service Schemes and Slum Rehabilitation Schemes?' 'What interventions can we make in the city planning which involves physical access, economic access and social access?'

There are three approaches adopted by people-oriented architects to handle the issue of shelter.

1. *Legal approach:* It deals with ownership rights and tenure, right to matrimonial property of married women, right to ancestral home for an unmarried daughter. Hema Dandekar's study of Charcop's Sight and Service Scheme reveals that in this scheme there is no bar against women owning a house. Loan facilities given for buying a flat depend upon the repaying capacity of women.
2. *Social Approach:* House as a unit is related to family structure. It gets reflected in a housing policy. Women and Shelter Group had done advocacy work in these regards. After 1993, some of us made interventions in changing the scenario. We took responsibility to reconstruct the destroyed homes in the riot-affected areas near Mahim utilising Times of India funds. For this we had to run from pillar to post. We had to face an extremely communal attitude of the entire bureaucracy. After three-four months, we managed to get a plot of land/*pattas* in Dindoshi. We had to meet the collector a couple of times to see to it that the *pattas* given to riot-affected people are in the name of women because women use these *pattas* for subsistence while men use them as commodity in the market.
3. *Physical planning of a house:* Patriarchal values get reflected in the physical planning of a house. Rules and regulations, by-laws have been stipulated by the Urban Development Department. In BDD chawls, all spaces allocated for community have been used by men where women feel constrained. In slum projects and sight and service projects, kitchen and toilets are clubbed together 'Kitchen and toilet' are treated as isolated spaces while women beneficiaries of slum development projects don't like it. Architects from MHADA don't listen to the women's point

of view. Ventilation is not considered to be all that important. A small study of slums and chawls in Bombay showed that women emphasized a separate space in the community that is exclusively used for washing clothes and making *chapatis* (Collective kitchen). *Nagari Nivara* Trust headed by Mrunal Gore and Baburao Sawant is dealing with a mass housing project for five thousand people. In this, we have made a provision for a space in the community, which is exclusively used, for women's activities. Even, the ownership titles are made in the name of women. There is a need for a shelter home for women in distress and a *creche* within each plot. SPARC, Bombay has managed to get *balwadi* and community hall included in their project areas. As per the FSI regulation, while zoning and city planning, 'public' is separated from 'private' but in actual reality women's lives are not compartmentalised like this. We need to critique the existing housing policies, demystify technical language and conduct surveys to understand how women's lives are affected by the urban development. To bring changes in the by-laws which are gender sensitive and people friendly, the lawyers and architect will have to work in collaboration. We need to raise consciousness among the students of architecture, more than fifty percent of who are women. When I ask the students of architecture the question regarding home –based professions, they identify women home-based professionals as providers of *crèche* facilities, dance-teachers or beauticians, while male home-based professionals are identified as engineers, doctors, chartered accountants and management consultants. Many women architects are going to be home-based professionals and they have to redesign the existing patterns of houses, keeping in mind both house-work and professional duties. The same applies to their women clients who are shouldering double burden. Advantages of keeping kitchen-space near drawing/ living room are many:

a. Women don't feel isolated from rest of the happenings in the outside world.

b. All members of the family start taking interest in kitchen cabinet. They get encouraged to share housework.

c. It ensures cleanliness of the kitchen area, as it is visible.

Ms. Sara Samuel, Executive Committee member, YWCA, Bombay

YWCA has been active in India since 1875. It is a national and an international establishment. Its global agenda emerges from local initiatives. We are active in 80 countries. We have 61 local organisations in India. Our national headquarter is in Delhi. World YWCA's headquarter is in Geneva, Switzerland. It believes in a democratic process and is a membership organisation. It has a special concern for young working women. It took part in the nationalist movement. In the post-independence period, YWCA built 61 hostels for working women and students in different parts of India. 1975 onwards, YWCA has been actively involved in collaborative ventures with several women's rights organisations. In Bombay, YWCA consolidated its ties with the women activists after taking part in a campaign for 24-hour women's compartment in the local suburban trains in 1982, for gender-just family laws and relief work for riot victims in Bhiwandi in 1984.

YWCA's international assignments are decided in the world council meeting, once in 4 years. This meeting reviews/evaluates it's past and elects the members of the executive council to carry out the work of world YWCA. At present, the priority area of the world YWCA is domestic violence. It is networking with other organisations.

Patriarchal setup has so marginalised women that they have become non-entity. Women's work is not recognised. Male-oriented planners and policy makers in the planning commission and other global and national organisations are oblivious of women's reality. Hence, we need to get into decision making processes. We need to push ourselves into those positions of power, which can enable us to improve women's condition. For this, we need to make ourselves aware of the contemporary reality through seminars and workshops. Only when we gain full-proof knowledge, we can be effective in our work. YWCA's work on nuclear and peace initiatives in Palestine and Namibia has been recognised by the UN.

Ms. Ulka Mahajan, Trainer, Samarthan, Bombay

Samarthan is an advocacy group of *Vidhayak Sansad*, which is directly working with the grass root organisations that send their issues to us. We take up only those issues, which have policy implications. We identify right persons at right level to get quick response. We work with government institute for policy-making, with the legislature and in *Vidhan Bhavan*. We frame questions after getting the first hand information on the subject. We brief individual MLA's. We go through performance budgets of all the departments. To understand technical subjects, we invite experts to conduct the study classes. We organise meetings of the grass-root workers with PA's of legislature. We need to have proper understanding of all democratic systems. We must acquire the expertise of strategic planning. Activists of the NGOs must be able to identify star question and calling attention motion. For training them in this direction, we take them to *Vidhan Sabha* to attend the session.

These case studies bring out 4 different perspectives on decision-making processes by professional social worker who works among the socially disadvantaged groups, an architect faced with conceptual and operational biases in her profession, head of pioneering women's institutions executing welfare schemes, a representative of non-government organisation working closely with the government structures .

Conclusion

At present, most of the women's organisations are demanding 33 per cent reservation of seats in the electoral bodies. But if they don't acquire sufficient skills and abilities to handle unfolding reality with efficiency and harmony, they will be the objects of jest. Without popular mandate if women are selected for the top positions, they will have to face non-cooperation from the administration and the law and order machinery. Women in the public life need a protective shield of popular support and tremendous good will so that they can execute a development agenda more meaningfully. If we don't want to be puppets in the hands of different power-blocks, we will have to empower ourselves with the first hand experience of the operational reality.

We should consolidate our experience gained during Training of the Trainers (TOT) workshops of different types of the decision-making bodies to evolve our day-to-day tactics and long term strategies (Devaki Jain, 2000). There is no short cut to field-work and efficient handing of the crisis situation. We also need to see ourselves as change-agents and not as beneficiaries of the welfare departments of the government structures and private foundations. Women in the public life need to create their own support-structures for safe night-halts, safe transport and clean toilets. Constant up-gradation of skills and knowledge base is a must for each and every woman decision-maker to survive in a public life for a long term. Ability to handle more than one portfolio is a key to success in this rapidly changing socio- economic and political environment. Women in public life must give up phobia for modern equipments for better communication such as computers (internet), cell phones and advanced technologies, which reduce human drudgery. Majority of Indian women are seeking protection of the benevolent patriarchs and only 11 per cent women (widows, separated, divorced, deserted and single) are actual/ nominal heads of the households. Hence it is unrealistic to seek women's liberation without active support of sympathetic men. The 21st century is going to unfold an era of partnership between men and women dedicated to the cause of liberation of humankind which will ensure social justice, safe environment, communal harmony and world peace in an era of terrorism in the name of religion that has upset the power relations in the world.

References

Devaki Jain (2000), *The Vocabulary of Women's Politics*, Fredrich Ebert Stiftung, Delhi .

Indian Association for Women's Studies, "Indian Women in Political Process", Special issue, Women's Studies Centre, Dr. Babasaheb Ambedkar Bhavan, University of Pune, January, 2002.

Institute of Social Studies Trust (2001), Uma Prachar, A Resource Letter on Panchayat Raj, Vol.8, No.4, December.

Raunaq Jahan (1987), "Women in South Asian Politics", **Mainstream, Delhi,** August 15, pp.35-44.

Review of Women's Studies (2000), "Reservations and Women's Movement", Economic and Political Weekly, Bombay, Vol. XXXV, Numbers 43-44, pp.ws 22-ws 60. See article by Mary John, p. 3828.

Subhashini Mahapatra (2001), *Women and Politics*, Rajat Publications, Delhi.

Vibhuti Patel (1987), "Adivasi Women on the Warpath" ', Miranda Davies (ed) *Third World- Second Sex*, Zed Press.

Vibhuti Patel (1988), "Emergence and Proliferation of Autonomous Women's Groups in India: 1974-1984" in Rehana Ghadiali (ed) *Women and Society in India*, Sage Publications.

Vibhuti Patel (1988), "Emergence and Proliferation of Autonomous Women's Groups (1974-1984) in Neera Desai (ed) *A Decade of Women's Movement in India*, Himalaya Publishing House.

Vibhuti Patel (1991), "Women's Action Groups and the State Machinery", in Maithreyi Krishnaraj (ed) Women and Violence, Research Centre for Women's Studies, SNDT Women's University, Bombay.

Vibhuti Patel (1993), "Ideological Debates Among Autonomous Women's Groups in India" in Susheela Kaushik (ed) *Women's Participation in Politics*, Indian Association for Women's Studies, Vikas Publishing House.

Vibhuti Patel (1994), "Women's Movement in India and Anti-rape Campaign", in J.P. Singh(ed) *The Indian Women-Myth and Reality*, Gyan Publishing House, Delhi.

Footnote

1. Armaity S. Desai " Challenges for the Voluntary Sector in India at the Beginning of the Twenty-first Century", Perspectives in Social Work, Vol. XVI, No. 3, Sept.-Dec., 2001, p. 11.

Fifteen

Evolution of Women's Studies in India

TOWARDS EQUALITY Report prepared by the Committee on Status of Women in India appointed by Government of India and published in 1974 acted as a catalyst for foundation and promotion of women's studies in India. This report was debated in the parliament and served as a focal point around which most of the programmes to celebrate the International Women's year (declared by the UN) were organised. Three shocking aspects of Indian Women's reality:

(a) declining sex ratio, high mortality and morbidity rates among Indian women;
(b) extremely low level of female literacy;
(c) marginalisation of women from the Indian economy made our policy-makers alarmed.

Major policy level decisions on women's studies were taken in 1975 because the Government of India had signed the UN charter of EQUALITY, DEVELOPMENT and PEACE on the eve of International Women's year (IWY). As IWY coincided with an emergency rule in India, most of the women activists involved in the militant mass movements of the early seventies were silenced with the help of state repression. In the post-emergency period, several of them became pioneers of the women's rights groups in India.[1] Their dialogue and collaborative ventures with women's studies academicians, mainstream research organisations, government departments and pioneer women's organisations like AIWC, YWCA, NFIW and women's wings of different political parties enriched women's studies as a discipline. Declaration of International Women's Decade (1975- 1985) created a conducive atmosphere for women's studies researches by establishment of women's studies unit in the universities, autonomous women's studies centers and the provision of massive research grants by the international aid organisations to women's studies scholars and women's rights activists.

Landmark Contribution of Towards Equality Report

The most important features of Towards Equality report were its analytical vision, its authentic database and all India coverage. The report-examined women's material reality from inter-disciplinary perspective. It helped Indian decision-makers to come out of their complacency regarding "high social status accorded to Indian women by goddess worshipping Indian culture". In the post-independence period, visibility of highly educated upper and middle class women in the educational institutions and elite organisations had blurred the vision of Indian Policy makers regarding acute survival struggle of mass of Indian women in the poverty groups. Comprehensive picture of socio-economic-legal-educational-cultural life of women given by the report were followed by concrete suggestions/ recommendations and guidelines for the government. Official meetings, seminars, conferences to debate different chapters of this report set the agenda for experts in different fields. The report was translated into several Indian languages and widely circulated in all those states where pioneer women's organisations and women's wings of political parties were active. As the middle class, educated women were actively involved in this effort, the newspapers and magazines gave massive coverage to this report. University Grants Commission established the first Research Unit on Women's Studies (RCWS)[2] and Tata Institute of Social Science (TISS) established its women's unit in 1974.[3] RCWS concentrated its efforts in commissioning primary research and TISS women's unit focused on teaching and training. National Council for Education, Research and Training (NCERT) started special cell to focus on women's education and to eliminate sexist biases in the existing syllabi.

Indian Council of Social Science Research Directive (1975)

Landmark decision of ICSSR in 1975 in terms of prioritising researches on women in poverty groups[4] helped committed social scientists to closely examine crucial problems faced by working class women in the urban, rural, tribal areas in the changing socio-economic and cultural contexts in different parts of India. Workload of cashew and coir workers in Kerala,[5] plight of paddy workers of Kerala,[6] implication of land-reforms on land-rights of women,[7] Worsening survival struggle of women due to shortage of fuel-wood, fodder and water[8], interplay of caste, class and gender among sweeper/scavenger women,[9] condition of dalit tobacco worker women and temple prostitution[10] relationship of purdah with female literacy[11] made many social scientists give up their approach of maintaining 'academic distance' and 'value neutrality' in social science researches. Stark reality of discrimination against girl-child in terms of nurturance, educational opportunities, health-care, child-marriage, segregation of women, condition of dalit tobacco worker women and temple-prostitution, repeated pregnancies-miscarriages/child-births, ill-health of women, domestic and societal violence faced by women forced women's studies scholars to declare WS as a partisan discipline wedded to the cause of women's rights/gender justice and empowerment of women. Use of term 'feminism' implied assertion of women's rights. 'Patriarchy' as an analytical category was gaining increasing popularity in WS researches to signify 'control over women's sexuality, fertility and labour'. 'Culture'-mainstream Brahminical and popular/folk culture representing women's spiritual, material and survival needs became important areas of scrutiny as they played extremely crucial role in determining 'autonomy' versus 'control' in women's lives.[12]

Researches With Interdisciplinary Perspective

Because of live contact of women's studies with the unfolding reality of women's struggles, theoretical framework and analytical tools used by WS did not fit into straight- jackets of any particular mainstream disciplines which are either gender-blind or gender-biased. During seventies, radical intellectuals had exposed elitist biases of the academic institutions.[13] Autonomous bodies specialising on dalit, tribal, peasant and labour studies were established.[14] Their booklets, pamphlets, leaflets, reports, manifestoes, declarations, creative writings enhanced confidence of women's studies scholars to make similar efforts to build women-specific knowledge system that would draw from the existing body of knowledge in the mainstream academia and would enrich its fossilised structure by fresh and realistic insights of women's studies researches.[15] Analytical categories such as, *segmentation in the labour- market, product market and factor market* to examine nature of marginalisation of women from the economy, *female headed households* to understand acuteness of survival struggles of single women, *visibility of women* in every area of human existence, deconstruction of patriarchy to understand power-relations between men and women in different socio-economic formations, use of terminologies like 'sex' to indicate biological difference between men and women and 'gender' to signify social relationships based on subordination of women and male domination. Rejection of approach which perceives women as 'beneficiaries', 'dependents', 'subordinate', 'just housewives' in the official discourses and examining women's performance in terms of human development index have been the outcome of interdisciplinary approach adopted by women's studies[16].

Discipline-wise Contribution in Women's Studies

(a) Sociology

Women's Studies scholars with intellectual investment of sociology have been pioneers in providing alternate analytical tools to overcome much touted 'structural functional analysis', 'role conflict' theory which individualise women's oppression by overlooking larger social reality and resort to victim-baiting by perpetuating the *status quo*. They examined processes of urbanisation, career development, women in household, kinship network in the context of interplay of class, caste, ethnicity, religion and gender. Their researches have provided guidance to the state and civil society for affirmative action for the development of women. During the seventies, sociologists in women's studies focused on 'marginalisation of women from the industrial and agrarian sectors' and suggested that integration of women in the labour market was possible by specially envisaged development programmes- employment generation activities, skill training and credit facilities. This suggestion suited the patriarchal class system as women could be involved in drudgery-prone, monotonous, highly labour intensive tasks for subsistence wages. We can call this path of women's development as "From starvation to subsistence". During the eighties women's studies scholars got extensive global exposure resulting into new confidence/gusto to shake the international financial bodies, the UN system, industry and trade so that women can get larger share of the cake and don't get wiped out in the name of structural adjustment programmes.

(b) Economics

Results of 1971 Census regarding sex-ratio, literacy, life expectancy, mortality, morbidity and work-force participation rate of women had made many economists sensitive about women's status in the Indian socio- economic set-up. In this context, when Indian Social Studies Trust (Delhi) took initiative in launching a special interest group to focus on special problems faced by women, it received enthusiastic response from both men and women economists. During First National Conference on Women's Studies in 1981, the group acquired a systematic shape in the form of Economist Interested in Women's Issues Group. Four workshops organised by EIWIG, 1. Technical Workshop on women and work, 1982, 2. Women and Poverty, 1983,[17] 3. Impact of Technological Changes on Women's Work and Wages, 1984, 4. Occupational Diversification of women in the Indian Economy, 1986- were extremely educative as they provided opportunities to economists to interact with grass-root activists, policy planners, international funding agencies, representatives of the UN system and social scientists from different disciplines. Those who were capable of only abstract thinking were forced to deal with the ground reality. Those who were used to remaining in the realm of ideas and intellectual jugglary had to reexamine veracity of their economic models, axiomatic formulations and Europocentric presumptions about dynamics of economic development. During the last two decades, women's studies scholars (both men and women) with background in economics have played crucial role in training decision- makers of the state apparatus, financial institutions, corporate bodies, labour institutes, development organisations and non-government organisations. "Economics" is the only discipline, which has managed to involve large number of men scholars for conducting primary researches and for analysis of existing data-system from women's perspective. [18]

(c) Education

Low literacy level of Indian women has been one of the major impediments in the way of women's empowerment. Illiteracy and semi-illiteracy keep women in perpetual state of assetlessness. Even for an effective implementation of innumerable development programmes sponsored by the government and non-government sector, the educated women in the work-force are a must. Conventional approach of imparting education through schools and colleges has declared its bankruptcy as it perpetuated class, caste, ethnicity and religion-based discrimination against the marginalised sections. Experiments in non-formal education are extremely useful in terms of their course-content/ syllabi as they capture genuine needs and aspirations of women. But their outreach is limited. Pathetic condition of million of women who are roped in for extremely demanding domestic chores as well as underpaid wage-work make it imperative to evolve multiple and flexible approaches in imparting women-specific education. Vedic/ Islamic/Judao-Christian scholastic traditions of chanting and rot-learning, memorising, choice of simplified and uniform written scripts, radio script, radio-programmes, multi-media channels, on the job training have to be tried simultaneously instead of pitting one against the other as women from different occupations and cultural backgrounds have different types of skills, aptitudes and abilities. Women's studies programmes which are action-oriented have tried multiple methods in their training programmes[19]. In the national gatherings of Indian Association of Women's Studies (IAWS) women participants from different parts of India pick up different dialects, folk-songs, stories and new phraseologies within 4-5 days as the atmosphere in this gathering is non-threatening and democratic space is provided for special interest groups. Moreover, distribution of audio and video cassettes of women's studies issues at cost-price have heiped a great deal in inculcating leadership qualities among mass of women spread across the country.[20]

(d) Literature

Women's Studies has been influential mainly in the English literature departments of some prestigious universities, though individual women scholars have made landmark contributions in Malayalam, Kannada, Hindi, Gujarati, Assamese and Marathi literature departments.[21]

Feminist literary criticism has gained respectability in the eyes of younger generation of academicians, film-makers, painters, singer, dancers, poets, writers and communication media persons. It has provided intellectual tools and developed sensitivity of new generation of creative artists to critically examine 'male gaze' which objectifies women and resorts to victim-baiting.[22] At the same time, it has developed sensibility to focus on women's agency in the midst of extreme form of depravity and dehumanisation. Influence of post-modernism in women's studies literature departments has questioned hegemonic presence of male-dominated discourses which dichotomise women as 'corrupting influence' or 'objects of pity'. By creating their own/autonomous space, WS in literature has legitimised experiences of both 'extra-ordinary' and 'ordinary' women.[23] They have brought to the fore women's agency by focusing on the knowledge of the subjugated sections of society and by tapping totally ignored areas such as women's diaries, devotional songs, work-related folk-songs, folk-paintings, embroidery work, quilts, drawings, personal diaries and photographs. Because of their multicultural background, they have been able to reach out to different parts of India.

(e) History

Initially, the major concern of WS scholars in history was to incorporate HER-STORY in history. Invisibility of 'women as subjects' and occasional mention of individual women as scheming, manipulating consorts/concubines/rulers were criticized vehemently in WS historical writings. Contribution of women in home-based life and in the public arena were and are delineated by them through alternate sources such as generational analysis, oral history records, folk-songs, scriptural analysis, examination of art-forms, music, traditional dances, folk-lores, analysis of village-goddesses, local deities and historically renowned women.

Among religious reformers, Meerabai has fascinated several WS scholars.[24] Discourses of social reform movements of the 19th century,[25] nationalist movements,[26] peasant and tribal struggles[27], industrial working class struggles[28], political participation of Women[29], have been extremely useful to understand patriarchal anxiety and women's resilience in the midst of crisis situation. WS researches have also shown that, in the absence of collective strength and independent politics of women, women become pawns in power politics controlled by men. This can happen in both, electoral politics [30] and politics of social movements[31]. Analysis of Nationalist movement has revolved around the role of All India Women's Council's work among the upper caste Hindu women, Anjuman Trusts work among Muslim women and contribution of charismatic personalities like Pandita Ramabai, Madam Cama, Cornelia Sorabjee and Mahatma Gandhi. Contribution of women workers in the economy has been highlighted with special focus on women in jute industry of Calcutta[32], women textile workers in Bombay[33], retrenchment of women in the Ahmedabad Textile industry[34], women cotton textile workers in Calcutta[35]. Historical narratives of female infanticide, sati, age of consent debate, women's education have been constructed by analysis of demographic data, discourses of male social reformers with the colonial administration and the responses of the patriarchs of the caste organisations and religious leaders[36].

(f) Demography and Health

WS scholars with technical expertise in demography have used their knowledge-base of parent discipline in demystifying official population policy and exposed its class, racist and gender biases.[37] Social, economic and cultural implications of family planning policies - use of coercion in mass sterilisation programmes, targeting poor women for compulsory IUD insertion, unsafe contraceptives and anti-pregnancy vaccines have been exposed by feminist health activists.[38] Support to ante-natal sex-determination tests resulting into abortion of female fetuses in the name of population stabilisation (by achieving Net Reproduction Rate of 1) had been criticized vehemently.[39] Health Researchers specialising on public health issues have exposed anti-women biases in the existing health care system.[40] Their studies on menstruation, abortion, backache, reproductive tract infections, low nutritional status of women, energy expenditure of Indian women, maternal mortality patterns, morbidity among Indian girls and women, occupational health problems faced by women, ill health of women due to absence of safe drinking water and inadequate sanitary facilities, miscarriages and repeated pregnancies among child-brides and young women[41] have enriched the understanding of the policy planners, health practitioners and women's groups working with mass of women. Research material generated by feminist doctors is now incorporated into training programmes of college and school teachers, health workers and ICDS staff.[42] Problems faced by women health workers have been examined by medical anthropologists.[43] There is only one study on 'women and sports' with WS perspective.[44]

(g) Social Work

TISS and Nirmala Niketan are the only two social work institutions in India which have made contributions in women's studies. They have conducted researches on their lives and survival struggles of 'socially wronged sections of society such as 'illegal' slum-dwellers, domestic workers, commercial sex-workers, aids-patients, displaced population due to Narmada dam, drought, earthquake in Latur. Audio-visual unit of TISS has prepared documentary films on survival struggles of tribal, peasant and working class women. Both of them organise training programmes on development and human rights issues faced by women while dealing with the criminal justice system, legal apparatus, women and shelter, cases of communal and caste violence, violence in matrimonial life. They have introduced WS in their syllabi.

(h) Anthropology

WS scholars have challenged androcentric world-view in anthropological writings. They have also questioned racist and class biases of mainstream anthropologists who stereotype tribal, peasant, oriental, ethnic, native women to serve the interest of the dominant sections of society. Glorification of *status quo* in the name of culture has been questioned by women's studies anthropologists. Their contributions on women's work in subsistence economy, practices of child marriage, polygamy and polyandry, different forms of control exercised over women's sexuality, fertility have helped the policy-makers to identify methods of social change through public education. Debate on ante-natal sex-determination tests got academic legitimacy because of timely intervention of WS anthropologists who took stand on this issue.[45]

(i) Home Science

This discipline is undergoing major changes due to global level interactions and active collaborations of scholars in home science and WS with the UN system. Women professionals in home science have come out with field-based insights on child development, food and nutrition, food processing and food-preservation, deviant behaviour of neglected children, communalism, domestic violence, etc. Practical orientation of its course content makes its faculty members more efficient in bringing about realistic changes in the lives of women with the help of networking with the state apparatus, industry and community. Women's Studies Research Centre of Faculty of Home Science, M.S. university, Baroda and Faculty of Home Science, SNDT Women's University conduct researches, maintain close contacts with women's groups, organise training programmes and provide consultancy services to the corporate world on women's issues.

(j) Law

Law teachers of Delhi University took initiative in WS by providing feminist perspective on criminal justice system by taking up specific incidents of custodial rape[46], dowry, sati and discrimination in the family laws.[47] WS had benefited from the material generated by legal activists in Delhi, Bombay, Pune, Bangalore and Madras.[48] Practical guidance about the legal system is provided in *Journey to Justice series* by Majlis[49]. Shah Bano controversy motivated several scholars to examine Muslim personal law with fresh insights.[50] WS has provided thread-bare examination of gender-biases in the existing legal system and suggested concrete provisions for legal reform based on gender justice. For the labour laws affecting mass of working women, the only reference material is provided by Sramshakti Report [51] and National Perspective Plan for Women, 1988- 2000 AD[52]

Grey Areas in WS Teaching and Research:

Seasoned scholars in WS have started focusing their attention on gender studies (GS) so that they can be effective in their educational work in the class-rooms and extension educational work in the communities. WS and GS have to gear their research endeavour to train their cadre for policy planning and effective execution of development agenda in today's multicultural context. Gender-blindness of most of the decision-making institutions and professional bodies demands intervention of WS scholars. Converting WS researches into textbooks and training material is an uphill task. Introduction of WS as a compulsory or optional subject in the university system without adequate teaching material has caused lot of inconvenience to teachers and students.

Structural Adjustment Programme is a *fate accompli* and we have to prepare our educational institutions to face global competition and international collaborations. India has a highest number of highly disciplined, educated and professionally competent pool of women. WS scholars must stop approaching decision-makers with begging bowls as we have enough experience of loopholes in the 'safety-net'. By involving economically and professionally powerful women and men in WS, we can generate multiple sources for women's development rather than involving women in low productivity economic activities or killing ourselves by individual counseling. WS scholars need to interact with industrial, financial, political and religious bodies to bend the existing power structure in favour of distributive justice, secularism and human rights.

Humanisation of the Labour Processes through technological interventions: From the beginning, WS movement has been global. In the last 25 years, WS scholars have become powerful in global decision-making bodies. If they get united they can bend the existing power-structure by changing the agenda of R & D. WS researches should be geared in the direction of humanisation of labour processes, environment friendly lifestyles.

WS activities must ensure empowerment of women from all sections of society, plural belief system, multicultural lifestyles and egalitarian and non-exploitative rural-urban exchange.

Concluding Remarks

Knowledge- base created by WS needs to be disseminated in a decentralised manner. Most of the publications in WS are in English. ICSSR, UGC and funding organizations should allocate funds for translations, textbook preparation and teaching aids. As the existing staff of the WS centers has enjoyed protection for more than 20 years, they need to face intellectual challenges from the mainstream academia, professional bodies and policy makers.

References

Eleanor B. Amico(1998), *Readers' Guide to Women's Studies*, Fitzroy Dearborn Publications, Chicago and London.

Ellen B. Kimnel and Mary Crawford (2001), "Method for Studying Gender" in *Encyclopedia of Women and Gender*, Academic Press, London.

Kanwar Sonali Jolly- Wadhawa (2000), *Gender- A Cross Cultural Perspective*, Gyan Publishing House, New Delhi.

Footnotes

1. Neera Desai (ED): *A Decade of Women's Movement in India*, Himalaya Publishing House, Bombay, 1988.
2. Maithreyi Krishnaraj: *Women's Studies in India*, Himalaya Publishing House, Bombay, 1988.
3. Suma Chitnis: *Review of Status of Women in India* (Mimeo), Tata Institute of Social Sciences, Bombay, 1974.
4. Neera Desai and Vibhuti Patel: *Critical Evaluation of Women's Studies Researches in India, 1974-1988*, Indian Council of Social Science Research, Delhi, 1990.
5. Molly Mathew: a. *Women in Coir Industry in Kerala*, b. *Women in Cashew Industry in Kerala* Centre for Regional Development Studies, Kottayam, Kerala, 1984.
6. Joan Mencher and Sardamony: *Muddy Feet, Dirty Hands*, ICSSR, 1982.
7. Sardamoni: *Land Reforms in Kerala*, ICSSR, 1983.
8. Bina Aggarwal: *Cold Hearth and Barren Land*, Kali for Women, 1988.
9. Malvika Karlekar: *Sweeper Women of Balmiki Community*, ICSSR, 1985.
10. a. C. S. Laxmi: *Women Workers in Nipani*, Women's Diary, Reaching Out, Bombay, 1982.

    b. Prabha Mahale: *Tobacco Workers of Nipani*, Research Centre for Women's Studies, Dharwad University, Dharwad, 1987.

c. Chhaya Datar: *Women in Belgaon Beedi Workers Union*, Kali for Women, 1990.

11. Kalpana Shah: *Women's Liberation and Voluntary Action*, Ajanta Publications, Delhi, 1984.
12. a. Veena Mazumdar: *Symbols of Power*, Allied Publications, New Delhi, 1979. b. Rehana Ghadiali : *Women in Indian Society- A Reader*, Sage Publications, Delhi, 1988.
13. Series of articles in *Economic and Political Weekly* and *Frontier* during 1969 and 1985.
14. a. Centre for Regional Development Studies, Kottayam. b. CROSS, Bangalore. c. Indian Social Institute, Delhi and Bangalore d. Indian School of Political Economy, Social Scientist, Trivandrum. e. Centre for Social Studies, Surat. f. A. N. Sinha Institute, Patna. h. Dalit Sahitya Academy, Bangalore. i. Indian Social Action, Bangalore, Centre for Informal Education and Development Studies, Bangalore.
15. Publications of Centre for Women's Development Studies are guided by this ethos. As a result, their researches have direct relevance for Government and Global Policies.
16. Development Alternatives With Women (DAWN) has been able to mobilize public opinion in favour of women's development agenda by efficient social marketing on this line.
17. Some papers of the first and second workshops are published in a book edited by Devaki Jain and Nirmala Banerjee: *Tyranny of Household* ,Vikas Pub. House, Delhi, 1985.
18. Prof. Asok Mitra, Prof. Amartya Sen, Prof. Parthsarathy, Prof. Sarathy Acharya, Prof. B. B. Patel, Prof. Pravin Visaria, Prof. Vaidyanathan, Prof. Amitabh Kundu, Prof. Mahendra Premi, Prof. Ashish Bose have played crucial role in creating favourable climate for women's cause at a policy level.
19. Foundation Course, 'Women in Changing India' introduced by SNDT Women's University at an undergraduate level is designed in this manner. It has proved to be successful both for class-room teaching and field-workers, Balwadi teacher, auxiliary nurses and mid-wives. YWCA is also using the textbooks of the Foundation course in Marathi, Gujarati, Hindi and English for its women's studies programme for women trainees of Vocational Training Institute. College of Social Work , Nirmala Niketan use this method with their own course content on area-based development issues for training elected members of the local self-government bodies-members of gram-panchayats, Zilla Panchayats and corporators. Stree-vani in Pune and SEVA in Ahmedabad use A-V materials for training of illiterate and semi-literate activists in development programmes of poor women.
20. A-V material produced by CENDIT and Jagori (Delhi); Stree Mukti Sangathana, Avehi and A-V unit of TISS in Bombay are used by different state government bodies, academic institutions and NGOs.
21. Writings of Sarah Joseph in Malayalam, 18 issues of *Narimukti* in Gujarati published by Sahiar-Baroda, publications in Kannada supported by

streelekha, volume released on March 8 by *Stree Uvach* in Marathi contain creative writings, translations from other languages and literary criticism by women literateurs. Sahitya Academy has promoted WS in literature by bringing out special numbers (on women and by women writers) of its periodical, *Indian Literature*.

22. C.S. Laxmi: *The Face Behind the Mask* (Women in Tamil Literature), Vikas Publications, New Delhi, 1984.
    Economic and Political Weekly has published dozens of articles on this line during last one decade in its special numbers on Review of Women's Studies. Recently *Social Scientist* has also started publishing articles on feminist literary criticism.
23. a. Suzie Tharu and K. Lalitha (Ed): *Women's Writings in India-From 600 BC to the Present*, Oxford University Publications, 1990. b. Viney Kripal (ed.): *The Girl Child in 20th Century Indian Literature*, Sterling Pub. Pvt. Ltd., 1992. c. Veena Poonacha (ed.): Short Stories on GIRL CHILD, Research Centre for Women's Studies, Bombay, 1993.
24. Parita Mukta: *Saint Poetess- Mirabai*, OUP, 1993.
25. Review of Women's Studies, EPW, Bombay, October 26, 1985/April 26, 1985/ December 19,1987/ April 30,1988/ October 29,1988.
26. Gail Minault : *The Extended Family- Women and Political Participation in India and Pakistan*, Chanakya Publication, Delhi, 1981.
27. a. Gail Omvedt : *We will Smash This Prison*, Orient Longman, Delhi, 1979. b. Stree Shakti Sangathana: *We Were Making History- Women in Telangana Uprising*, Kali for women, Delhi, 1990.
28. Sujata Gothoskar (Ed).: *Struggles of Women at Work*, Vikas Pub. House, 1992.
29. Susheela Kaushik (Ed) *Women's Participation in Politics*, Indian Association of Women's Studies, Vikas Publishing House, 1993.
30. Hazel D'lima: *Women in Local Government-A Study of Maharashtra*, Concept Publications, New Delhi, 1983.
31. Ilina Sen (Ed): *Space Within Struggle*, Kali For Women, Delhi, 1990.
32. Samita Sen: Women Workers in the Jute Textile Industry, Cambridge University, 1993.
33. Meera Savara : *Changing Trends in Women's Employment*, Himalaya Publishing House, Bombay, 1985.
34. Renana Jhabwala, *Closing Doors*, SETU, Ahmedabad, 1985.
35. Nirmal Banerjee : *Women in the Unorganised Sector, The Calcutta Experience*, Orient Longman, Hyderabad, 1984.
36. Review of Women's Studies, Economic and Political Weekly, Bombay, 1985-1995.
37. Malini Karkal and Divya Pandey: *Studies on Women and Population: A Critique*, Himalaya Publishing House, Bombay, 1989.
38. C. Satyamala, Nirmala Sundram and Nalini Bhanot: *Taking Sides- Choices Before Health Workers*, ANITRA, Madras, 1986.
39. Ravindra R.P.: *Scarcer Half*, Centre for Education and Documentation, Bombay, 1986.
40. Special No. on Women and Health, Socialist Health Review, Bombay, 1984.

Several articles in Radical Journal of Health and Medico Friends Circle Bulletin.

41. Manisha Gupte and Anita Borkar : Women's Work, Fertility and Access to Health Care- A Socio-economic Study of Two Villages in Pune District, The Foundation for Research in Community Health, Bombay, October, 1987.
42. Dr. Mira Shiva, Dr. Rani Bang, Dr. Veena Shatrugna and Dr. Mira Sadgopal have made pioneering contribution by demystifying medical knowledge concerning reproductive rights of women.
43. Aditi Iyer and Amar Jesani: *Women in Health Care: Auxiliary Nurse Midwives*, Foundation for Research in Community Health, Bombay, 1996.
44. Padma Prakash: Women and Sports, Research Centre for Women's Studies, Bombay, 1987.
45. Seminar: Special number on Femicide, No. 331, March 1987. Sex-determination and Female Foeticide, Voluntary Health Association of India, 1999.
46. Open letter to the Supreme Court of India regarding its judgment on gang-rape of a tribal girl, Mathura by two policemen and in the police station by four law teachers Latika Sarkar, Upendra Baxi, Kelkar and Vasudha Dhagamwar in 1980. This letter became a catalyst for a nation-wide anti-rape agitation in India.
47. Satya Ranjan Sathe: *Gender Justice*, Research Centre for Women's Studies, SNDT Women's University, Bombay, 1993.
48. Publications of Lawyers Collective and Majlis, Bombay; Indian Law Institute, Bangalore; Legal Perspective, Madras and a pictorial publication of Nandita Haksar: *Demystification of Laws for Women in India*, Inter India Publication, New Delhi, 1986 and writings and resolutions on controversy about family laws edited by A.R. Desai: *Women's Liberation and Politics of Religious Personal Laws*, C. G. Shah Memorial Trust Publication, 1990 are found useful for training programmes and class-room teaching.
49. Flavia Agnes has dealt with issues like rape, family courts and maintenance rights in this series.
50. Asghar Ali Engineer: *The Shah Bano Controversy*, Orient Longman, Hyderabad, 1987.
51. prepared by National Commission on Self Employed women and Women in the Unorganised Sector, Government of India, 1988.
52. Government of India, Delhi, 1988.

Sixteen

The Dynamics of Women's Studies and the Women's Movement in India

Introduction

When analysing the origin, development and direction of women's studies (WS) in India; it is important to understand its relationship with the Indian women's movement (WM). The dialectical relationship between 'pedagogy' and 'praxis', vis-à-vis the 'women's question', has been a matter of great concern for pioneers of Women's Studies (WS). The need to study women's issues in academic institutions and to conduct research based on experiential material and affirmative action was beginning to be discussed among Indian women's studies scholars by the early eighties.[1] The discourse on this subject has proved to be a fruitful exercise for activists, academics, researchers, policy planners and the UN system. This paper tries to examine the following issues: the genesis of interaction between WS and the WM in India; the contribution of WS to mainstream academia-economics, political science, sociology, literature, history, education, psychology; the analytical tools and the theoretical insights provided by WS and the WM in India; the research methodology and agenda of the WS, ongoing debates on the scope and limitations of WS within institutionalised structures, the shift of focus from WS to gender studies; the economics and politics of funding, consultancy and priorities in research.

Pioneers of WS in India defined it as a discipline that involved research, documentation, teaching, training and action. It is understood that women have subordinate status in our society so the knowledge-base created by WS should be used for empowerment of women and there is a need to examine to what extent WS in India have served this purpose.

Genesis of WS in India

Unlike its western counterpart, WS in India evolved as a result of state patronage after the declaration of the United Nations International Women's Year (UN-IWY) in 1975.

In the pre-independence period, academics were concerned with the status of women in the higher castes and classes. The reasons for widow-burning, child-marriage, purdah and illiteracy among women found extensive reference in their works. In the post -independence period, two distinct periods can be discerned: that up to 1974 and the years thereafter. Before 1974, the focus of scholars interested in women's question was on the role-conflict of middle class women. Very few studies situated the problems of Indian women in the context of the macro forces of the developmental process. The only exceptions were the scholarly works of Neera Desai (1954) and D.R. Gadgil (1965).

Towards Equality (1974) was prepared by the scholars with an interdisciplinary perspective and was presented in Parliament, where it received a tremendous response from the decision-making bodies, the state apparatus and the print media. Principal research bodies, like the Indian Council of Social Science Research (ICSSR), provided financial support to scholars committed to the women's cause, to conduct research into problems faced by women in poverty.

The Genesis of Women's Movement in India

The birth of the women's liberation movement in India was a result of the radicalisation of Indian politics in the late 1960s and the early 1970s. In the late 1960s there was an upsurge internationally of the black movement, the women's movement, the anti-war movement and the working class movement. These were independent, self-determining and democratic movements, which questioned all hierarchical structures. In India, young people of that period had not participated in the dreams of the nationalist movement. Faced with multiple crises: - economic, social and political, together with corruption, drought, inflation, unemployment, pauperisation of the rural poor - the disenchanted youth responded with protest. Widespread, open discontent, was expressed in action and consolidation of the action developed into powerful organisations throughout the country. These movements raised a number of diverse issues-land-rights, wages, employment security, water availability, destruction of nature, oppression and exploitation of the Dalits (the untouchables) and the working masses. Many women participated in these struggles with enthusiasm, responsibility and creativity.[2]

The UN Declaration of 1975 as an International Women's Year coincided with the Emergency Rule in India. By the time the Emergency was lifted in 1977, several women's groups had developed around democratic rights issues. The press swung into "action" after the imposed silence of nearly two years. Atrocities committed against women during the Emergency were openly documented and reported in the press. These atrocities struck a chord in most women's own experience of life in the family, in the streets, in the workplace and in political groups. The culmination of this process was reached in 1980 when many women's groups took to the street to protest. During the 1980s the issue of women's oppression was depicted not only in discussion forums, seminars and `serious' articles but also in the popular media. Women who had on their own identified the sources of their problems and indignity, began to acquire a language, an organisational platform, a collective identity and a legitimacy they did not have earlier.

Dialogue Between WS and WM

It was in the early 1980s that women's studies' centres, functioning autonomously or within the university system, started accepting empirical and experimental evidence from the women's movement. It was a time when participatory research, action research and subaltern studies were gaining ground in the field of social sciences. This process indirectly facilitated the interaction of WS and the WM.

In the first National Conference of Women's Studies in 1981, a wide variety of issues were discussed by activists, researchers, academicians and policy makers. These included the developmental process which bypassed women, the gender bias in textbooks, sexism in the media, gender blindness in science and technology, health needs of women and violence against them (rape, domestic violence and prostitution. The general consensus among the participants (both women and men) was that WS was pro-women and not neutral. It was seen that WS would build a knowledge base for empowering women by pressing for change at policy level and in curriculum development, by criticising gender-blindness as well as gender-bias within mainstream academia, by creating alternative analytical tools and visions and by advocacy for women's developmental needs in the economy and in society. This Conference established a new trend by which, gradually, women activists were invited, as resource persons and participants, to academic seminars, consultations and training workshops.

Activist Researchers

During the 1980s, an increasing number of women's rights activists became involved in WS either as independent researchers, consultants, trainers and resource-persons for seminars and workshops - or as guest faculty members in higher education institutions which specialised in mass communication or government training. At places such as Anveshi in Hyderabad and Alochana in Pune, women activists collectively formed WS groups. Anveshi made a major contribution through its collective research projects, "We Were Making History" (1998). It was based on interviews with women whose contributions in the peasant uprising in the late 1940s (which was crushed ruthlessly by the post-colonial state), up till that time had been invisible. Their second project, "Women's Writings in India" (1990), was based on women's creative writing in more than a dozen languages, mostly from India's diverse folk tradition, from 600 B.C. to the present.

The dual role in WS of theory and praxis, or academic exercise and action, has been articulated by the current president of Indian Association of Women's Studies (IAWS): "Women's studies provides contextualisation of knowledge in the process of both understanding and changing women's reality. As a movement it emphasizes the need for providing material basis for equality and independence of women." (Krishnaraj, 1986). This approach accepts the dual role of WS as a discourse and as a movement. There have been critics of this approach who think that if WS has to be part of the educational system, it should retain its dispassionate features of rigorous intellectual activity, and objectivity. But IAWS counters this argument and stresses that rigour can be retained even if WS takes an interventionist approach. It is this contact with the real situation, which provides insights, which, may not be obtained by sitting in a 'distant' university chair. Hence IAWS provides a platform to discuss the issues confronting contemporary reality.

Curriculum Development

In the last 15 years, the principal body of higher education, the University Grants Commission (UGC), has given primary attention to WS. SNDT Women's University in Bombay was the first to establish a WS unit, in 1974. Now it has a fully established Research Centre for Women's Studies (RCWS) and the UGC has accorded it the status of a Centre for Advanced Research in Women's Studies. The UGC has supported over 25 universities in different parts of the country in starting WS centres. The National Policy for Education, 1987 (NPE) also incorporated WS in its curriculum development. Mainstream disciplines now are introducing optional or compulsory papers. Gender Economics, Sociology of Women, Women and Development, Women and Literature, Women and Psychology, Women and Education, Women in History, Reproductive Rights of Women are being offered at Delhi University, Pune University, Calcutta University, Jadhavpur University and five women's universities. SNDT Women's University was the first to introduce a foundation course, "Women's Rights in Changing India", a compulsory paper for all undergraduate students in each discipline.[3]

The response of academics to WS in mainstream academia is mixed. Interest in studying women from a feminist perspective has been more of a concern to some individuals in the university system. The majority of sociologists continue with the structural functional theory and consensual model; economists continue with their neo-classical paradigm and psychologists continue with quantitative analyses that have misogynist implications. Even radical historiography/subaltern studies are not immune from stereotypical representation of women. (Desai and Patel, 1993).

The IAWS, which was established in 1981, has provided an arena for brainstorming and discussing women's issues, new perspectives, innovative methodologies and theoretical insights. Contributions made at its biannual conferences include task forces like "Education for Women's Equality" in the NPE (1986), "The Role of Science and Technology", "Reviewing and Planning WS" for the UGC, collective research projects by WS centres on "Girl Child and the Family". These, together with working groups like Economists Interested in Women's Issues Group (EIWIG) have resulted in a vast body of literature for classroom teaching as well as for policy dialogue. (Mazumdar, 1991).

The Search for a New Paradigm

An approach was accepted which considers that WS is both for understanding the situation of women's lives and consciousness raising for social change. This resulted in a serious search for a new paradigm. The first step in this direction was to make women visible in various disciplines, highlighting their role and contribution and capturing their experience. By creating legitimacy for WS as a 'researchable' area, efforts were made to break the silence surrounding the role of women and the silence of women themselves. Thus WS became a process of unfoldment of women. Making women visible is not an additive process where earlier women were not seen but are now visible - a kind of tokenism that exists in the power structures or some history textbooks. The WS approach implies challenging the dominant notion of knowledge, methodology and data sources based on class, ethnic/caste/ religious and gender biases. Another related problem with visibility is about new indicators, new standards and new criteria for visibility creation. WS makes women visible not as sex-objects but as active agents in socio-economic, cultural and political processes. WS looks at gender "not as a collection of psychological traits but as a basic element of social structure especially of sexual division of labour which is tied to gender division and male dominance." (Kalpagam, 1986, p.8). WS attempt towards visibility of women in statistics and indicators by questioning the concepts of 'work', 'productive labour', 'head of the household' led to the process of deconstructing patriarchy.

WS and the Construction of Knowledge

Radical scholars in various disciplines-sociology, history, economics, psychology, political science and literature have raised questions about objectivity, value neutrality, consensual model, demystification with survey research and quantitative analysis, the elitist bias of the disciplines and other such issues. However, they have ignored women's dimension. Hence the need for WS to go beyond both the mainstream and male critiques of the mainstream disciplines. For the construction of knowledge, WS in India began by re-examining prevalent concepts on household, economic activity, work-force and using new concepts such as patriarchy, sex-segregation, gender, oppression and exploitation. Several studies pointed to the biases and lacunae in the existing methods of data-collection, faulty definitions and ideological constraints especially in the large-scale sample surveys and in the census. (EIWIG, 1982; Sardamoni, 1992). Women's studies have evolved a new source of data-base and a new approach of analysing the existing data-base. WS scholarship has analysed the interaction between women's productive and reproductive roles in the market economy as well as in the subsistence production by unearthing cultural, historical and social contexts of construction of female identity and reorganisation of gender-based division of labour. (Mies, Lalitha, Kumar, 1986; Singh and Kelles-Viitanen, 1987; Agarwal, 1988; Dube and Parliwala, 1990; Krishnaraj and Channa, 1990; Banerjee, 1984). WS historians have looked at non-conventional data sources like reinterpretation of mythologies, scanning of short-stories, autobiographies, biographies, novels, poems and folk-songs. Attempts at rewriting the history of women in ancient India raise serious questions as to why was there marginalised representation of women? Was it due to limited concerns of traditional historian or was it due to the kind of tools employed? Why there is a heavy reliance on literary texts? In India, the early literary sources being literary texts, the problem is further compounded. (Chakravarty and Roy, 1987). Chakravarti has imaginatively used both the Buddhist and the Brahminical sources to focus on women in servitude. Here the attempt has been to use a non-Brahminical source. Lata Mani uses historical documents to question the motives of the British rulers in enacting the law of Sati. (Mani, EPW, April, 1986). Landmark contributions on different aspects of Indian women's survival struggles in colonial India have been made by during the last decade. (Sangari and Vaid, 1989; Krishnamurty, 1989; Sarkar, 1987). Identification and removal of sexist-bias in the textbooks and formulation of gender-just curriculum development have been a major concern of women's studies scholar. In psychology, discourse analysis and qualitative analysis have contributed new insights to understand complexities of gender relations. (Parkar, 1992). In the field of literary criticism new inroads have been made by women's studies scholars who have examined the mainstream literature with women's perspective and generated a new theoretical understanding to capture intricacy of man-woman relationship. (Radha, 1987; Tharu and Lalitha, 1991).

New Tools of Analysis

Women's studies begin by re-examining concepts and using new concepts to understand women. Role theory as used in conventional researches in sociology to study working women, has been questioned as it concentrates more on women rather than men and role conflict indicates a fact and not explanation. Further it confirms the role relationships but does not question it. (Krishnaraj, EPW, 1986). Similarly conventional concepts of household, family, housework, and male-headship have been modified while understanding women's reality. In the earlier sections of review of substantive researches various illustrations of such modifications and even radical departures have been mentioned.

WS scholars have started using the concepts of patriarchy, sex-segregation, discrimination and gender in their various studies. Several studies point to the biases and lacunae in existing methods of data collection, especially in large-scale sample surveys and in the census. (Jain, 1982; Agarwal, 1982; Mencher and Sardamoni, 1982; Mitra, 1980).

Case Studies

The WS researchers have been quite adept in using the case history or case study methods. When researcher found that secondary sources were unable to provide insights into the problem, case studies were taken up. For a long time it was thought that case study is a method used by the anthropologists, to study in detail the tribal life situations. Leela Gulati has described how she proceeds with case study when she wanted to understand the life of women in poverty. (Gulati, 1982; Karlekar, 1982; Banerjee, 1990).

Similarly those who are involved in ICSSR studies on the family strategies have used case studies method to understand how families try to cope with the larger needs of survival through the control or promotion of women's education and works. In one of the studies in Gujarat, case studies not only helped understand the strategies but how caste norms affected family decisions were brought out in the in-depth interviews. Similarly, the participation of the tribal women in the earlier protest struggle surfaced during the discussion. (Desai, 1987).

Oral History - Case History

When written records to grapple with the experiences of women are not available, oral testimonies of women's experiences have been very useful. (Stree Shakti Sangathana, 1989; Sen, 1990). The folk literature, particularly proverbs, myths, songs and folk tales are beginning to be used by WS researchers to understand the inner stirrings of women and society's attitude to women. Leela Dube has very ably used the folk material to examine social construction of gender. (Dube, EPW, 1988). Dube believes that in WS the use of oral history is convenient because while dealing with illiterate and semiliterate women, it helps the latter to become articulate, thereby enabling the researcher to obtain information and perception.

Autobiographies, Biographies and the 3 Generations Studies

The study of autobiographies, biographies and the 3 generations studies have proved to be useful to understand how some of the women grew from traditional background to forming their own identities. For getting authenticity and first person perception, autobiographies and diaries prove very useful. Autobiographies, of course, have to be cautiously handled, as many a times, romanticised picture is portrayed or certain vital facts are omitted because they might bring stigma to the person. Nostalgic memories of the past are many a times seen in romantic perspective. A study of 20 autobiographies of Maharashtrian women analyses the issues like child marriage, widow remarriage, family conflicts, struggle for education, participation in the nationalist movement and even opting for unconventional careers like cineartists have been covered. (Mehta and Vaidya, 1985, RCWS).

Quite a few seminars have been held where the focus of discussion is oral history, study of autobiographies and use of photographs and three generational studies to evolve an understanding of women's identity. Unfortunately the papers of such seminars are not available, with the result that much useful material and experience fail to reach larger community.

Content Analysis

WS has been using content analysis, particularly for media studies. Almost all researches on media (including in the literature) have tried to understand society's perception of women through the content analysis of film, television serial, tabloid journals, radio programmes, advertisements and dramas. Content analysis of literature has also been used to understand the motives of the ruling class, the ideology of social reformers and philosophies such as liberalism and feminism.

Participatory Technique

Participatory technique is more used in training development personnel and organising awareness programmes. Action being an important constituent of WS, this technique is used to conduct researches on the existing movements and developmental projects. Those who have been working with women at grass- roots have felt the need of using various techniques to break the silence of women, to get their participation and eventually generate a climate of equality. The hiatus between the trainer and the trainee, needs to be obliterated; the gap between producer of knowledge and user of knowledge has to be removed.

In WS, we have been saying that women's voices have to be

heard; how they perceive dowry or a violent situation is very crucial. While studying objective reality and micro forces, WS also examines subjective reactions, psycho related issues. To understand social oppression, personal involvement provides a deeper understanding of the problem. Hence WS recognises the role of personal data and personal accounts in highlighting the dynamics of women's oppression in situations like draught, communal riots, caste riots, Bhopal gas tragedy, ecological policies and others. (Omvedt, 1978; D'mello, 1988; Patel, 1988).

A nagging question invariably crops up whether these individual accounts are sufficient to infer general trends? Whether they have really helped in understanding women's lives? Whether the rigour in the studies could be maintained when subjective experiences are used as data sources?

WS in India has been a decade old phenomenon. It is too early to evaluate the efficacy of the tools and methods. What is very significant is that, after the eighties, more and more innovative approaches are being used by WS scholars. Information on experiences in various facets of life is growing. At a future date, effort will have to be made to provide a cohesive or not so cohesive picture of a woman's life as manifested in different spheres. Importantly enough it is recognised by researchers that subjective tools have to be handled very cautiously and they need constant checking and rechecking through other evidences. Further it is also accepted that WS by definition is interdisciplinary, hence it will have to borrow tools and methods from various disciplines. Further a versatile mind and not a specialist approach to grasp the problems of women is necessary. It is important to note that studies based on experimenting with new tools or new concepts have yet to emerge.

Shift in the Thrust of Areas

In the context of development debate which had been going on at that time, the glaring decline in work participation of women and growing experiments of income generating activities for poor women, the studies on work are likely to be more. However, with more and more data coming out emphasising marginalisation of women in the development activities, employment is no guarantee against ill-treatment of women as revealed in dowry deaths, wife-beating, sexual harassment and attitude to girl child, explorations into the causes for such occurrences, the role of superstructure and ideology was realised. Patriarchal overtones in the institutional structures of family, education, economy, law and others are being examined.

From Descriptive to Analytical Approach

Absence of analytical approach has been due to very faulty research training and lack of perspective. In women's studies, we have been shouting from the housetops that we do not wish to sacrifice rigour, nor do we want women's studies to be a 'soft discipline'. Frequent workshops on training in methodology and exposure to more and more innovative techniques will be prerequisites for making women's studies researches more analytical and not superficial.

Research and Action

During the decade for quite some time researches on women and action on women were moving parallel. After the eighties the chasm between the researcher and the activist sharpened, as funds started pouring into women's research. The government through its ministries, such as labour, Rural Development and Social Welfare sponsored studies initially to academics, which might have resulted into a hierarchical situation. Simultaneously with the growth of grassroots work and autonomous women's groups organising campaigns and lobbying for political action, a necessity to study the problem arose. Foreign funders started supporting such actions or activists resulted in debates on whether one should take foreign fund or not? It was believed to have implications of unequal power dimensions, apart from the fact that research priorities might be determined.

Another dimension of this issue is concerning role of the researcher. If women's studies is both understanding and action, then commitment to social change is essential. Women's oppressive reality has not to be merely studied in a classroom but has to be eliminated. The logic of adopting innovative techniques like life history, autobiography, experiential data is self-awareness and then the need to change. Articulation of one's experiences in terms of oppression or growing identity on the one hand indicates a changed situation wherein a woman is able to indicate a changed situation where in a woman is able to frankly and honestly express her inner tribulations and a critique of the most private relationship. On the other hand this realisation some day ought to lead to action for changing this relationship. It could come more rapidly if there is support available through the women's movement. Of course, there are levels and levels of action, but activity and empathy are of prime significance in women's studies.

Institutionalising Women's Studies - A Few Hurdles

With the UGC legitimising women's studies by encouraging the building up of centres, cells, programmes, courses in the university system; many concerned women's studies protagonists have been anxious about implications of such steps. On the one hand, unless women's studies get into the mainstream of education, the transformation in attitude, behaviour or perception is not possible. Apart from the danger of using Women's Studies as spring board for one's own career promotion, there is also a serious danger of supporting status-quo, through mystical and ideological explanations. By highlighting the 'inner strength' or 'shakti' of women, contending that 'fire' is a purifier or eulogising 'mother earth' and 'motherhood, the scholars many times hide the acceptance of women's oppressive situation. Similarly, attempts are also made to justify female foeticide on the ground that it will end ill-treatment and discrimination of female child, which leads eventually to female mortality. There is a very thin line between understanding women's oppressive situation and recommending adjustment to the situation in the name of 'purity', 'inner strength' or 'lesser evil'.

From WS to Gender Studies

A move from women's studies to gender studies has been a demand of the day in the mainstream academia. While justifying WS as a felt-need for a new epistemology, the basic understanding was that male dominant ideology and sexism in the social sciences and humanities were unable to capture women's perceptions and it was necessary to decentre a patriarchal discourse. Justification for Gender Studies comes from an understanding that both men and women are constructed and constrained by the unequal power relations based on class, caste/race/ethnicity and gender.

Future of Women's Studies and Women's Movement in India

The state of art profile of WS at the end of this exercise is not neat and clear, as women's life is also not simple. It is full of contradictions. The research activity and the debates generated in women's studies have reached the levels of compensatory research where women's perspective has been added to the conventional discipline. We need more systematic work to challenge the mainstream discipline, build new paradigms and provide significant theoretical understanding. On the contrary, women's movement in India is far more creative, courageous and vibrant in terms of its research agenda, advocacy and policy oriented research and action plans. As a result, all those who used to say "Women's issues can wait" are forced to accept "Every issue is a women's issue".

References

Agarwal, Bina (1983), "Report on the Current Status and Needed Priorities of Women's Studies in Asia and the Pacific", *APDC*, Malaysia.

Agarwal, Bina (ed.)(1988), *Structures of Patriarchy- State, Community and Household in Modernising Asia* London: Zed Books.

Banerjee, Nirmala (1984), *Women in the Unorganised Sector- The Calcutta Experience* London: Orient Longman.

Banerjee, Nirmala (1992), *Indian Women in a Changing Industrial Scenario*, Sage Publications, London.

Chakravarty, Uma and Roy, Kumkum (1987), "In Search of Our Past- A Review of the Limitations and Possibilities of the Historiography of Women in Early India", *Economic and Political Weekly*, April 30.

Desai, Neera (1977), *Women in Modern India*, Vora & co, Bombay.

Desai, Neera (1978), *Social Change in Gujarat- A Study of Nineteenth Century Gujarati Society*, Bombay: Vora & co.

Desai, Neera and Patel, Vibhuti(1990), *Indian Women - Change and Challenge*, Bombay: Popular Publications.

Desai, Neera and Patel, Vibhuti (1993), *Critical Evaluation of Women's Studies Researches in India, 1974-1993*, ICSSR, Delhi.

D'mello, Flavia (1988), " Our Fight Against Wifebeating" in Ghadiali, Rehana, *Women in Indian Society- A Reader*, New Delhi: Sage Publications.

Dube, Leela and Parliwala, Rajni (eds.) (1990), *Structures and Strategies-Women, Work and Family* London: Sage.

Eisenstein, Zilla (ed.) (1979), *Capitalist Patriarchy and the Case for Socialist Feminism* New York: Monthly Review Press.

Gadgil, D. R. (1965), 'Women in the Working Force in India', Delhi: University of Delhi.

Gulati, Leela (1981), *Profiles of Female Poverty: Study of Five Poor Working Women in Kerala*, New Delhi: Hindustan Publications.

Jain, Devaki and Banerjee, Nirmala (Eds) (1985), *Women in Poverty - the Tyranny of the Household*. New Delhi, Vikas Publications.

Kalpagam, U. (1986), 'Gender in Economics - the Indian Experience', Economic and Political Weekly, October 23.

Karlekar, Malvika (1982), *Poverty and Women's Work*, New Delhi: Vikas Publishing House.

Krishnamurty, J. (1989), *Women in Colonial India- Essays on Survival, Work and the State* Delhi: Oxford University Press.

Krishnaraj, Maithreyi (1986), Women's *Studies in India - Some Perspectives*, Bombay, Popular Prakashan.

Krishnaraj, Maithreyi and Channa Karuna (eds.) (1990), *Gender and the Household Domain - Social and Cultural Dimensions* London: Sage.

Mani, Lata (1986), "Production of an Official Discourse on Sati in Early Nineteenth Century Bengal", Economic and Political Weekly.

Mazumdar, Veena (1991), "Emergence of the Indian Association for Women's Studies", IAW Newsletter, No. 12, January 1991. pp. 1-6.

Mencher, Joan and Sardamoni, K. (1982), "Muddy Feet, Dirty Hands - Rice Production and Female Agricultural Labour", EPW, Review of Agriculture, Vol. 17, No. 52, December.

Mies, Maria assisted by Lalitha, K. and Krishna Kumar (1986), *Indian Women in Subsistence and Agriculture Labour* Geneva: International Labour Organisation.

Minault, Gail (ed.) (1981), *The Extended Family - Women and Political Participation in India and Pakistan*, Delhi: Chanakya Publications.

Mitra, Asok (1980), *The Status of Women - Household and Non-household Economic Activity*, New Delhi: Allied Publications.

Moore, Henrietta (1988), *Feminism and Anthropology*, Oxford: Polity Press.

Omvedt, Gail (1978), *We Shall Smash This Prison*, Delhi, Orient Longman.

Parker, Ian (1992), *Discourse Dynamics - Critical Analysis for Social and Individual Psychology*. London: Routledge.

Patel, Sujata (1987), *The Making of Industrial Relations- The Ahmedabad Textile Industry, 1918-1939*, Delhi: Oxford University Press.

Patel, Vibhuti (1985), 'Emergence and Proliferation of Autonomous Women's Organisations in India' in Ghadiali, Rehana, 1988, *Women in Indian Society*, Delhi: Sage Publications.

Patel, Vibhuti (1989), "Recent Debates on Concepts of Paid- Unpaid Work, Domestic Work and Employment of Women", *UN-INSTRAW and SNDT Women's University*, Bombay, 1989.

Radha, K. (ed.) (1987), *Feminism and Literature*, Trivandrum: Institute of English, University of Kerala.

Sanghari, Kumkum and Vaid, Sudesh (Eds) (1990), *Recasting Women - Essays in Indian Colonial History*, Rutgers: Rutgers University Press.

Sardamoni, K. (ed.) (1992), *Finding the Household- Conceptual and Methodological Issues*. London: Sage.

Sarkar, Tanika (1987), *Bengal 1928-1934, The Politics of Protest*, Delhi: Oxford University Press.

Sen, Ilina (1989), *Space Within Struggle*, Delhi: Kali for Women.

Sharma, Ursula (1980), *Women, Work and Property in Northwest India*. London: Tavistock Publications.

Singh, Andrea Menefee and Kelles-Viitanen, Anita (eds.) (1987), *Invisible Hands- Women in Home-based Production*. London: Sage.

Stree Shakti Sangathana (1988), *We Were Making History*, Delhi: Kali for Women.

Tharu, Susie and Lalitha K. (eds.) (1990), *Women Writing in India- 600 B.C. to the Present, Vol. I: 600 B.C. to the Early Twentieth Century*. Delhi: Oxford University Press.

Walby, Sylvia (1990), *Theorizing Patriarchy*, Oxford: Basil Blackwell.

Footnotes

1. See Neera Desai and Vibhuti Patel (1988) *'Critical Review of Researches in Women's Studies'*, India council of Social Science Research (ICSSR), Delhi. Also see, a state of art report prepared by Neera Desai, Leela Dube and Veena Mazumdar (1982) *'Women's Studies and Social Sciences in India'*, UNESCO Regional Expert Meeting, Delhi.
2. For detailed description of this process see Vibhuti Patel, 'Women's Liberation in India', *New Left Review*, 153, August, 1985, pp.75-86; Sujata Gotoskar and Vibhuti Patel, 'Documents From the Indian Women's Movement', *Feminist Review*, 1982, No. 12, pp.92-103.
3. For further details of the course content, see *An Overview, 1993* SNDT Women's University, Bombay.

Seventeen

Conclusion

Indian women will be facing multifaceted challenges in the millennium era as a result of simultaneous working of economic liberalisation, globalisation, women's participation in the Panchayati Raj institutions and predominance of identity politics in the day to day governance of civil society.

Adverse sex ratio of women to men has put the Indian women in the category of "Endangered species". Worsening socio-political, cultural and economic situation has made Indian women, targets of varied forms of covert and overt violence. The state response in terms of Domestic Violence Bill is a slap on the face of Indian women as it does not take cognisance of 'casual beating', though state sponsored National Commission of Women and State Commissions of Women are showing willingness to work with women's rights groups on issue-to-issue basis.

Health profile of mass of Indian women will demand urgent attention in the areas of nutrition, reproductive rights and mental health. New reproductive technologies with harmful impact on women's physical and mental well being will have to be opposed in collaboration with women's groups in other developing countries.

Indian women's movement will have to play prominent role in the peace initiatives in the subcontinent. Networking with the South, the South-East and the East Asian countries will gain ground among women as the diplomatic ties and trade relations among these countries get strengthened.

As awareness about women's rights is increasing day by day, matters relating to religion-based family laws which govern important areas of women's lives such as marriage, divorce, custody of children, maintenance, property, alimony, right to live in matrimonial or parental home, land rights will gain prominence in the public debate.

Because women are considered to be the repositories of culture and tradition, women will have to evolve creative ways of dealing with identity politics. Symbols, imagery, dress code of Indian women will be defined according to influence of interplay between identity politics and multicultural ethos.

Global cosmetic industries are using adolescent girls' bodies to create a monolithic model of beauty so that they can capture world market. As against that, the educational institutions, socially committed voluntary organisations will have to make serious efforts to visibalise women as subjects, individuals making productive contributions to the economy as well as to the society at large. Alternate media generated by the people's movements which highlight developmental issues of women will have to be empowered and will have to be given place of prominence by the electronic and print media.

Legal system will have to be responsive to gender justice. Judicial activism by women's rights organisations will get momentum and will take a shape of popular movement in the coming time. Sexual harassment at workplace will be opposed publicly by women as a result of its meticulous codification by the human rights groups.

Worsening environmental crisis will throw up new leadership of indigenous women working in collaboration with social movements spearheading the cause of judicious distribution of land, water, bio-mass, energy resources. Debate on bio-technology will sharpen.

To analyse complex realities so that appropriate policies can be derived, more and more women's studies will have to be established to promote area studies. Emergence and proliferation of women's studies centres in smaller town will encourage debates in the regional languages. In place of elitist concern, women studies will have mass appeal. More and more women's studies units and centres will be established at udergraduate level. More and more educational material on women studies will come out in regional languages.

Professional bodies of women administrators, managers, executives, teachers, researchers, scientists, engineers, politicians will have to establish global contacts to take maximum advantage of globalisation. More and more women entrepreneurs will expand their business ventures and will also provide umbrella to self help groups of women.

Major Changes in geo-politics as well as industrial and agrarian development will pose equally major Challenges for Indian women. In this context, engendering health, education, employment and political fields with long-term perspective will become important matter for women's agenda.

Index

T

U

V

W

Y

Z